ANTHROPOLOGICAL PAPERS

MUSEUM OF ANTHROPOLOGY, UNIVERSITY OF MICHIGAN

NO. 41

THE ARCHAEOLOGY OF SUMMER ISLAND: CHANGING SETTLEMENT SYSTEMS IN NORTHERN LAKE MICHIGAN

BY

DAVID S. BROSE

ANN ARBOR

THE UNIVERSITY OF MICHIGAN, 1970

ISBN (print): 978-0-932206-39-8
ISBN (ebook): 978-1-951519-29-2

Browse all of our books at
sites.lsa.umich.edu/archaeology-books.

Order our books from the University of Michigan
Press at www.press.umich.edu.

For permissions, questions, or manuscript queries,
contact Museum publications by email at umma-
pubs@umich.edu or visit the Museum website at
lsa.umich.edu/ummaa.

PREFACE

THE present work, a revised version of a doctoral dissertation, represents an attempt to interpret some aspects of the prehistory of the basin of northern Lake Michigan, especially in its western portions. The key to this interpretation was provided by the excavation and analysis of the Summer Island site. Much of this work and part of the publication cost was supported by the National Science Foundation Grant GS-1486 "Archaeological Investigations in Michigan" awarded to Dr. James E. Fitting of The University of Michigan. Needless to say, the work of previous archaeologists in this area was indispensable in the formulation of many of the hypotheses. Chief among these were George I. Quimby, James E. Fitting, Ronald J. Mason, and Alan McPherron. In a wider context the work of James V. Wright, James B. Stoltman, Warren Wittry, William A. Ritchie, James B. Griffin, Charles Cleland, and Robert L. Hall provided the necessary framework in which these hypotheses could be applied to the archaeological data of the Great Lakes area. Many of the conclusions reached in this report are at variance with those reached by these scholars. Those presented here are also subject to the same type of criticism I have leveled against earlier interpretations and by such dialogue some approximation of "what really happened" may be construed. Certainly such criticism is not directed at the individuals, but rather to the archaeological issues involved.

Many of these people have generously examined some of the materials from Summer Island and shared their interpretations with me for which I am grateful. I would also like to thank my doctoral committee and especially the chairman, for having read and commented upon earlier versions of this paper. The committee consisted of James E. Fitting, chairman, with James B. Griffin, Volney H. Jones, Robert M. Warner, and Aram Yengoyan as members.

Gratitude is also expressed for the help given to me by the following individuals: Dr. Charles A. Reed of the University of Northern Illinois for faunal identification in the field; Dr. Hugh C. Cutler of the Missouri Botanical Garden, for botanical identifications on the island; Gerald Wiggers, of the U. S. Forest Service, for his helpfulness in the identification and classification of soils on the island; Barbara (Bird) Luxenberg and Elizabeth Butch for laboratory analysis of faunal remains; Daniel Caister and Volney H. Jones, for laboratory analysis of floral remains; James H. Robertson of The University of Michigan, Department of Mineralogy, for his help in identifying mineral specimens, The University of Michigan Institute for Social Research and The University of Michigan Computing Center, for access to their programs; and to Robert E. Whallon for his help in modifying these; Dan Stevens and Terry Brooks, of Summer Science Incorporated, for their encouragement and logistic support during the six weeks spent in excavations on the island, and to Mrs. Charles P. Wilkinson for her conscientious efforts as typist and spelling consultant. Last, but certainly far from least, were the efforts of my wife, Barbara, who helped in the analysis and cataloging of artifacts, and their photography. She also composed the photographic plates, read, edited, and corrected the final version of the manuscript.

TABLE OF CONTENTS

INTRODUCTION

WITHIN the upper Great Lakes region the northern Lake Michigan basin has received the greatest amount of recent archaeological attention. In northeastern Wisconsin Mason (1966, 1967) excavated and reported three sites that clearly demonstrate the chronological sequence from Middle Woodland through early Late Woodland to a final Upper Mississippian. His Middle Woodland North Bay culture at the Mero and the Porte des Morts sites was seen to be related to late Illinois Hopewellian cultures as well as to the more northern Laurel—Saugeen—Point Peninsula complexes. The early Late Woodland occupations at the Mero and Heins Creek sites were closely related to developments in eastern Wisconsin and northern Michigan. The Oneota component at the Mero site was related to developments in eastern Wisconsin whose chronological placement was somewhat uncertain.

On Bois Blanc Island McPherron (1967) excavated the Juntunen site which demonstrated the Late Woodland chronological sequence in the region of Mackinac Straits. The earliest (Mackinac) phase was seen to be closely related to the Heins Creek complex in Wisconsin while later phases seemed oriented to developments to the east.

Binford and Quimby (1963) analyzed the lithic industries from several sites in the northern Lake Michigan area and came to the conclusion that a rather specialized bipolar core technique was characteristic of the Late Woodland Period (p. 306).

Fitting (1968*b*) analyzed several sites from the Garden Peninsula and concluded that within this region many of the differences displayed by the lithic industry were a function of site utilization as much as chronological placement.

The investigation of several sites along the north shore of Lake Michigan (Fitting, 1968*b*; Janzen, 1968; Cleland and Peske, 1968; Brose, 1968; Prahl and Brose, n.d.) clearly revealed that at any period of time several different types of sites could be found within this area. Many of the differences between these sites were clearly due to differing functions, and Fitting (1968*b*) was able to interpret these as an indication that the economic adaptation in this area produced seasonally occupied sites with distinct characteristics.

In attempting a synthesis of these data it became clear that several crucial pieces of information were lacking. No major settlement attributable to the Middle Woodland period had been analyzed hampering any reconstruction of the economic adaptation. The precise cultural relationships between the North Bay culture and the Laurel occupations to the north were poorly understood and no acceptable processual explanation for their chronological placement or ceramic similarity was available. Neither was any explanation available for the apparent lithic similarities in the Late Woodland period in this area.

Several archaeological surveys indicated the possibility of a large, well-stratified site on Summer Island that contained Middle Woodland, Oneota, and Late Woodland components. I undertook the excavation of the site and the subsequent analysis of materials from July, 1967 to June, 1968. It was hoped that these analyses would provide answers to some questions regarding the nature of the Oneota adaptation to the agriculturally marginal environment of northern Lake Michigan as well as aiding in the solution of these other problems. The results of these analyses, and the inferences drawn from them, are contained in this thesis. To some extent the initial problems are still unanswered. Only further archaeological work on small single component or stratified sites in this area can test the derived hypotheses concerning the full seasonal cycle of economic utilization of the land, the water, and their resources.

PART I

DESCRIPTION OF THE SITE

I

ENVIRONMENTAL SETTING

BEDROCK GEOLOGY

THE major physiographic feature of the northern Lake Michigan basin is the Niagara Escarpment. This geological formation can be traced from the type locality at Niagara Falls, New York, through the Bruce Peninsula of Ontario and the Manitoulin Islands of Lake Huron, across the Straits of Mackinac and down the Garden Peninsula of Michigan to the Door Peninsula of Wisconsin (Hough, 1958: 14). The high bluffs which form the western shore of the Garden Peninsula and the chain of outlying islands spanning the mouth of the Green Bay are composed of hard, resistant limestone and dolomite formations of the Niagara series (Fig. 1). The soft gypsum and shaly dolomite, Richmond and Black River members of the Cataract Formation, which have been eroded to about two hundred feet below lake level, form the trough presently occupied by Big Bay de Noc (Sinclair, 1960: 11). During the Pleistocene a discontinuous mantle of glacial drift of varying thickness was deposited on the bedrock surface. On the Garden Peninsula glacial deposits form highlands and ridges of some height. Low swamps occur frequently, as drainage is in an early stage of development. These Pleistocene formations are thinnest on the channel islands lying directly south of the Garden Peninsula where bedrock frequently outcrops or lies directly below the surface.

Nearly all of Summer Island, and the entire western shore of the Garden Peninsula as far south as Sand Bay, is composed of, or directly underlain by, the lowest formation of the Middle Silurian Niagara series (Fig. 2). This Burnt Bluff Formation is a thinly bedded to massive, light gray to buff colored, calcitic dolomite approximately two hundred fifty feet thick. The southeastern tip of Little Summer Island, the northwest half of Summer Island, and the Sand Bay region on the Garden Peninsula, are composed of the overlying Middle Silurian Manistique Dolomite, a thinly bedded to massive, light buff to brownish-gray cherty dolomite about one hundred fifty feet thick. This Manistique Dolomite forms the east shore of the Garden Peninsula. Point Detour, the

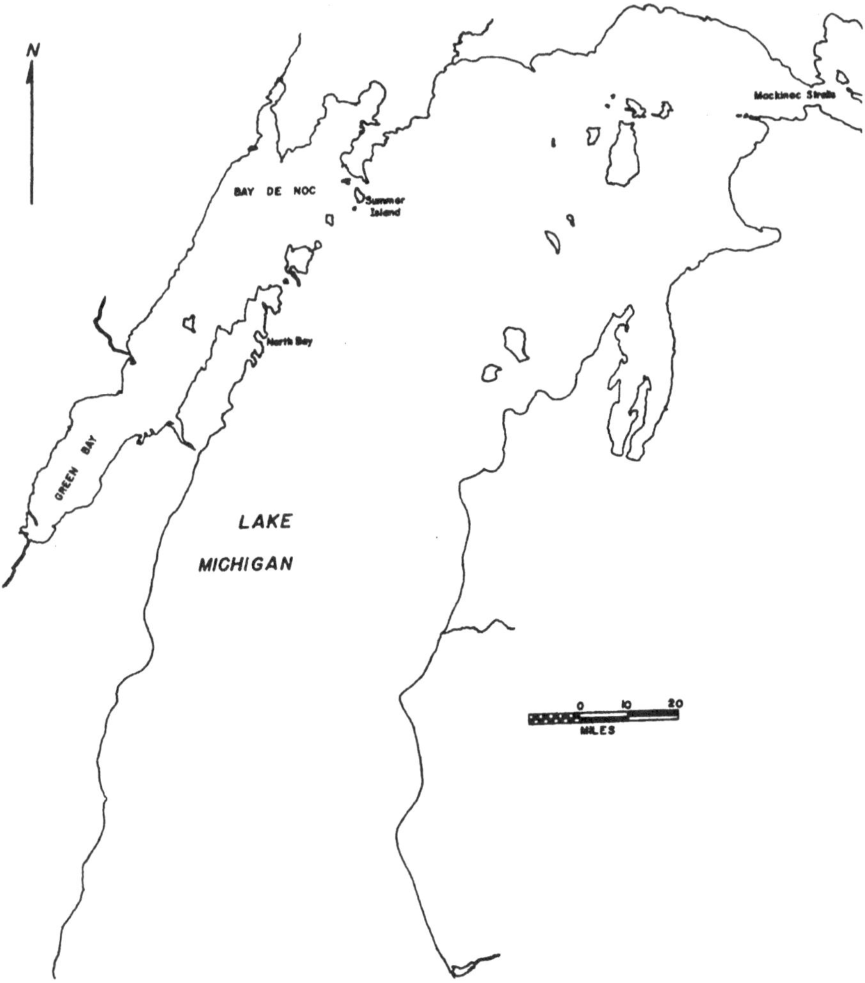

FIG. 1. Map of northern Lake Michigan.

southeast half of Summer Island, and all of Poverty Island are composed of the upper member of the Middle Silurian series, Engadine Dolomite. This formation is a massive, hard, bluish-white dolomite approximately ten to twenty feet thick. All of these formations have a strike N10°E and a southeast dip of about forty feet per mile (ibid.: 17).

During the Pleistocene epoch, ice of the Nebraskan, Kansan, and Illinoian stages covered the area of Summer Island (Flint, 1957: Fig. 20-21, p. 338). Any interglacial soils developed in this

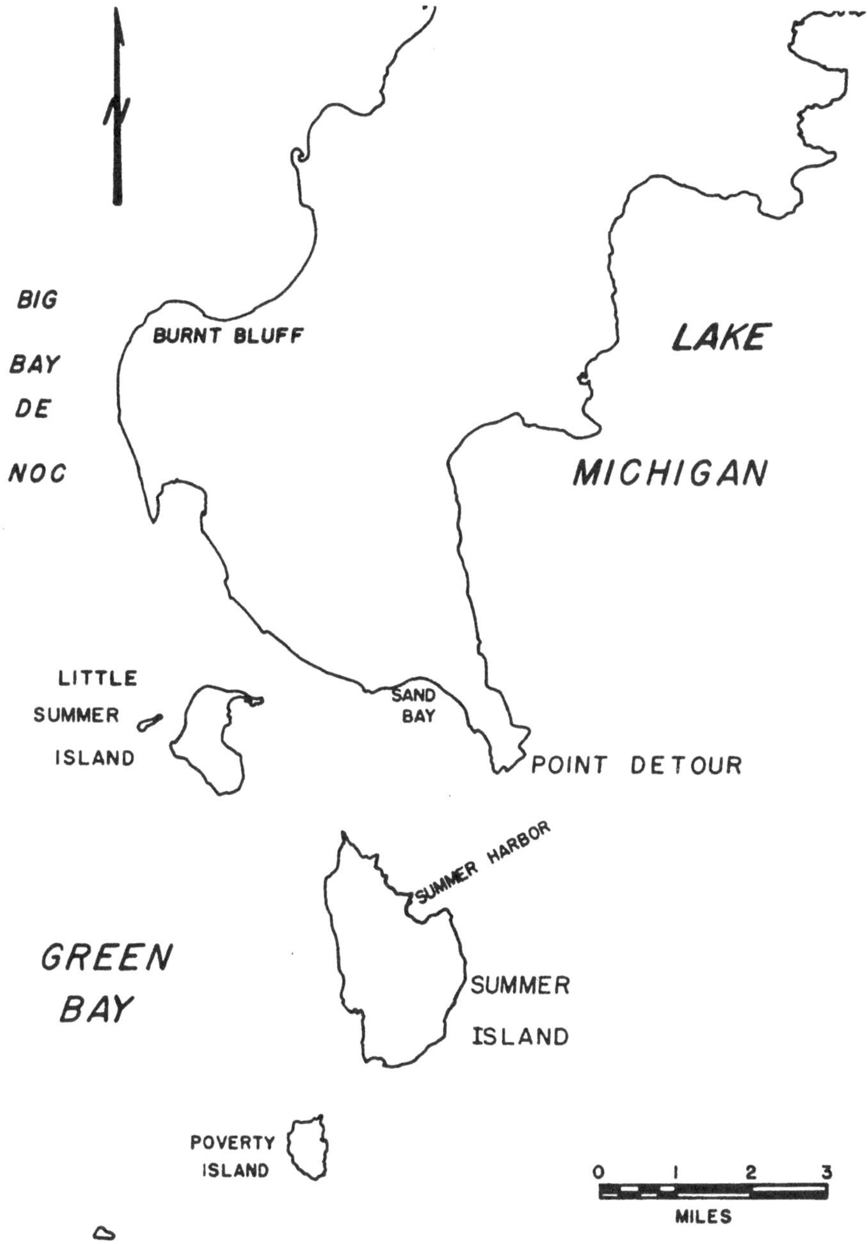

FIG. 2. Map of southern Delta County.

area during Sangamon times were removed by the successive stages of the Wisconsin glaciers. While the region was free from ice during the Two Creeks Interstadial (Flint, 1957: Fig. 20-24, p. 344) any soil formations attributable to this period were removed by the subsequent Valders advance which clearly overrode this area (Frye, Willman, and Black, *in* Wright and Frey, 1965: Fig. 1, p. 43). This Valders invasion was the last glacial event in the northern Lake Michigan basin and by 11,000 to 10,000 B.P. this area was free from all ice (Wayne and Zumberge, *in* Wright and Frey, 1965: 73).

The Valders till was rapidly deposited in this last glacial retreat (Frye, Willman, and Black, *in* Wright and Frey, 1965: 73). Wayne and Zumberge (1965: 72) state that "The most distinguishing feature of the Valders drift in both Wisconsin and Michigan is its red or pink color. . . ." Black, however, says that in the northern Lake Michigan area of drift, Valders till may not be red and clayey, but rather brownish, stoney, and sandy (1966: 69). Black further indicates that the Valders till should be found on Summer Island (1966: Fig. 1, pp. 170, 173).

Following the retreat of the Valders ice the Summer Island-Garden Peninsula area was innundated by waters of the proglacial Lake Algonquin (605 feet A.T.), several stages of which cut beaches into the limestone bluffs along the west shore of the Garden Peninsula and the central highlands of Summer Island. A rather strong wave-cut beach was surveyed along Burnt Bluff at 650 feet (Prahl and Farrand, 1968: 7) that is assigned to the Wyebridge Stage (dated at sometime after 9,000 B.C.). This correlates with a wave-cut beach observed along the limestone bluffs on the southwest side of Summer Island, surveyed at 650 feet by our 1967 field crews. The post-Algonquin uplift in this area is estimated at about one hundred twenty feet (Farrand, 1962: 185). With the opening of the North Bay (Ontario) outlet sometime prior to 9,500 B.P. the lake levels dropped to the Chippewa-Stanley low stages and rose again to the Nipissing Lake Stage (605 feet A.T.) as crustal rebound lifted that same outlet (Hough, 1963: 103). Lake Nipissing probably reached the 605 foot level at about 4,000-4,500 B.P. (ibid.: 106), but "it is important to recognize that the maximum Nipissing level was short-lived and that there were probably short term fluctuations at this level" (Griffin, 1965*a*: 662-63). There is a clear Nipissing-cut beach at Burnt Bluff at 600-605 feet above sea level (Prahl and Farrand, 1968). On Summer Island a sandy beach ridge was surveyed running northeast-southwest across the back of a clearing about 280 feet west of the shore of Summer Harbor. This ridge rose about 1.2 feet above the lakeward sands and stood at 603 feet above sea level. Post-Nipissing crustal upwarping in this region is minimal (MacLean, 1963), as the stated elevations indicate. From the Nipissing Stage the water in the Lake Michigan basin has dropped to the present lake stage of 580 feet with a brief pause at the Algoma Stage (595 feet A.T.) during the second millennium B.C. Present lake levels seem to have been reached by 3,000 B.P. (Hough, 1963: 106) in the Michigan-Huron basin. Certainly the present lake levels had been reached by the time of the Early Woodland occupation at the Schultz site, Saginaw County, dated at 530 B.C. and 540 B.C. (Crane and Griffin, 1966: 262-63).

TOPOGRAPHY

At the present time Summer Island lies 2.0 miles south of Point Detour, the southeasternmost point of the Garden Peninsula. The island is 1.84 miles wide (northeast-southwest) and 3.15 miles long (northwest-southeast) and has a coastline of approximately 10.3 miles. It is the northernmost of a chain of eight islands that lie across the mouth of Green Bay and separate it from Lake Michigan north of Wisconsin's Door Peninsula. Poverty Island lies 1.3 miles south of Summer Island. St. Martins, the next island to the south, is 3.9 miles from Poverty. By such island-hopping the 28 miles between the Garden and Door peninsulas can be crossed with no point of the journey being more than 2.1 miles from land.

The waters of Lake Michigan to the east of Summer Island lie over jointed blocks of Engadine Dolomite shoaling out for a thousand feet to a depth of 16 feet. Thereafter the floor drops off sharply to depths between 124 feet and 192 feet within a mile of shore. The waters of Green Bay to the southwest of Summer Island also shoal out over jointed blocks of Engadine and Manistique Dolomite so that between Summer and Poverty islands the depth nowhere exceeds 19 feet. West of Summer Island the Manistique Dolomite shelves gently outward into the northern Green Bay basin reaching bottom depths of 30 feet at an average distance of three-quarters of a mile. To the northwest and north of Summer Island, as far as Sand Bay and Little Summer Island, the bottom consists of bedded limestone of the Manistique formation with some pockets of sandy gravel. Depths in this sector nowhere exceed 12 feet and are often considerably less. The water between Summer and Little Summer islands averages 4.0 feet in depth and limestone shoals break the water in a number of places. It is possible to walk from one island to the other in dry years, and often hazardous to take a boat between them. Between Summer Harbor and Point Detour the bottom slopes to 40 feet and is mainly jointed Engadine Dolomite.

Approaching from the north Summer Island appears as a low two-tiered mass. The central wave-cut heights rise abruptly to over 700 feet above sea level, while the western half of the island and the entire shoreline lies below 640 feet above sea level. From about half a mile out Summer Island seems to offer no suitable harbor for any kind of boat. At this distance from shore, within the mouth of Summer Harbor itself, the depth is 20 feet with a blocky limestone bottom. Toward either side of the harbor the bottom projects upward unevenly, often breaking the surface in gull-covered limestone shoals several hundred feet from shore. The shore along the entire island presents the appearance of jumbled blocks of limestone dropping a sheer ten or twelve feet onto the more broken limestone shelf which forms the bottom. There are two exceptions to this picture: the extreme northwestern point of Summer Island is a low, gravelly bar extending several thousand feet north and gently dipping to lie about four feet below the water midway between the Summer Islands. Toward the foot of Summer Harbor where the bottom is less than eight feet in depth, it is composed of a rather clean sand which extends shoreward to the beach. Nonetheless, scattered blocks of dolomite often lie inches below the surface of the water and along the sand beach. The beach itself runs along the southwestern shore of Summer Harbor for about nine hundred to a thousand feet. To either side the limestone rises directly from the water to heights of from four to seven feet. Behind the sand beach and the twenty-six foot wide sand and gravel shingle the land slopes steeply upward in a high sand bank reaching a rather sudden plateau about twenty feet above the lake. This sandy plain forms a clearing, erratically covered with thin vegetation. The clearing runs along the harbor for about 650 feet north and south and is about 250 feet wide at the center. It is crescentic, following the shoreline, each tapered end meeting a limestone ledge and, immediately beyond, the forest. These two limestone ledges, surveyed at an elevation of 605 feet above sea level, are rather perpendicular and probably meet in the woods which borders them some distance inland from the clearing. They are conncected across the back of the clearing by a low sandy ridge (elev. 602-5 feet above sea level) representing the Lake Nipissing beach. The Summer Island site, 20 DE 4, is located within the southern half of the area bounded by the harbor, the sand ridge, and the limestone shelves.

CLIMATE

The climate of southern Delta County is described in a brochure published in 1925 by the Escanaba Chamber of Commerce as follows:

The summers are most delightful. The days are comfortably warm, but, being tempered by the cooling breezes from the three bays, the temperature rarely ever rises above 90 degrees. . . . Winter comes about the first of December and is followed by three to four months of crisp, invigorating weather. The snowfall averages from eight to fifteen inches.

TABLE 1

CLIMATE OF SOUTHERN GARDEN PENINSULA AND SUMMER ISLAND

Average annual temperature	40-45° F.
Average January temperature	15-20° F.
Average July temperature	65° F.
Average annual minimum temperature	-20° F.
Average annual maximum temperature	95° F.
Lowest temperature observed	-40° F.
Highest temperature observed	105° F.
Average annual precipitation	25-30"
Period of maximum precipitation	April-Sept.
Average annual snowfall	80"
Average annual number of days with snow cover	120-140
Average annual number of days with cloud cover	140-60
Average annual number of frost-free days	120-40

Source: U.S. Weather Station, Garden, Michigan, 1889-1938 (U.S.D.A. Yearbook, 1941: 703-46).

While this picture is, predictably, optimistic (see Table 1), it is reasonably accurate. The "crisp, invigorating" winter is, however, far more severe than indicated above. There is some good evidence showing that northern Lake Michigan produces increased storm activity in the fall and winter and decreased storm frequency in spring and summer (Changnon, 1966: 233). A recent study indicates that the four months from mid-November to mid-March produced 49 per cent of all storms during the period A.D. 1889-1961 (Ayers, 1965: 60-61). In winter northern Lake Michigan is covered by ice building out from shore so that 60 to 90 per cent of the water surface may be covered.

Freezing may be a smooth process, or it may be a result of the piling-up of ice in ridges and windrows that may rise from 10 to 20 feet above water level, making any transit hazardous. Lake shipping is usually suspended by the first of December and opens again between the middle of March (in the South) and early April or even early May (in Lake Superior) [Powers, *in* Ayers *et al.*, 1958: 37].

While the ice separating Summer Island from the Garden Peninsula is often thick enough to support a bulldozer ("ten to twenty inches" [Edwin Palmcook: personal communication]), it is subject to variable winds and currents so that sections only a few yards distant may be less than one inch thick. Needless to say, this does little to decrease the hazards of winter travel. Considering all factors, the period from mid-November to mid-March is quite inhospitable on the offshore islands of Delta County.

SOILS AND VEGETATION

Summer Island lies in that part of the upper Great Lakes best characterized ecologically as a transition zone (Cleland, 1966: 5). Dice has shown that his "Canadian Biotic Province" is a zone where Carolinian and Hudsonian fauna overlap (1938: 512) and Cleland notes that Summer Island lies just within the southern limits of a "pure" Canadian Biotic Province (1966: Fig. 1, p. 6). Both would describe the flora of Summer Island as mixed hardwood-conifer forest (Dice, 1938: 503-5; Cleland, 1966: 9-10). Cushing, however, makes the point that within this vegetation community, composition varies with time and space to produce a series of communities grading into one another, no one of which is by itself characteristic (1965: 407). It seems necessary therefore to characterize the flora of the island with more precision than would be gained from inclusion in continental-sized zones alone.

A soil survey of the Manistique River State Forest on Summer Island was undertaken in June, 1967, by Mr. G. Wiggers of the Hiawatha National Forest staff. Fortunately, I was on the island at the time and thus able to accompany and make notes of the survey while in progress.

The interior central highlands of the island are rather gently sloping to level areas lying above 660 feet above sea level. This area has been undergoing soil genesis since the dropping of Lake Algonquin below the Wyebridge Stage at least 9,000 years ago. Soils in this area are uniformly classified as Summerville Sandy Loam and are developed on slopes of less than 6 per cent. These soils have a pH of 6.0 to 6.5. The extreme northern portion of the island is a sloping plain dissected by numerous shallow ravines and large outcrops of dolomite. Soils are characterized by low, poorly drained patches of shallow Rapid River Sandy Loam and loam (with pH values of 6.0 to 7.0) alternating with Bonduel Sandy Loam (pH 6.5 to 7.5) in the flatter areas and Alpena Loamy Sands (pH 6.5 to 7.5) on the somewhat steeper slopes. The southwestern Poverty Lookout Harbor area of steep limestone bluffs and broken terrain is characterized as Duel Sands (pH 7.0 to 7.5). The remainder of the island, fully 75 per cent, is described by the Forest Service as Rock Land, being broken and jointed surface outcrops of Manistique Dolomite in the north and Engadine Dolomite in the south. No surface peats or clays are known on the island.

With the aid of Dr. H. Cutler of the Missouri Botanical Gardens, The University of Michigan Museum of Anthropology field crew compiled the following initial botanical survey of Summer Island in late July of 1967. Forest cover on the interior Summerville Sandy Loam was characterized by a dominance of hemlock (*Tsuga canadensis*), balsam fir (*Abies balsamea*), beech (*Fagus grandifola*), sugar maple (*Acer saccharum*), paper and yellow birch (*Betula papyrifera, B. allegheniensis*). Other trees in this area were red maple (*Acer rubrum*), white oak (*Querus alba*), white pine (*Pinus strobus*), and basswood (*Tilia americana*). There was little undergrowth in this forest, and only two species, hazelnut (*Corylus americana*) and goldenrod (*Solidago*), were identified in any numbers. The Rapid River and Bonduel Sandy Loams were dominated by sugar maple, yellow birch, beech, and hemlock, with some basswood, quaking aspen (*Populus tremuloides*), red maple, rock maple (*Acer spicatum*), white pine, and a few examples of black cherry (*Prunus serotina*). Undergrowth in these areas was quite thick and the following species were identified: black huckleberry (*Gaylussacia baccata*), red currant (*Ribes triste*), gooseberry (*Ribes oxyancanthoides*), blackberry (*Rubus occidentalis*), chokecherry (*Prunus virginiana*), and blueberry (*Vaccinium angustifolium*). Occasional flat clearings in these areas would be covered with goldenrod and milkweed (*Asclepias syriaca*). The slopes in these areas, where not bare rock, would generally be Alpena Loamy Sand and had a cover of jack pine (*Pinus banksiana*), quaking aspen, paper birch, and occasional red oak (*Querus rubra*) and fire cherry (*Prunus pensylvanicus*). On the Rock Lands, where little in the way of soils had developed, the weathered, jointed limestone supported a forest cover dominated by balsalm fir and white spruce, although hemlock, black spruce (*Picea mariana*), quaking aspen, white pine, red maple, red pine (*Pinus resinosa*), and occasionally northern cedar (*Thuja occidentalis*) occurred. There was little undergrowth, although there were dense windfalls; the damper low areas supported some blueberry. With the exception of the Duel Sand area, the entire coast was covered with a dense tangle of northern cedar and with occasional balsalm fir and black spruce. The edges of the Duel Sand area, in which the site is located, were covered by paper birch and quaking aspen, with northern cedar along the lakeward portions of the clearing. Directly behind this "screen," the spruce-fir forest characteristic of the Rock Lands occurred mixed with paper birch and aspen. The clearing itself showed alternating areas of sand blow out, grass, blueberry, raspberry (*Rubus strigosus*), milkweed, goldenrod, sweet fern, (*Comptonia peregrina*), scouring rush (*Equisetum arvense*), and black-eyed Susan (*Rudbeckia hirta*). Some chokecherry grew along the edge of the sand bluff at the southern edge of the clearing with several large northern cedar and hemlock trees in the north-central portion.

The several cladistic communities enumerated above can together be taken to represent the character of the "Lake Forest" (Cushing, 1965: 406-7) of the Canadian Province. It should be clear from the foregoing that although Summer Island can be characterized as "northern hardwood-fir forest," discrete topographical areas of the island could be called northern hardwoods, Great Lakes pine forest, or spruce-fir forest. It should be repeated that while the Rock Lands spruce-fir forest is distinctly Hudsonian, such minor Hudsonian communities within the Canadian Province lack many, if not most, of the characteristic Hudsonian mammal fauna (Dice, 1938: 509). It is finally noted that in addition to being located in a transition zone, numerous "transition zones" exist upon the island itself so far as floral communities are concerned. While the haphazard hardwood logging operations on the island in the 1870s and 1900s have no doubt contributed to the decimation of the original beech-maple interior forests, the present situation should not be materially different from the aboriginal one.

FAUNA

The mammal species that would be expected on Summer Island, are noted by Burt (1954), Burt and Grossenheider (1956), Cleland (1966), and Murie (1958). Of this Canadian fauna porcupine, raccoon, wolf, woodchuck, skunk, red fox, gray fox, eastern chipmunk, least chipmunk, red squirrel, long-tailed weasel, black bear, moose, and elk were not observed by any of our field crew during ten weeks of camping on the island. While it is possible to miss small insectivores such as shrews and voles, the fact that several species of each were identified by tracks or by sight gives more weight to the negative evidence concerning those unobserved species. There is no record, nor can any of the residents of Fairport who hunt on Summer Island regularly, recall any bear, elk or moose on the island. The total presently known mammal fauna on Big Summer Island thus consists of several insectivores, a small number of fur-bearing rodents, eastern cottontail, coyote, and whitetail deer.

A richer avian fauna is present, but of these the only seasonally available birds of economic importance are the Canadian goose, mallard, black duck, wood duck, pintail, and blue wing teal. The island does not lie directly on any well traveled migration route (Hawkins, 1964: 206-7), and local residents make no attempt to do their duck hunting there.

Although the pine snake is not indicated for the Canadian Biotic Province (Cleland, 1966: 243), it does in fact occur in rather large numbers on Summer Island. With this exception, even the herpetological population is rather meager. Paradoxically, the major faunal resource on Summer Island is the fish offshore.

Rostlund (1952: 73) has described the Great Lakes as a province,

> formed by the overlapping of the Mississippian and Canadian faunas, and therefore northern and southern fish intermingle in the region. Whitefishes, lake herrings, lake trout and pikeperch constitute the bulk of the resource which consequently is high in quality, for these fish are all prime food fishes. Other important fish are . . . pike, muskellunge, sauger, and lake sturgeon.
>
> In the smaller waters tributary to the main lakes or in narrow passages, such as the Straits of Mackinac, or at Sault Ste. Marie, the fish are seasonally highly available . . . aboriginal fishing in the main lakes may even be called an inland fishery.

Scott (1954) and Hubbs and Lagler (1961) have indicated that lake sturgeon, yellow walleye, sauger, freshwater drum, and burbot may also be found on shallow gravel bottoms or rocky shoals.

In discussing the availability of fish within the Great Lakes province, Rostlund makes the following points; alkaline waters, especially those deriving their basic quality from limestone beds, are by far the most productive. Warmer waters are, on the whole, more conducive to maximum growth of fish than are very cold waters; the most productive part of any lake is the shoal water zone near the shore. And, while an abundant supply of plankton cannot be said to be sufficient for high fish productivity, Rostlund cites several icthyological authorities to the effect that a low production of plankton (invariably) implies a low fish production (1952: 44-47).

Summer Island, with its limestone shoals, clearly occupies one of the best topographical areas for high fish production in the Lake Michigan basin. The spring-to-fall water temperatures off Summer Island are determined by the interplay of the deeper bottom currents originating at the 200 foot deep contour of Lake Michigan and the surface currents which seem to follow the prevailing west winds out of Big Bay de Noc. To the southwest of Summer Island and to the northeast of Point Detour there are two areas of "probable bottom upwelling" that produce deep bottom currents which move to the west-southwest and southwest respectively, sweeping the east and south shores of the island (Ayers, Chandler, *et al.*, 1958: Fig. 11, p. 28; Fig. 12, p. 29). Surface currents flow south along the east side of Summer Island from the Point Detour area and join a second set of surface currents moving south-southeast out of Bay de Noc passing just south of the island (Ayers, Chandler, *et al.*, 1958: Fig. 13, p. 30). The combined effect of this set of currents is to temper the extremes of any one of them. From early June through late July the surface temperature of Summer Harbor is 15 to 16 degrees centigrade (ibid.: 21), which could be considered warm water. In the waters west and north of Summer Island these temperatures decrease rapidly with depth, and most water below eight feet ranges from 10 to 12 degrees centigrade (ibid.: 143). No data are available for the waters just south or west of Summer Island.

While these deep water temperatures seem cold enough to prevent maximum girth for individual fish (Rostlund, 1952: 45), they may be responsible for the high productivity of this area within the Great Lakes province. Damann's recent work shows a great increase in the volume of plankton per volume of water off Chicago from mid-April to May and again from early October to November. At Milwaukee this spring rise in plankton endures until late June (Damann, 1966: 11-13). A simple linear regression shows a clear positive correlation between the rise of plankton and temperatures below 54 degrees Fahrenheit (13 degrees centigrade). Damann concludes (1966: 16) that maximum plankton populations in Lake Michigan (where total plankton is composed primarily of diatoms) occur in months with average water temperatures in the vicinity of 50 to 54 degrees Fahrenheit (10 to 12 degrees centigrade). By interpolation, the basic Summer Island shoal waters should exhibit a quite high production of plankton from mid-May through late October.

The shallow gravel to the north and northwest of Summer Island is the preferred bottom for such early spring-spawning fish as lake sturgeon (*Acipenser fulvescens*), yellow walleye (*Stizosted-*

ion vitreum), sauger (*S. canadense*) and burbot (*Lota [lota] lacustris*) (Scott, 1954: 7, 84, 86, 119). Northern pike (*Esox lucius*) and muskellunge (*E. masquinongy*) spawn in midspring in shallow bays, such as Summer Harbor (Scott, 1954: 75-77). The lake whitefish (*Coregonus clupeaformis*) and cisco and menominee (*Leucicthys artedi*) (*L.* sp.) spawn in November, preferably on rocky or gravelly shoals where large numbers of these species are commonly captured (Scott, 1954: 19-22). The various lake trout (*Salvelinus ramaycush*) also spawn on rocky shoals in early November, and are generally found in these same shallow waters with the spring thaw (ibid.: 34-35). To conclude, I would reiterate: Summer Island is unusually poor in terrestrial fauna year round, but has unusually rich lacustrine faunal resources from early spring to November.

II

DESCRIPTION OF EXCAVATIONS

HISTORY OF INVESTIGATIONS

THE Summer Island site, 20 DE 4, is located in the SW 1/4 of the NW 1/4 of Section 27, Township 37 North, Range 19 West in Fairbanks Township, Delta County, Michigan. Geographical coordinates of the site are 45 degrees 34 minutes 14 seconds North Latitude 86 degrees 38 minutes 30 seconds West Longitude.

The land upon which the site is located was originally sold by the United States Government to Thomas Farrell of Escanaba in 1884 and timber rights were given to the Jackson Iron Company in 1885. The land passed through a series of receiverships, mostly for unpaid taxes, but timber rights were sold by the Jackson Company to Cleveland Cliffs Corporation in 1914. In 1948 the land and all rights were purchased for unpaid taxes from the State of Michigan by Percy Penfold of East Jordan, Michigan. As of the summer of 1967 the land was held in probate for the Penfold estate with an option to the property purchased by the Summer Science Corporation, a group of high school and university teachers building a science camp on the island.

The earliest direct reference to the aboriginal site on the island is a passing reference to an extinct village at the mouth of Green Bay on Summer Island (Schoolcraft, 1851) supposedly occupied as late as 1770. A reference to an Indian village site, unoccupied in 1830, is made in the Michigan Pioneer and Historical Collection (MPHC, 1890-1921: XVI, 3). A 1927 copy of a map made by Lucius Lyon, Surveyor General, on September 21, 1848 is located in the Department of Conservation, Lansing. This map indicates a fishing settlement located on the site, but whether occupied or not, whether aboriginal or not, is unstated. None of the subsequent state surveys of Summer Island indicate any site. Hinsdale (1931: 19) mentions a village site at Summer Harbor, but does not specify any archaeological materials and seems to have relied on the information enumerated above.

The earliest archaeological reconaissance of the Summer Island site was by George I. Quimby in the summer of 1959 (Binford and Quimby, 1963: 277-307). Surface collections were made from deflated areas along the north edge of the clearing (Fig. 3) and several test pits were dug to recover aboriginal materials in stratigraphic sequence (Binford and Quimby, 1963: 282). In the summer of 1963 two survey parties from the Museum of Anthropology, The University of Michigan visited the site independently as part of an Upper Peninsula Archaeological Survey. The first party, consisting of Barry Kent and David Griffin, excavated three 5 by 5 foot test pits at various locations throughout the clearing. The second party, consisting of G. Richard Peske and Dan Higgins, excavated a 5 by 10 foot profile trench along the southern edge of the clearing, and also two 3 by 5 foot test pits further north. All three reports (Binford and Quimby, 1963; Kent and Griffin, n.d.; Peske and Higgins, n.d.) indicated that the site appeared to be stratified with the major component being Upper Mississippian similar to that reported by Mason (1966) on the Door Peninsula, Wisconsin. Earlier materials were mentioned by Quimby (Binford and Quimbly, 1963) and stressed by Peske and Higgins (n.d.). In the summer of 1965 James Fitting and John Speth, with a University of Michigan field crew then engaged in excavation of the limestone caves along Burnt Bluff, spent an afternoon making surface collections of lithic material from deflated areas within the Summer Island site. In the late spring of 1967, aided by my wife, I spent a day on Summer Island in preliminary site survey prior to the extensive excavations to be undertaken that summer.

Formal excavations were undertaken at the Summer Island site from July 2 through August 25, 1967, under the sponsorship of a National Science Foundation Grant (GS-1486), "Archaeological Investigations in Michigan" awarded to Dr. James E. Fitting of The University of Michigan. The University of Michigan's Museum of Anthropology field crew, under my direction, consisted of Burton Barnard, Kenneth Carstens, James Driskell, Paul Fellows, and Victor Fitting. We were assisted during the month of August by Robert Luton. From the second to the eleventh of August, twenty high school students, Summer Science Campers, spent four hours a day working on the site under the close supervision of the University field crew. At first this addition to the field crew was more hinderance than assistance but by the end of the period many of these students had acquired proficiency in many excavation techniques and were of real value on the site.

During the fifty-two days the crew was in the field six full days were lost because of rain. A total of four days were lost to excavation in setting up and taking down our camp at the beginning and end of the season, in back-filling the excavations, and in

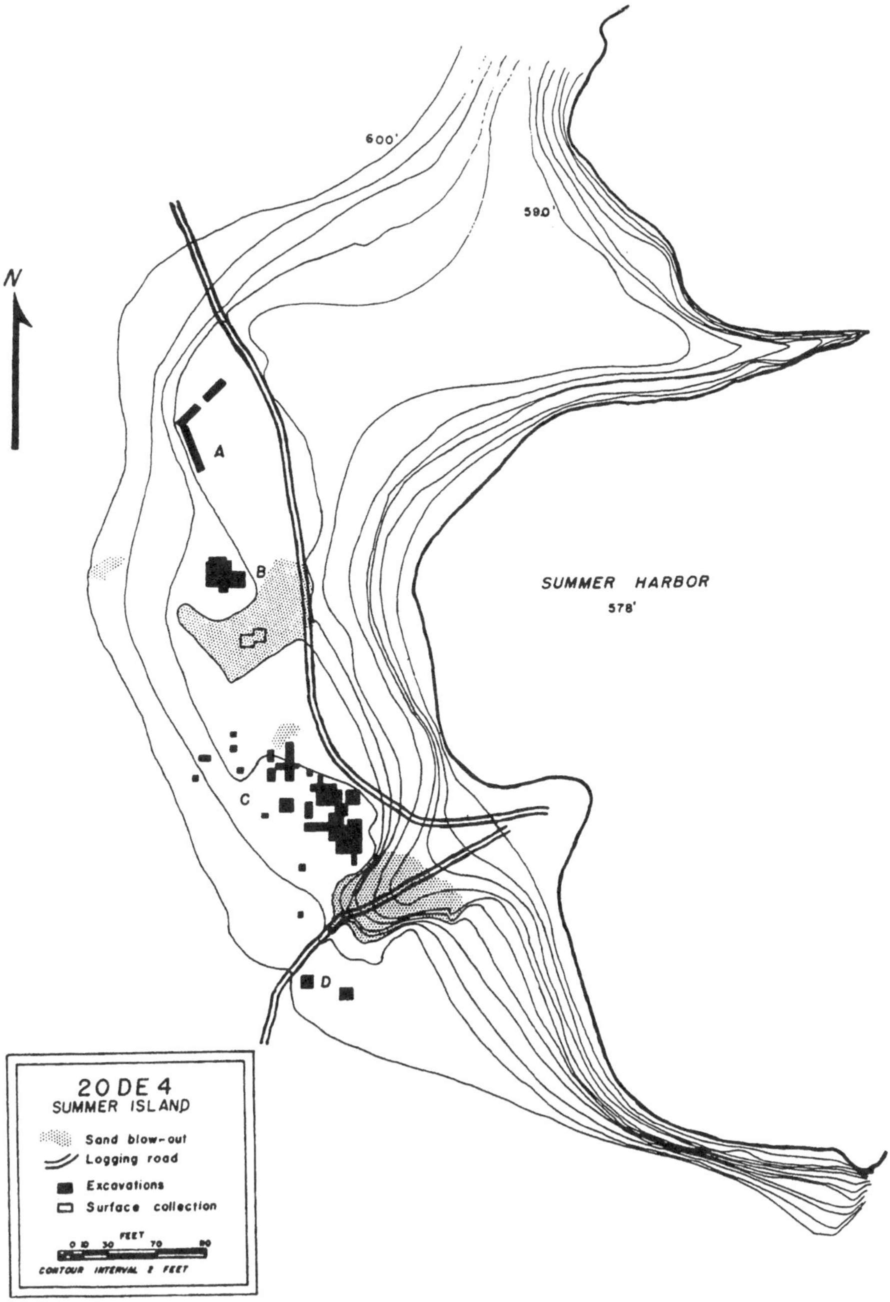

FIG. 3. Map of the Summer Island site.

packing samples for shipment. Several days were virtually lost in an orientation session for the Summer Science Campers, but the camp agreed to take care of dining facilities while the camp was in session and the exchange was considered mutually agreeable.

Of the forty days the full University of Michigan crew spent in the field, the average workday was nine to ten hours long. During that time over 6,500 cubic feet of soils were excavated and sifted, representing about 2.7 cubic feet per man/hour. This figure does not take into account the two weeks' assistance of Robert Luton or the work accomplished with the help of the twenty campers.

Since the time required to dig and sift 2.7 cubic feet of unconsolidated sands is normally under three minutes, it should be apparent that note-taking, profiling, and painstaking troweling occupied most of the time. Perhaps the 20:1 ratio for possible to actual dirt removed is some index of the care taken in excavation.

LOCATION OF SITE AREA

The nature of the clearing within which the Summer Island site is situated limited the choices for locating the initial excavation units. All elevations below 584 feet above sea level along the shore of Summer Harbor were covered with driftwood, dead shad (*Pomolobus pseudoharengus*), and other flotsam, clearly indicating a storm beach. Directly west of this shingle the sand ridges rose rather abruptly to an elevation of 590 feet above sea level. On this 10 per cent grade test pits revealed no artifactual material, either aboriginal or historic. Quimby had stated that the lakeward border of the site was 125 feet inland (Binford and Quimby, 1963: 282) and on my initial survey of the island in early June I had recovered some materials from deflated areas along the southern logging road 120 to 200 feet inland. Following this road to the southwest and testing along its sand banks clearly indicated a decrease in the frequency of aboriginal materials from east to west after a distance of 150 feet from the harbor. The logging road running to the north paralleled the shoreline for about 300 feet at a distance of about 80 feet inland. Several test pits from the 1963 survey crews had indicated that no aboriginal material was located to the east of this road. I found large amounts of aboriginal material on deflated surfaces immediately to the west of this road, and in the northern bank of the southern roadcut at a distance of about 100 feet from the lake. The discrepancy between Quimby's figures and mine may be due to the lowered lake level in August, 1959 (U.S. Army Lake Survey: 577 feet) as the elevations cited (Binford and Quimby, 1963: 282) might indicate.

From these indications, it appeared clear that the site lay to the west of the north logging road. A surface collection of several deflated areas along the 603 foot Nipissing beach (just inside the woods, 200 to 250 feet from the harbor beach) revealed only historic material. A series of historic foundations at the northern edge of the clearing (Fig. 3, Area "A") were tested and revealed sterile sands overlying the bedrock less than one foot below the floors. A large sandblow located about halfway between the southern logging road and the historic foundations yielded a scattering of aboriginal materials.

While the southern roadcut produced prehistoric materials, this was confined to its northern bank and even here was restricted to those portions lying 80 to 150 feet from Summer Harbor. The main prehistoric occupation would thus seem to be located in the 180 by 400 foot area northwest of the logging roads, east of the 603 foot beach ridge, and south of the historic foundations. Within this area were several deep sandblows where surface collections had been made by all the field parties since 1959. A small test pit dug into each of these blows revealed that deflation had removed all overburden above the sterile sands. Since no occupation could be encountered in these blowouts excavations were confined to the vegetation-stabilized surfaces (Fig. 3, Areas "B" and "C") within the area designated above.

SURVEY TECHNIQUE AND RATIONALE

With the aid of a chain saw, a small grove of aspen was cleared from the southwest portion of Area "C" and several cedars were removed between Area "A" and Area "B." A point in the center of Area "C" was chosen to be the basic datum point for elevation and a ten-foot steel rod two inches in diameter, was driven vertically into the ground at this point with much straining and cursing. When the rod encountered increased resistance at a depth of about 8.5 feet a sixteen-pound sledge hammer was used to drive it six inches farther into the ground. The foot of steel rod projecting above the surface resisted any side-to-side movement and, as it could not, at this point, be retracted, the burred end became our bench mark. All depth measurements were tied into the tip of this stake as directly as possible. The true elevation of this bench mark was shot in from lake level on two separate occasions when the winds were minimal. The water table of the Green Bay-Bay de Noc region was obtained from the U.S. Coast Guard Station at Escanaba on both occasions. Subsequent to the field season the Green Bay-Lake Michigan levels for those days and hours were obtained from the U.S. Army Corps of Engineers, U.S. Lake Survey Division, Water Level Section, Detroit. All four figures (which were within 0.15 foot of each other) were averaged to compute the true elevation of our bench mark. In retrospect, our method for creating an artificial datum point was extremely clumsy: only good luck located it in a sterile area of the site.

Prior to any further excavations the site was topographically surveyed with a transit and Philadelphia Rod. With the tripod set up over our bench mark the entire site area could easily be surveyed after cutting a dozen sighting lines through the woods to the west as far as the limestone ridges bounding the site area.

With the transit and a steel tape two three hundred-foot lines were laid out at right angles. These lines ran magnetic north-south and east-west and crossed in the center over the bench mark. This point was given the description 500E500, thus indicating that the origin of the Cartesian coordinate system in which it was located lay 500 feet to the south and 500 feet to the west. Every point on the site could thus be designated by coordinates indicating its distance north and east of the 0-0 point without the confusion of left-right or negative prefixes. Surveyor's stakes were placed along the axes at twenty-foot intervals and a secondary series of perpendicular lines were laid out along these with the transit. All excavation units were subsequently laid out from these twenty-foot points with the aid of the transit, set over one of the stakes, and the one hundred-foot steel tape. It must be emphasized that the use of this coordinate system in no way dictated the location of excavation units as it might appear to some (Mason, 1966: 31). It did provide a system whereby any point on the site could easily be identified as to horizontal location. That is, it provided both a reference for measuring areal distributions within the occupation, as well as providing a number of arbitrary points of elevation for filling in contours on the topographic map.

All excavation units were identified by reference to the coordinates of their southwest corner. The location and elevation of this designator stake was also surveyed in with the transit and rod and all depth measurements within that unit were taken from a line marked on the stake at ground level. Each excavation unit was dug as a vertical-sided 5 by 5, 5 by 10, or 10 by 10 foot unit. Within the larger units all material was segregated in separate 5 by 5 foot squares, so that all excavation units represent a 25 square foot area.

EXCAVATION TECHNIQUE

All units were due to remove each different stratum within the 5 by 5 as a discrete provenience unit. That this ideal was not always attained is principally due to the extremely homogeneous nature of the several strata immediately below the sod. Where any change of soil texture or color was perceived in excavating a unit the surface of the new stratum was not violated and the floor was cleaned horizontally to reveal its extent. All artifacts were left in place on this interface and a plan drawing ("square sheet") of the unit at that depth was made to one-twelfth scale. Depth, below ground level at the southwest corner, was measured for all corners and any other points higher or lower than the rest of the floor. The locations of all in situ artifacts were measured, and they were recorded by separate item numbers on this plan. The floor was watered down with a three gallon garden sprayer and soil colors were compared to those in the Munsell color charts (Munsell, 1954) and the hue and chroma value was then entered on this plan map to indicate differential coloration within the stratum. All post molds and features were measured, recorded, and generally pedestaled until the next level or lower. If it seemed worthwhile the floor was then rewet and a series of two and one-quarter by two and one-quarter inch black-and-white and 35mm diapositive photographs were taken.

All excavated material other than the midden levels and feature contents, was sifted through quarter-inch hardware cloth. The only exception to this was the twelve-foot geological test pit that was dug through the bottom of a previously excavated 10 by 10 foot excavation unit (495E490). The dense middens were sifted through eighth-inch hardware cloth. In both cases, all material remaining in the screens was recovered except for living flora and occasional insect larvae. The entire contents of all features (pits, hearths, large post molds) was subjected to flotation (as suggested by Dr. Hugh C. Cutler) using nearby Summer Harbor for a water source and a 2 and one-half gallon bucket with a bottom of three-sixty-fourths inch brass screening. All flotation material and seventeen 500cc unsifted soil samples were recovered for microscopic analysis.

Wherever a change in soil color or texture indicated that a new stratum had been reached, the material recovered from the surface of the previous stratum to the surface of the newly exposed one was bagged separately and the provenience unit was closed. All provenience units were designed to include material from a single layer of soil within a 5 by 5 foot square. All features or concentrations of bone, chippage, sherds, etc. were given individual provenience designations. Where the edge of the midden cut across a level within an excavation unit, materials from inside and outside the midden area were given separate provenience designations. Where excavation cut down 0.3 feet without encountering any soil change an arbitrary level floor was cut, a square sheet drawn, and a new provenience unit begun. All excavation units were carried down at least 1.5 feet into sterile sands; the early units were cut down over three feet into the sterile sands underlying the site. After each excavation unit had been carried down into the sterile sands the walls were shaved smooth, one-twelfth scale stratigraphic profile drawings were made, and photographs were taken on at least two contiguous walls.

Because of the instability of the drying sand, sections of the wall frequently would slump when depths greater than three feet were reached. This made speed essential in profile drawing. As several units were often being prepared for profile photographs simultaneously it was often impossible to obtain photographs of all profiles. On one occasion I had taken a bracketed series of black-and-white photographs of a section of wall in the 450E540 area, turned around to pick up the slide camera, and turned back to find the wall lying in the bottom of the unit. Because of this tendency to slump, profiles were often drawn during the course of excavation and subsequently corrected against the clean wall upon completion of the unit.

It was this factor that also argued against any attempt to leave large excavated areas of the site open and clean for medium-altitude comprehensive photographs of the house floors. As we were opening new excavation units by following the house patterns encountered previously, disposition of back dirt was also a constant problem. The solution decided upon was to place the sifter tripods over the nearest excavated unit and thus avoid the problem of moving our back dirt piles to excavate the areas beneath them.

LOCATION OF EXCAVATION UNITS

Excavations were begun in Area "C." Two 5 by 10 foot units were opened running north-south at 490E510 and 520E480 in an attempt to locate the midden first encountered in the 1963 surveys. A corner of this occupation was encountered in the north end of 520E480 only. Two 10 by 10 foot units were then excavated at 470E530 and 500E545. The latter unit produced several features containing Oneota-like ceramics, but not a trace of midden. In 470E530 all but the extreme southwest corner yielded a densely occupied midden at a depth of about 1.5 feet. The edges of this midden were quite easy to see (Pl. I, *a*) as they showed black against the underlying light gray or very pale brown sands; furthermore, the midden produced large amounts of artifacts, fire-cracted rock, and animal bone, while the surrounding sands were nearly sterile. A series of 10 by 10 foot units was excavated following this dark midden stratum to the north and east. While these excavations were in progress in the large block of eastern Area "C," test pits were excavated to the south of the logging road (Fig. 3, Area "D"). These excavations, like those in Area "A," recovered no aboriginal material in situ. A series of 5 by 5 foot units were excavated to the west of and upon the Nipissing beach ridge (not indicated on map). These units, as well as units in the southwestern portion of Area "C," produced a thin mixture of Oneota and historic artifacts but no indications of the midden or earlier-looking materials. A 5 by 30 trench was opened running north from 520E480 in the northwestern part of Area "C," uncovering a second area of midden. This northern midden area was traced to the west through a series of 5 by 5 and 5 by 10 foot units, but time did not permit intensive excavation.

To the north of the surface-collected blow out, a 10 by 10 foot excavation unit was opened on a level portion of vegetation-stabilized dune sand (Area "B"). A hearth (Feature 30) and a double line of post molds were encountered in a quasi-midden level at a depth of 1.0 ft. This post mold line was followed to the east and then to the north where it recurved upon itself to form an oval, approximately 12 by 20 feet in size, enclosing two hearths and a shallow pit. Lack of time and personnel prevented extensive excavation in the area immediately northwest of this structure in Area "B," but several 3 by 5 foot test pits located between Area "B" and the Nipissing beach to the west, and between Areas "A" and "B," proved sterile beneath the historic artifact-filled humus.

In general, excavations were concentrated in Area "C" where the largest vegetation-stabilized surface existed, and where the early occupation of the site was found to be most intensive. The ultimate objective was to define the limits of the site by extensive small-sized test excavations while large-scale, intensive excavation was undertaken in those areas of the site which showed promise of revealing complete structures and living areas with large quantities of in situ material. It was hoped that such an excavation program would lend itself to the analysis of horizontal as well as vertical distribution of artifacts at the site. It is these analyses that occupy much of this thesis.

III

GEOMORPHOLOGY OF THE SITE

METHODS OF COLLECTION AND ANALYSIS

WHILE complete excavation profiles were never open simultaneously across the entire site, linear serial samples were taken at 0.2 foot intervals from a number of excavation units along the same north-south or east-west axis as these units were excavated. A geological test pit, 10 by 10 feet, was excavated through the floor of excavation unit 495E490. Because of the danger of slumping the geological test pit was stepped-down to 5 by 5 feet below depths of six feet (Fig. 4). Due to the narrowness of this excavation the soil samples, taken vertically every half foot, actually represent an unmixed number of channel samples which is preferable where average characteristics of several superimposed formations are to be determined (Krumbein and Pettijohn, 1938: 14-16). Samples consisted of two 500cc volumes from different portions of the same stratum or one liter samples in the dipping bedded sands. This is the sample size advised by Wentworth for sediments ranging from 0.0625mm to 4.0mm (ibid.: 32). Following Krumbein's suggestion, each field sample was air-dried for several weeks in a warm open oven, then crushed with a rubber-tipped pestle and "hand-quartered" to obtain an acceptable test sample size without introducing any bias (ibid.: 44, 70-75). Each test sample was then shaken for 10 minutes on an automatic Ro-Tap shaker through a column of woven wire mesh sieves, stacked so as to conform to the $\sqrt{2}$ modified Wentworth (1922) grade scale with the coarsest mesh at the top of the column and a pan at the base (ibid.: 124-26, 138, 139). This modified grade scale has class limits which agree well with certain distinctions between traction and suspension loads (ibid.: 80). The results of these tests are shown in Table II by percentage of total sample weight.

Readings of pH were obtained on The University of Michigan's School of Natural Resources' pH meter but are probably not accurate to more than two-tenths. If the geological profile of the deep unit can be taken as representative of the entire site (or at least of Area "C") the soils seem to range from medium acid to

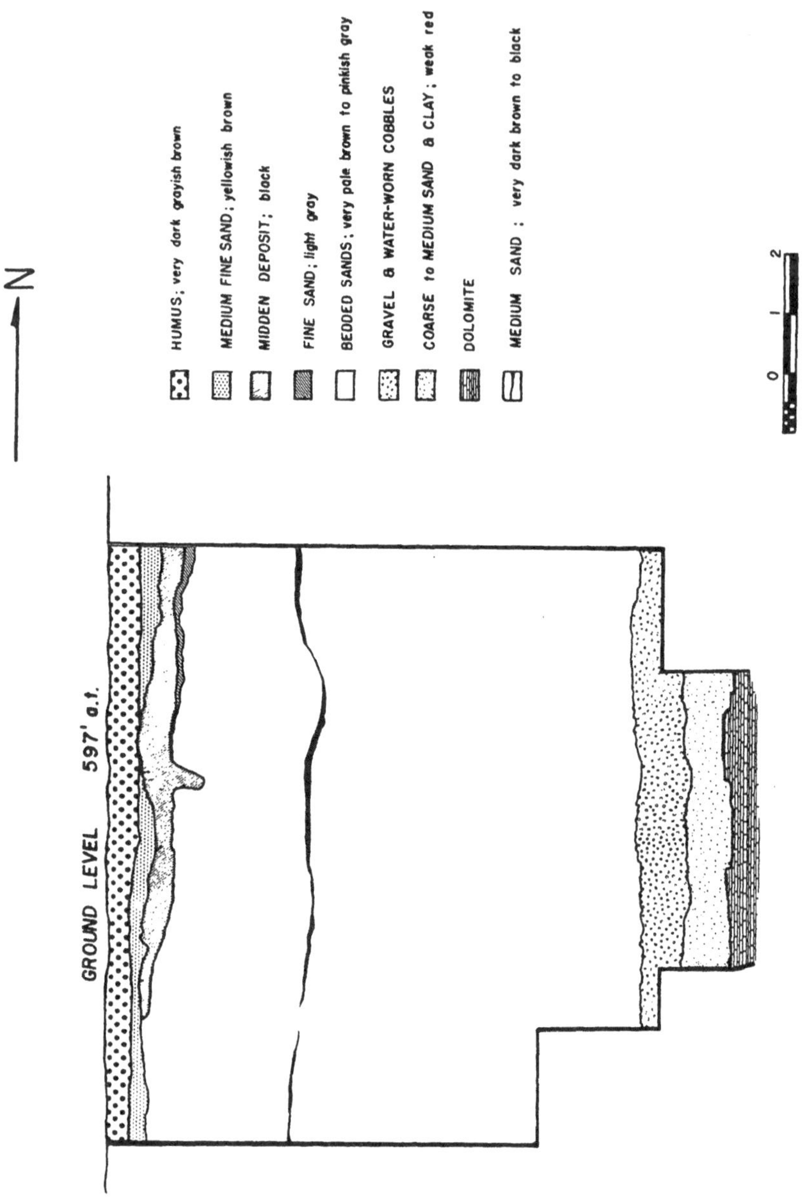

FIG. 4. Stratigraphic profile of geological test pit.

moderately alkaline (*USDA*, 1962: 235). Three distinct areas of acidity were noted. These occurred at the surface and at depths of about one foot and three feet. These correspond to the present thin meadow humus, the earliest occupational level, and the thin intermittent lens of very dark brown to black sands. The highest alkalinity occurred at the base of the column, where the sediments contain fair amounts of limestone pebbles.

Microscopic analysis of each test sample was carried out with a binocular microscope and a 150x lens. In each sample 100 grains were counted and examined to determine the ratio of quartz to non-quartz minerals, analysis of shape, degree of roundness, and surface texture based on visual comparison with a simplified set of standards as described by Trowbridge and Mortimore (*in* Krumbein and Pettijohn, 1938: 280, 290). A detailed description of the mineralogical analyses can be found in Brose (n.d.). The results of these analyses will be referred to in the following description of depositional units.

SEQUENCE OF DEPOSITIONAL UNITS

Unit A.—Depth of sample: Below 10.0 feet at 500E500. This basal unit consisted of jointed blocks of Engadine Dolomite, the surface of the bedrock underlying Pleistocene deposits in this portion of Summer Island. The surface of the dolomite was rather smooth and showed no clear weathering interface although it appeared waterworn.

Unit B.—Depth of sample: 9.3 to 9.9 feet below ground surface at 500E500. This unit consisted of red to brownish pink coarse to medium sand and clay with some rounded pebbles and cobbles of exotic igneous rock and native dolomites and shales. The pH of this deposit was rather basic, probably due to the hydrolysis involving the very abundant alkaline dolomites (cf. Bunting, 1965: 92). The degree of sorting present in this unit closely approximated values derived from Valders drift in eastern Wisconsin (Lee, Janke and Beaver, 1962: 154-55) and was also quite close to particle-size distribution curves from other glacial drift samples in Delta County (Sinclair, 1960: 42-43). The lack of any definite skewness in sorting argued against water redeposition for this deposit. The deposit probably represented the truncated base of water-washed Valders till left by the retreat of this glacial stage at about B.P. 9500.

Unit C.—This unit consisted of gravel and water-worn cobbles of Engadine and Burnt Bluff Dolomite in a matrix of pinkish gray coarse to medium sands lying conformably upon the clayey till. No bedding was observable in this unit although several large flat cobbles all had similar orientation with their longest axis north-south, all dipping slightly to the east. Particle-size distribution curves from this unit (Fig. 5) indicated the median grain size is 0.50-0.250mm but highly skewed to the medium coarse grain size. Friedman (1961: 514-29) has shown that plotting mean grain size against skewness on a Phi Scale, results in a clear separation of beach and dune sands. In Figure 6 the culturally sterile test samples from 500E500 are so plotted. The sediments from depositional Unit C were clearly quite representative of beach sands. A test of these samples using settling velocities of light and heavy minerals (Hand, 1967: 514-20) confirmed this interpretation. The low frequencies of silts and clays confirmed the interpretation that this unit represented a near-beach deposit originating as an offshore bar derived from locally weathered dolomites and reworked glacial till. The surface of this deposit, at about 589 feet above sea level corresponds to no known beach line. It probably represents the truncated portion of a Lake Alqonquian deposit.

Unit D.—This unit consisted of foreset beds of very pale brown medium sands dipping to the east at about 15 to 25 degrees. As Figure 6 indicates, there are probably the result of the deposition of reworked Unit C deposits at some offshore point during the rise to Lake Nipissing maximum levels. These sediments were probably reworked and sorted by a rapid rise of lake waters from the Lake Chippewa low water stage rather than by erosional rainwater.

Unit E.—This depositional unit consisted of five to eight cross-bedded lenses of very pale brown medium sands lying conformably upon Unit D. The foreset beds of Unit E dipped gently to the east at less than a 10 degree angle from horizontal; the backset beds were practically level. All lenses within this unit represent reworked beach deposits (Fig. 6). The location of primary sediments was a sand dune upon which soil genesis was occurring. The nature of the bedding, the minerals present, the analysis of shape and surface texture, and the distribution of particle size all agree with the interpretation of this unit as an immediate offshore beach deposit during a period of minor water level fluctuations; probably deposited at the time of the Lake Nipissing maximum.

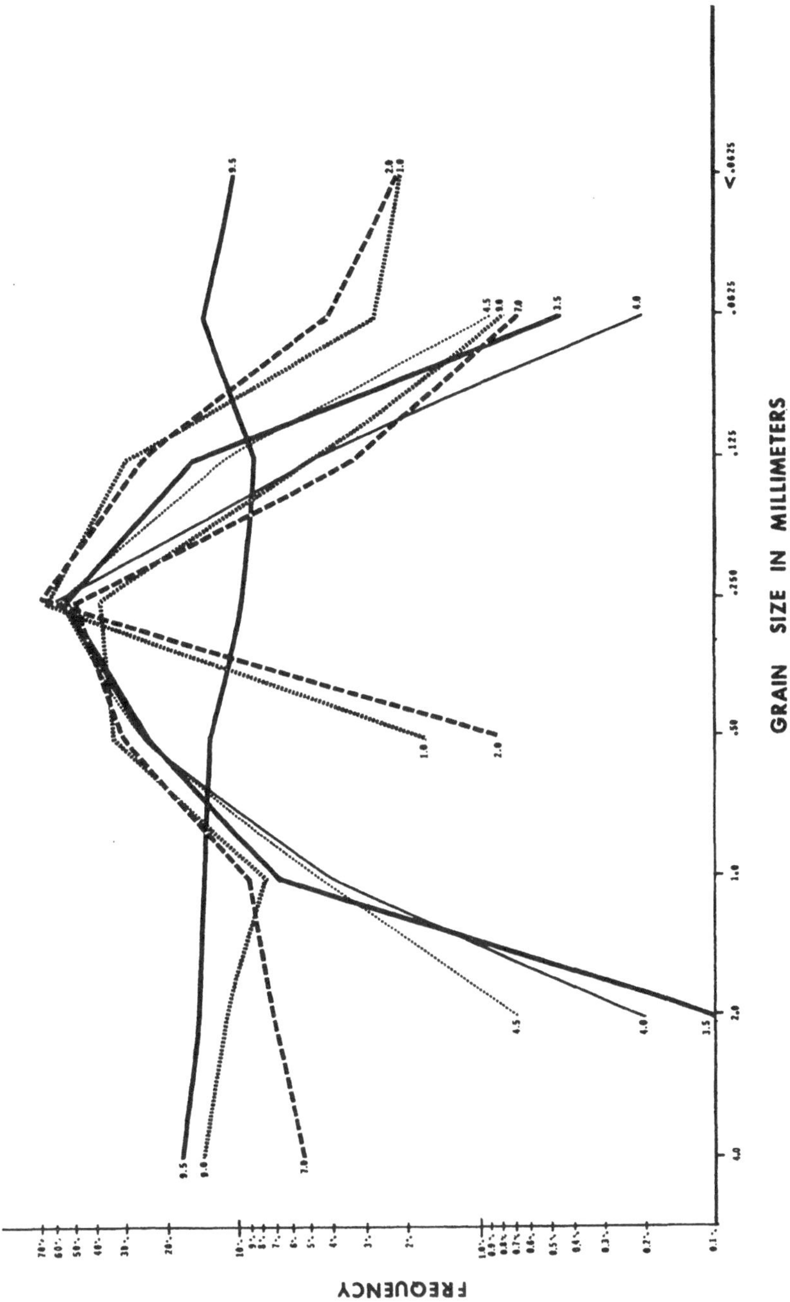

FIG. 5. Distribution of soil sample grain sizes.

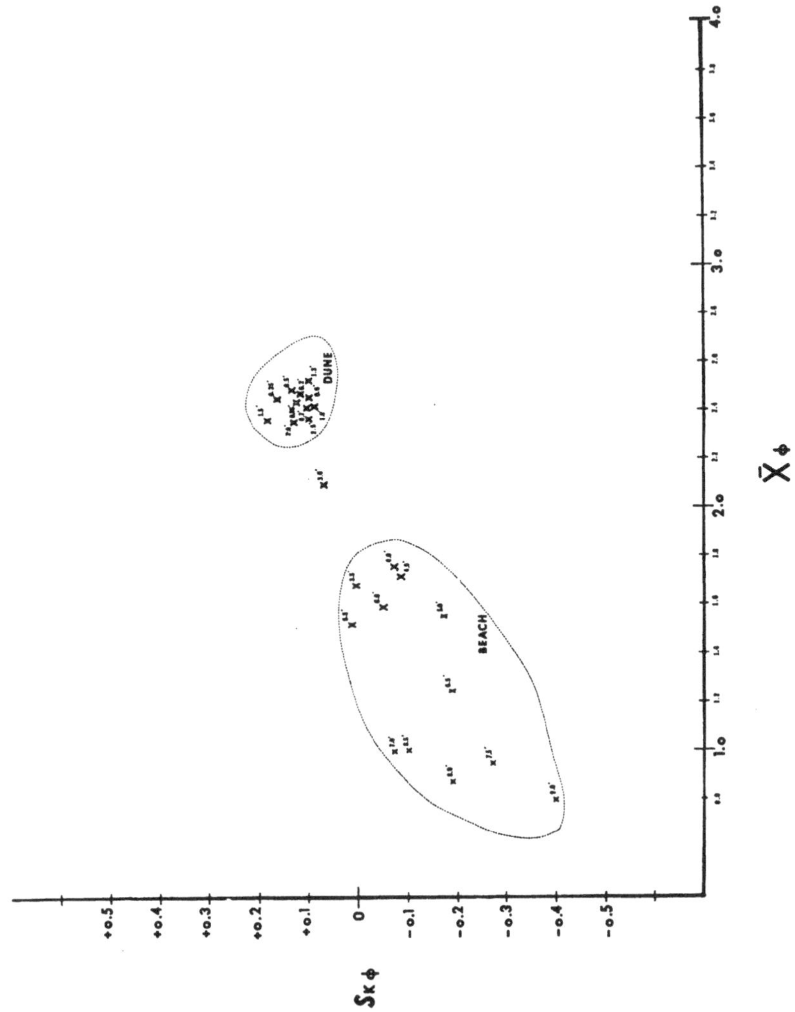

FIG. 6. Mean grain size plotted against skewness in soil samples.

Unit F.—This unit consisted of three to seven foreset beds of medium to medium-fine sands, dipping down to the east at about a 10 degree angle from horizontal. The upper portion of this unit was a pinkish gray which graded to a brownish gray at the bottom. This unit rested conformably upon depositional Unit E. This unit would seem to represent reworked sediments, originally deposited as an onshore dune, and subsequently redeposited just offshore as beach sands. With the lowering of lake levels to below 594 feet above sea level a period of soil genesis occurred with illuviation from the upper ($A2_b$) zone of this unit and illuviation in the lower (B_b) zone of water soluble alkaline and ferrous minerals. The secondary deposition of these sediments can thus be attributed to wave action of an Algoma Lake Stage, and the subsequent soil horizonation to a post-Algoma period some time after 1000 B.C.

Unit G.—This unit consisted of an intermittent lens of dark brown to black medium sands, all sloping up from a center located in mid-Area "B" which lay at an elevation of about 594 to 595 feet above sea level. Grain shapes seemed rather well distributed from angular to round and a plot of X against Sk did not clearly indicate beach or dune deposition. A reasonable interpretation of this unit would be that it represents the surface of secondary beach deposits (e.g., unit F) with some development of soil zoning as a podzolic $A1_b$ horizon, as vegetation colonized a damp depression on the backslopes of a beach dune. With further dropping of the water table the area was denuded of cover, some degree of aeolian sorting took place, and eventually deflation occurred on the higher or more exposed portions.

Unit H.--This unit consisted of four to five cross-bedded lenses of very pale light brown medium to medium-fine sands. Bedding was quite irregular across the site but all beds had a slope of 10-15 degrees from horizontal. Nearly three-fourths of all grains showed frosted or pitted surfaces and 70 per cent were angular to subangular. The unit overlay unit G where it existed, otherwise, it lay directly upon the surface of unit F. This unit clearly represents the deposition of shifting dune sands, derived from various sources, during a period of variable effective winds (see Flint, 1957: 178-80). It is not possible from the available data to determine either the shape of the resultant dunes or the direction of prevailing winds (ibid.). The deposition of this unit seems to have leveled the backslope depression evident during the deposition of unit G.

Unit I.—This unit consisted of light brown to yellowish brown cross-bedded sands. In all respects except non-quartz mineral frequencies it was virtually identical to unit H. In terms of depositional environment this unit would seem to represent a continuation of the shifting-dune formation evidenced by unit H. The mineralogical difference may further indicate that this unit represents an illuviation zone of B_{2b} horizon in the development of a podzolic soil (Bunting, 1965: 95-97).

Unit J.—This unit consisted of two foreset beds of light gray to very pale brown medium sands dipping down to the northeast at an angle of about five degrees. This depositional unit was practically neutral in acidity and seems to represent the illuviation zone of a soil profile. This is possibly an A_{2b} horizon of a podzolic soil (USDA, 1962: 175; Bunting, 1965: 148), but it may not be a natural soil horizon at all. Depositional units H, I, and J occurred at all areas of the site with similar scalar and vector characteristics (see Brose, 1965: 71). Their peculiar pH and mineralogical characteristics, indicative of some degree of soil genesis, were limited to their being overlain by depositional unit K. In terms of deposition, unit J was the last unit on the site that predated human occupation. It was not, however, unaltered by human activity. While no true A_o podzol horizon seems to have developed upon the surface of unit J, the cultural deposition of the highly organic midden (unit K) seems to have taken the place of an A_o or A_H horizon (Soil Survey Manual, 1962: 257; Bunting, 1965: 149) and initiated the podzolization of units H through J.

Unit K.—This unit consisted of three discontinuous but homogeneous levels of medium sands, overlying the aforementioned soil genesis in units H-J with some evidence of disconformity. The sands of unit K were stained black by organic materials and the unit showed a large amount of humic acid when treated with 3N sodium hydroxide solution. Examination with an 8x lens revealed fragments of bone, mollusk shell, charcoal, charred organic materials, small fragments of fire ceramics, granules of fire-cracked igneous rock, and very small chips of chert, flint, chalcedony, jasper, and agate.

Large amounts of grit-tempered pottery, worked and unworked animal bone, chipped-stone tools and debitage, fire-cracked igneous rock, and charcoal were found in this matrix, often in large concentrations but also randomly distributed throughout the unit. This depositional unit frequently intruded into units below as pits or postholes (Figs. 7, 8). In areal extent unit K was

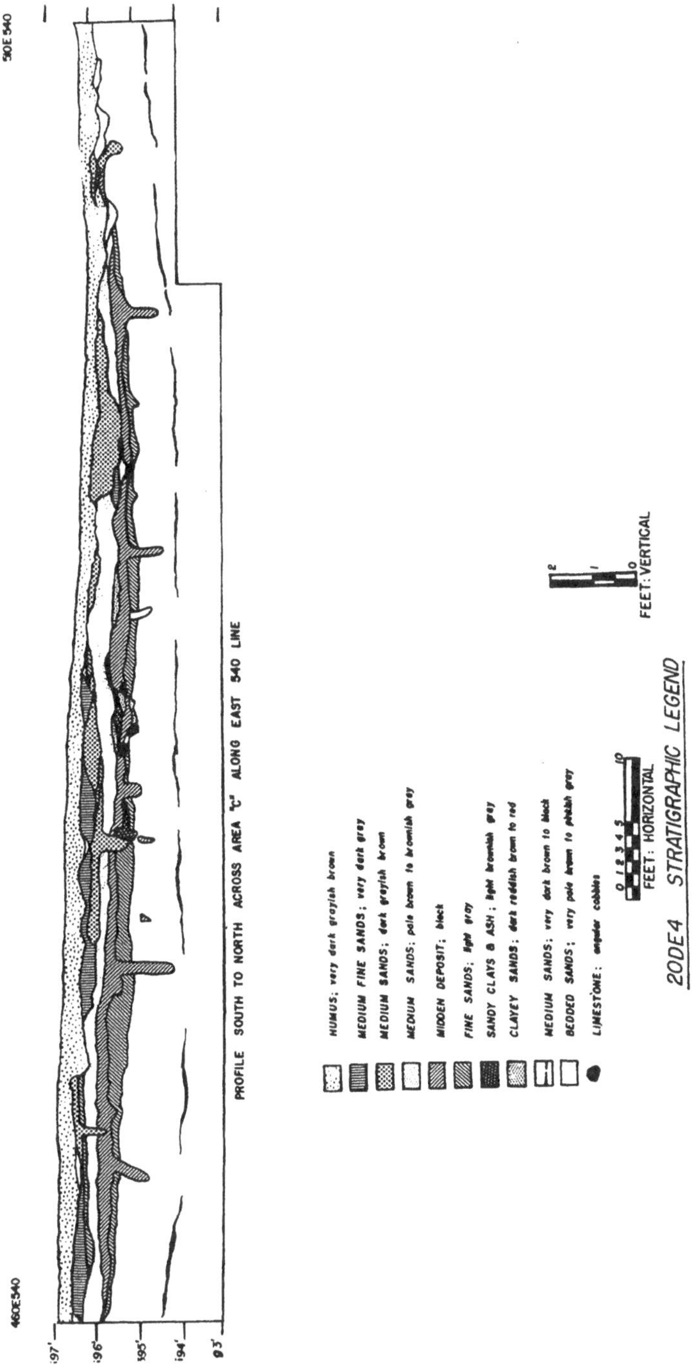

FIG. 7. North-South stratigraphic profile across Area "C."

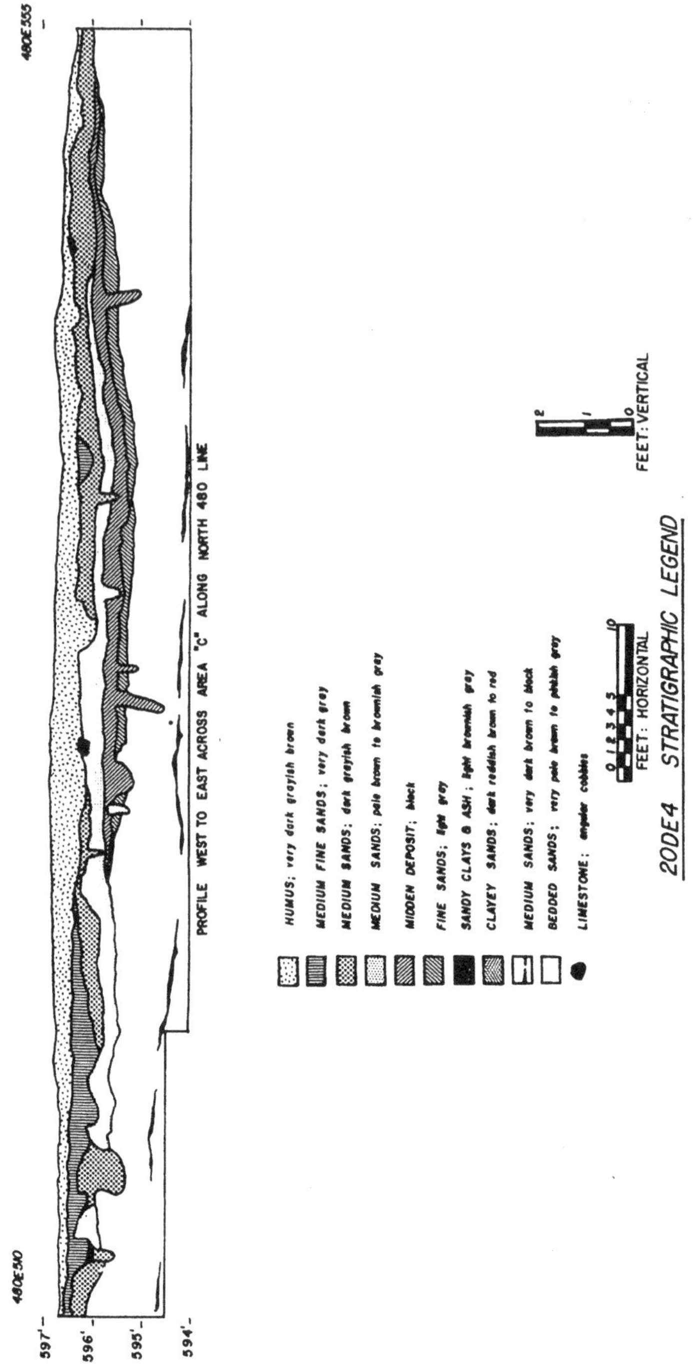

FIG. 8. East-West stratigraphic profile across Area "C."

found only in Area "C" of the site. Its maximum thickness was 0.4 feet in the centers of rather uniform level lenses which thinned out abruptly at the edges (Fig. 4).

It seems quite obvious that this unit does not represent a natural level of deposition: it is a sheet midden indicating the extent of intensive human occupation at the site. Windblown sand comprised about half of this deposit, the remainder being culturally introduced materials present in the form of refuse on the living-floors.

Unit L.—This unit consisted of a discontinuous level of pale brown to brownish gray medium sands occurring in thin lenses throughout Area "C." Although no bedding was evident the analysis of grain shape and surface texture agrees with the $X\phi$-$Sk\phi$ plot showing this unit had been deposited by wind action. Several lenses representing this depositional unit were thicker along their southeastern edges probably thus indicating the source of these sediments was the sand beach along Summer Harbor. The unit was generally culturally sterile and represents the formation of a backslope dune after the abandonment of the occupation of unit K, but with no major intervening erosional hiatus.

Unit M.—This unit consisted of several lenses of dark grayish-brown medium sands lying unconformably upon the surface of unit L. The pH was slightly acidic which, with the present carbonate and felspar clay minerals, indicated that this unit may have once represented an incipient podzolic A_3 horizon (Bunting, 1965: 151) which has since been subjected to an unusual amount of intrusive organic activity. This unit contained a fair amount of shell-tempered pottery, fire-cracked igneous rock, and chert implements and debitage. Very little worked bone was present in this unit and faunal remains, in general, were scanty. Pits and postholes originating in this unit intruded as deep as unit I in some cases.

Microscopic and distribution analyses of particles from this unit indicated aeolian redeposition of originally lacustrine deposits on the slightly deflated surface of unit L.

Unit N.—This unit consisted of yellowish-brown to very dark brown medium-fine sands occurring in cross-bedded lenses discontinuously across the site in both Area "B" and Area "C." The depositional environment seems to have been quite similar to the present sandy meadow with deflated areas, on the backslopes of the aeolian dune formation. Small dark lenses within this unit probably indicate local vegetation-stabilized areas. Cultural materials incorporated into this unit during its formation include both grit-tempered pottery, chipped flint projectile points and debitage, and historic trade goods. Few intrusions into lower levels originating in this unit were noted in Area "C" although both pits and postholes were plentiful in Area "B."

Immediately above depositional unit N (where it occurred) and across the entire site south of Area "A" at depths of 0.3 to 0.5 feet below present ground level, a clear plow scar interface had leveled the site area. At 490E540 this interface lay 0.4 feet below the ground surface. The plow scars were rather shallow with an average trough- to crest-height of 0.15 feet. The furrows ran northwest-southeast and frequently truncated higher portions of unit N.

Unit O.—This unit consisted of the present humus developing on dark brown medium sands. It represents the upper portions of units M and N disturbed by plowing with subsequent deflation, aeolian redeposition, and historic logging operations. Cultural materials in this matrix (from the base of the plow scars to the surface of the ground) include a mixture of all antecedent occupations and much nineteenth century material. These sediments are too badly disturbed to infer depositional environment but it should have been similar to present conditions. The surface of the ground is presently sporadically covered with thin meadow vegetation.

PART II

THE MIDDLE WOODLAND COMPONENT

IV

THE NATURE OF THE COMPONENT

PREDATING the first human occupation, the site must have looked topographically much as it does at present (Pl. I, *a*, *b*): a fairly level sandy meadow dipped down from the edge of the forest to the rather steep sand bank which dropped about twelve feet to a wide sand beach running for fifty yards along the harbor. It was on a sporadically herb stabilized dune surface (depositional unit J) along the southern margin of the meadow, that the initial occupation of the site took place.

This occupation is best evidenced by the deposition of a dense midden (unit K) which occurred as three separate lenses within Area "C" (Fig. 9). All of these midden lenses lay at elevations of from 595 to 596 feet above sea level, and appeared to occupy slight depressions on the surface of the culturally sterile meadow-covered sands (Figs. 7 and 8). Such areas often retain moisture slightly longer than the more elevated portions of well-drained sand dune deposits, and are commonly colonized by beach grasses and rushes (Odum, 1959: 260-61). The three definite midden lenses were all roughly oval shaped and lay in an arc of about 95 degrees running from southeast to northwest. The southeasternmost lens was the largest and averaged twenty-five feet east-west by sixty feet north-south. The central midden lens was not thoroughly excavated but seemed to be about twenty feet north-south by about fifteen feet east-west. The third midden lens associated with this component was defined by several test pits in northwestern Area "C" to be about fifteen feet east-west by about twenty feet north-south. All three occupied the same stratigraphic provenience and were remarkably similar in artifact content. All were sealed by the thin brown aeolian sands of depositional unit L and rested upon the sterile sands of unit J. No overlapping of midden lenses occurred, and since sherds recovered from one lens could often be fitted to shreds recovered from one of the other lenses their simultaneous occupation was postulated. All lenses were from 0.2 to 0.4 feet thick and ended rather abruptly on their margins. No stratigraphic break occurred within any of these lenses.

Within each of these midden lenses post molds originated. These stood out clearly from the underlying pale sands (Pl. II, *b*,

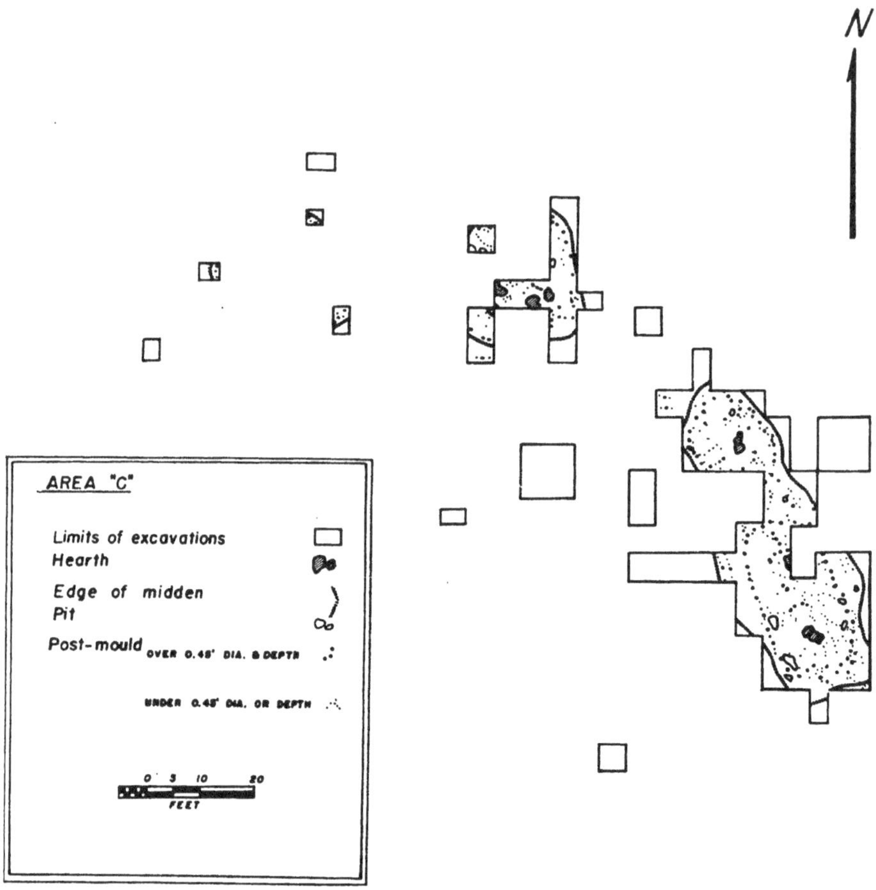

FIG. 9. Postmold patterns originating at the Middle Woodland level.

c). After the midden was removed by troweling the floor was shaved level to reveal the patterns taken by these post molds (Fig. 9). The post molds, caused by the in situ decay of wooden posts, are probably somewhat larger than the original size of the post because of organic staining of the surrounding sands. Some correction factor clearly should be applied to post mold measurements to obtain the actual dimensions of the post. In the absence of any reported experimental factor, I would estimate the true diameter of the post to be about 85 per cent that of the post mold diameter. This estimate is based on discussions with surveyors who have relocated old boundary marker stakes. It is not too reliable, however, and I will refer in all subsequent measurements to the post mold itself although the need for some correction should be kept in mind. The distribution of post mold

TABLE 2

DISTRIBUTION OF POST MOLD DIAMETERS IN THE MIDDLE WOODLAND COMPONENT

Class Limits (In Feet)	Number of Occurrences
< 0.16	9
0.16-0.25	47
0.26-0.35	89
0.36-0.45	23
0.46-0.55	24
0.56-0.65	49
0.66-0.75	33
0.76-0.85	10
0.86-0.95	3
0.96-1.05	2
> 1.06	1
	290

TABLE 3

MIDDLE WOODLAND POST MOLD SIZE AGAINST LOCATION

Post Mold	External Wall O/E	Other O/E	Total
Over 0.45 ft. in diameter and depth	96/48.3	26/73.7	122
Under 0.45 ft. in diameter or depth	19/66.5	149/101.5	168
TOTAL	115	175	290

$\chi^2 = 126.1$
df = 1
$p << .001$
$\phi^2 = .4358$

diameters in the Middle Woodland occupation at the site displayed a clear bimodality (Table 2). The two mean post mold diameters fall at 0.23 feet and 0.64 feet. The pattern made by the larger post molds was easiest to see in the southeastern lens where two oval structures could be traced. Although large post molds occasionally occurred in subsidiary structures or inside the large structures (Fig. 9), it is evident from Table 3 that there was a very definite tendency to use these large posts as external wall construction of the structures in the central and northwestern

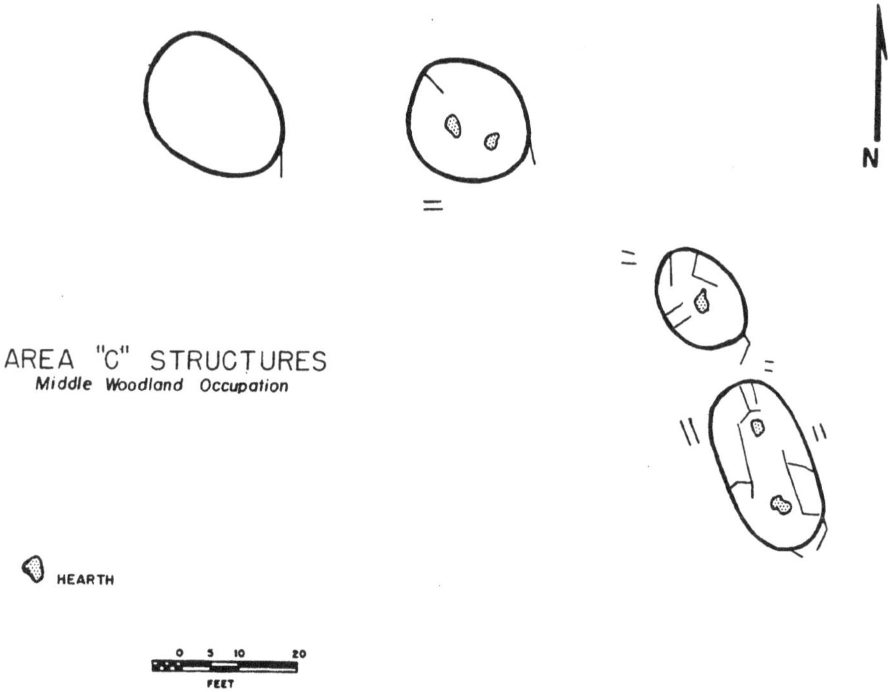

FIG. 10. Reconstruction of Middle Woodland structures.

midden lenses can be made. It seems reasonable to inrer that four closed structures with a number of smaller open structures existed during this period of occupation (Fig. 10). Only two post molds showed any signs of replacement of the original posts. Both involved the replacement of a small interior post by a larger one, and revealed a faint post mold about 0.35 feet in diameter resulting in a two-toned figure eight. The direct replacement of a smaller post for a larger one would have been totally unstable. It is possible that several other large-for-small post replacements took place with no subsequent archaeological traces. Such post replacement seems to be more in the nature of post-construction correction than repair that would probably have utilized replacement materials of similar size to the original. Accordingly, there is no evidence for replacement due to deterioration represented in these structures. Given the average figure of four or five years for the replacement of untreated fence posts on the Garden Peninsula, five miles away (Lester DeVet, personal communication), I would assume that this component at the site represents no more than two or three years' occupation.

With little difficulty the four enclosed structures of Area "C" can be considered houses. The southern house in the southeastern midden lens (house I) was elliptical with its northwest-southeast axis about twenty-nine feet long and about twelve feet wide. At the foci of this ellipse two hearths were located. Associated with this house were two parallel rows of posts to the east and northwest representing open structures designated ancillary structures I_A and I_B respectively. Structure I_A was four feet long and two feet wide. Structure I_B was five feet long and two feet wide.

Eight feet to the north-northwest of house I, within the same midden lens, was house II; it was oval in shape with a northwest-southeast axis eighteen feet long and about twelve feet wide. A single hearth was located just south of the center. Associated with this house to the southeast and northwest were ancillary structures II_A and II_B respectively. Structure II_A was two feet long and two feet wide. Structure II_B was four feet long and two feet wide.

Thirty-two feet to the northwest of house II, in the central midden lens, house III was located. This house seemed to be ellipsoid in shape with the northwest-southeast axis probably about twenty-two feet long and about sixteen feet wide. Two hearths were located just south of the foci of this ellipsoid. Associated with this house was ancillary structure III_A. Like the others, it was composed of a double line of posts about four feet long and two feet apart. While imperfectly known, structure IV was located in the northwestern midden lens about twenty feet west of structure III. No associated subsidiary structures were recovered. No hearths were found in the excavated marginal portions of this structure, nor are any to be expected so near an external wall. If size can be taken as any indication, this structure should contain one hearth.

It should occasion no great surprise that the limits of the midden did not correspond precisely with the house walls. Numerous examples of Upper Paleolithic settlements are known where there is a sharp "edge" to cultural materials lying outside the actual walls of a structure. In some places the midden outside the dwelling is denser than comparable areas within the structures (Grigor'ev, 1967: 346). The most acceptable explanation for the distribution of these midden lenses at the Summer

Island site is to be first sought in the distribution of the pre-occupation vegetation (see page 33). The higher areas between midden lenses would have been subjected to stronger winds as well as less moisture and therefore supported far less vegetation (see Odum, 1959; Grigor'ev, 1967). Second, Schoolcraft reports that among the Ojibwa the usual lodge was an eliptical/oval frame-work of poles tied together at the top and covered with bark. Around the border of the lodge on the ground, twigs of spruce or hemlock were strewn, upon which skins were often spread for beds (cited in Morgan, 1881: 113). Without implying any ethno-linguistic alignment, this seems to parallel the situation seen in the structures of Summer Island's Middle Woodland component. Add to this the tendency for sheet runoff to accumulate soluble organic compounds in depressions (USDA, 1962: 255), and the distribution of the midden lens edges beyond the borders of the houses is almost expectable. It may also be the case that these midden areas outside the houses represent the areas of the most intense human activity during this occupation. From this point of view they may serve to limit areas of constant traffic, crushing the extant vegetation and adding large amounts of exotic organic materials. This assumption will be returned to later when efforts are made to derive estimates of the population from the archae-ological remains along lines suggested by Cook and Heizer (1965).

V

CERAMICS

GENERAL APPROACH

FROM the 1967 excavations a total of 4451 sherds (wt. = 6347 grams) were recovered within the Middle Woodland levels of the site. An additional 163 rimsherds and 209 decorated bodysherds typologically assignable to this occupation were recovered from overlying levels. In the following discussions of horizontal distribution only those sherds recovered in position within their original levels of deposition will be considered. The distribution of ceramics from the Middle Woodland levels of the site are shown in Table 4 by types and varieties. As Table 5 demonstrates, the Middle Woodland ceramics from succeeding levels of the site do not differ significantly enough to raise any suggestion that they are not drawn from the same population.

In analyzing this sample, rim and bodysherds were merged to form a minimum number of vessels. Similar rimsherds and bodysherds were tested against these vessels and considered a separate vessel only if two or more attributes differed. This was considerably simplified by several characteristics exhibited by the ceramics from the Middle Woodland component at Summer Island: all vessels were plain-surfaced below the shoulder. Below the exterior lip all vessels exhibited only a single decorative technique exclusive of a single horizontal row of punctates just above the shoulder. Although angle and pressure of application varied, only a single implement seems to have been employed in the decoration of any one vessel. Finally, we were fortunate in being able to reconstruct at least one vessel, of almost all types, from the lip to well below the shoulder.

All vessels displaying similar rim profiles, lip treatment, decorative motif, decorative technique, and design element, were considered to represent a single type. Where only decorative motif or decorative technique differed varieties of this type were proposed. Where application of design elements seemed to show clear differences, separate groups within the variety were set up (Table 6). This method for segregating ceramic decoration may seem needlessly compartmentalized. Neither does it clearly

TABLE 4

CERAMICS FROM MIDDLE WOODLAND COMPONENT

Ceramic Variety	Rim-Sherds	Decorated Bodysherds	Minimal No. of Vessels	Percentage of Minimal Vessels	No. of All Assignable Sherds	Percentage of Assignable Sherds	Mean Vessel Occurrence Per Excavation Unit
Banked Stamp, plain	42	135	21	15.8	177	12.5	1.187
Banked Stamp, narrow	22	51	14	10.5	73	5.3	0.679
Plain, Unbossed, notched	89	---	13	9.8	89	6.3	0.418
Banked Stamp, dentate	28	87	13	9.8	105	7.3	0.396
Dragged Stamp, dentate	42	156	12	9.1	198	13.9	0.343
Dragged Stamp, plain	87	342	11	8.4	429	30.4	0.291
Banked Punctate, fingernail	7	26	11	8.4	33	2.3	0.261
Braided Cord linear stamped	15	37	8	5.9	52	3.9	0.269
Banked Stamp, plain, chevron	7	26	6	4.5	33	2.3	0.276
Dentate tool linear stamped	8	14	5	3.7	22	1.5	0.090
Banked Stamp, narrow, bedded	12	52	5	3.7	64	4.8	0.224
Linear Incised, interrupted	13	17	4	2.9	30	2.2	0.030
Miscellaneous Stamped	12	30	4	2.9	42	2.9	0.007

Linear Incised, simple criss-cross	3	32	3	2.2	22	1.5	0.090
Indeterminate	. . .	21	3	2.2	21	1.4	0.060
TOTALS	387	1026	133	99.8	1390	98.5	X = 0.309

Unassignable plain bodysherds—2989
Total sherds from component—4451

TABLE 5

MIDDLE WOODLAND CERAMICS BY PERCENTAGE OF VESSEL FROM COMPONENT

Ceramic Variety, O/E	Middle Woodland	Mississippian	Late Woodland	Historic	Total
Banked Stamp, plain	16/15.7	18/15.7	14/15.7	15/15.7	63
Banked stamp, narrow	11/12	12/12	12/12	13/12	48
Plain, unbossed, notched	10/10.3	11/10.3	9/10.3	11/.03	41
Banked Stamp, dentate	10/11.7	12/11.7	13/11.7	12/11.7	47
Dragged Stamp, dentate	9/8.3	8/8.3	8/8.3	10/8.7	35
Dragged Stamp, plain	9/7.2	6/7.2	8/7.2	7/7.2	30
Banked Punctate, fingernail	8/7.5	7/7.5	6/7.5	9/7.5	30
Braided Cord Linear Stamped	6/6	5/6	8/6	5/6	24
Banked Stamp, plain, chevron	5/4	4/4	4/4	3/4	16
Dentate Tool Linear Stamped	4/3.7	5/3.7	3/3.7	3/3.7	15
Other	13/11.7	12/11.7	15/11.7	12/11.7	52
TOTAL	100	100	100	100	400

$\chi^2 = 12.193$
df = 30
p > 90
$\phi^2 = .0303$

TABLE 6

SCHEMATIC REPRESENTATION OF MIDDLE WOODLAND CERAMIC TAXONOMY

Ware: Upper Peninsula

Banked Stamp	Plain tool	chevron
		oblique
	Dentate tool	oblique
	Narrow tool	vertical
		bedded
Banked Punctate	Fingernail	oblique
Dragged Stamp	Plain tool	oblique
	Dentate tool	oblique
Linear Impressed	Dentate tool	perpendicular
	Braided cord	vertical
Linear Incised	Interrupted	horizontal
		opposed
	Simple	crisscross
Plain	Unbossed	notched

follow any previous scheme for the classification or typology of ceramics. This was deemed necessary in view of the fact that practically every vessel from this component has counterparts recovered from other sites which have been illustrated under a plethora of type and variety names. In most cases these taxa have been rather loosely applied and the same material often falls into several different type-variety groups. Under the same name several different attribute combinations are unfortunately lumped together for purposes of discussion. James Wright (1967: 3) has claimed that short of a detailed description of each sherd such a method for attribute analysis is as good as any other. Spaulding, however, has demonstrated that certain combinations of attributes may be statistically more significant than others (1953: 305). In his application of Spaulding's methods to the Laurel ceramics of Minnesota, Stoltman (1962: 25-28) agreed that the recognition of the attributes to be tested still involved a subjective element. I would add that the discrimination of attributes may be as much a factor of application as of perception. In the reports cited above, a great variety of ceramic decoration was under analysis. Minor variations within the "type" or "variety" were considered of little moment as the primary objective seems to have been to compare a number of types from one site to similar descriptions from other sites. At the Summer Island site the ceramic population is of manageable size; the initial objective is to analyze differences in design elements and decorative motifs between areas within the site. Variation of style is quite limited. The range of variation is so limited in the Summer Island Middle Woodland component, that nearly 83 per cent of all vessels from these ceramics would be classified as two types by Stoltman (1962: 45, 55), by Mason (1966; 1967) or by J. Wright (1967). For these reasons the discussion of the Middle Woodland ceramic complex from Summer Island will be in terms of the taxonomy outlined herein. The names given to the types will have the meaning assigned to them as they are described. While some attempt will be made to conform to previous usage, I do not feel obligated to use misleading or ambiguous terms no matter how strongly entrenched in the literature they have become. This is especially evident with the use of "punctate" as a term to denote almost any noncontinuous decorative element, regardless of shape or size. I here have reserved "punctate" to refer to discrete, more-or-less circular, impressions which have been placed into the clay and withdrawn without any noticeable angle of dragging. I have also referred to fingernail impressions as punctates to avoid any implications of incising or deliberately-shaped tool use. All other noncontinuous impressions are considered stamping of some sort.

ANALYTICAL METHODS

The following section will present each of the ceramic types recovered from the Middle Woodland component ranked in order of decreasing frequency of vessels represented (Table 4). The range for every dimension given is based on at least one vernier caliper measurement on each sherd, with over five different measurements taken for each vessel. While extremely time-consuming, these fifteen hundred measurements lend some degree of accuracy to the mean dimensions listed for each type. One result of this labor was the confirmation of what had been assumed initially: that there was as great a range for any measurement on a single vessel as there was between several vessels of the same group. A second, less obvious result was the low degree of correlation observed between the mean vessel thickness and the mean rim diameter for all vessels within a single ceramic variety. This indicates that, within certain mechanical limits, vessel thickness is not determined by vessel size, and can probably be considered more of a stylistic than a functional variable.

Rim diameters were determined by comparing all rimsherds over 10 cm long from a single vessel to a sheet of cardboard inscribed with semicircles of known diameter. The mean rim diameter for each vessel was thus determined (Table 7). Then the mean rim diameter for the ceramic group was computed from the mean vessel diameters. This method was used to avoid biasing the estimated rim diameter of the ceramic group by incorporating the extremes often found on individual sherds due to differential postdepositional warping as the result of earth pressures. The stated range of rim diameter for any ceramic group indicates the range for individual rimsherds, while the stated mean rim diameter is based on the described secondary vessel diameter.

Several sherds were sent to Dr. James Porter of Winnipeg University for thin-section petrological analysis. His report was not available at the time this section was written. Microscopic or refractive mineralogical analyses of the tempering particles were not undertaken. The mineral identifications given are based on visual examination with a 15x hand lens and treatment with 20 per cent solution of hydrochloric acid.

In general, all of the ceramic types can be considered to represent the same ware (as utilized by Griffin [1952: 101, 114-16, 121]). All vessels seemed to have been constructed of the same slightly sandy clay. No surface deposits of clay were noted on Summer Island, but subsurface deposits should be nearly ubiquitous, and surface deposits exist on the Garden Peninsula within a hundred yards of shore. Measurements for hardness were taken on all sherds. Scratch tests were made on exterior and interior surfaces and on the edges of fresh breaks. All measurements indicated a hardness of 2.0 to 3.5 on the Mohs hardness scale and all but a dozen were between 2.5 and 3.0. Since hardness varied as much on any single sherd as it did within the entire sample, it seems doubtful that more refined techniques of testing would yield statistically significant results (as I had implied previously [Brose, 1966*a*]).

Paste texture was classified as either compact, laminar, or friable. These distinctions were observed to vary from one edge of a sherd to another. Due to their extremely subjective nature even a single observer could not maintain any real consistency

TABLE 7

MEAN RIM DIAMETERS FOR MIDDLE WOODLAND VESSELS

Ceramic Variety Observed/Expected	Class Limits for Rim Diameter 15.0-22.0 cm	22.1-28.0 cm	28.1-35.0 cm	Total
Banked Stamp, plain	2/3.5	6/12.3	19/11.2	27
Banked Stamp, narrow	2/2.4	15/8.6	2/8.0	19
Plain, Unbossed, notched	1/1.6	3/5.9	9/8.5	13
Banked Stamp, dentate	3/1.6	9/5.9	1/8.5	13
Dragged Stamp, dentate	1/1.5	2/5.5	9/5.0	12
Dragged Stamp, plain	1/1.4	9/5.0	1/4.6	11
Banked Punctate, fingernail	2/1.4	7/5.0	2/4.6	11
Linear Stamped	1/0.6	2/3.6	5/3.8	8
Linear Incised, interrupted	2/0.9	2/3.2	3/2.9	7
TOTAL	15	55	51	121

χ^2 with continuity correction = 36.91
df = 16
p < .01
ϕ^2 = 0.1757

Note:—Twelve vessels representing the three varieties; Linear impressed dentate stamped, Miscellaneous stamp, and Linear incised simple crisscross, could not be entered into this table due to expected cell frequencies of zero.

in his evaluation. Forty per cent of all sherds were described as compact textured, 35 per cent as laminar, and 25 per cent as friable. The thinner upper shoulder and neck portion of most vessels was more compact than other areas, while shoulders tended to display a higher frequency of laminar fracturing.

Colors were examined under a 3200 degrees Kelvin daylight type light and compared to hue/chroma values from the book of Munsell Soil Color Charts (Munsell, 1954). This precision was of little real value since color changes across the surface of a single sherd were common. Many of these color changes are due to differential firing conditions, but whether before or after breakage is impossible to say. Many of these color changes are also due to differential weathering, and post-depositional organic and mineral staining. There is no reasonable method that I am aware of for distinguishing between these very different causal factors. No significant color differences were consistantly observed between vessel surfaces and interiors. This may indicate that a fairly low degree firing took place in an oxidizing atmosphere (Matson, 1937: 116) since the range of color never approaches black on any portion of the sherd. The colors ranged from very pale brown or yellowish brown to dark grayish brown or dark reddish brown.

All vessels appear to have been manufactured by the coiling technique. Two ceramic fragments that were recovered from a fire pit at this level (F. No. 39) may represent pinched-off ends of such coils (Pl. III, *a*). There was no evidence from these ceramics of a mortise-and-tennon coiling technique such as Wright illustrates for Ontario (Wright and Anderson, 1963: 31-33; J. Wright, 1967: Pl. 3, Fig. 18). The five vessel bases recovered from this component are all conical (Pl. III, *b*), although the angle of their apex varies considerably. While only a single vessel could be restored from base to lip, there is no reason to believe that the other vessels deviated significantly from this shape. The vessels may then be characterized as conoidal in shape with a moderately constricted neck and a slightly everted rim (Pl. III, *c*).

Temper consisted primarily of crushed granitic grit averaging about 2.0 mm in diameter and making up about 25 to 30 per cent aplastic within the paste. Vessel thickness ranged from 4.0 mm to 9.8 mm, with a mean body thickness of about 7.0 mm and a lip thickness of about 5.1 mm. These last attributes, temper and thickness, will be dealt with in detail in the description of ceramic variety. They are included here only to complete the criteria necessary to define the ceramic ware to which those types belong.

With the exception of temper particle size and sherd thickness, factors that are functionally related, these ceramics can clearly be considered as related to the Laurel Wares of Minnesota (Wilford, 1952: 4-15; 1955: 133-34; Stoltman, 1962: 37-38), Manitoba (MacNeish, 1958: 138-54) and Ontario (J. Wright, 1967). In terms of the sherd thickness they seem to be more closely related to North Bay II Wares from the Door Peninsula of Wisconsin (Mason, 1966: 75:125; 1967: 280-302), the Saugeen Focus ceramics from Ontario (Wright and Anderson, 1963: 23-36), and the Au Sable Series from Michigan (Brose, n.d.*a*). In view of the unresolved relationships of these ceramics, and to avoid prejudice by a too-ready assignment to established groups, I would propose a provisional series to be called *Upper Peninsula Ware*. This would include the Middle Woodland ceramics from Summer Island and similar ceramics from sites along the north shore of Lake Michigan as far east as the Mackinac Straits. The similarity of this designation to the Point Peninsula Wares of eastern Ontario and upper New York State (Ritchie and MacNeish, 1949: 97-106) is not wholly coincidental, and is reflected in the ceramic complex as well as in the terminology. The relationships of these broad ceramic groups to each other will be explored in detail as each ceramic type is described. Some degree of synthesis will be attempted thereafter.

FORMAL ANALYSIS

Summer Island Banked Stamp; *Plain tool variety*, [*oblique group*] (Pls. IV, V) consisted of twenty-one vessels represented by forty-two rimsherds and 135 decorated bodysherds from the Middle Woodland levels. An additional 33 sherds were recovered from later deposits. Paste texture tended to be friable and coil breaks were clearly evident. Temper consisted of crushed granitic grit and some darker, basaltic minerals. Tempering-particle size ranged from 0.5 mm to 8.9 mm, with a mean diameter of 2.5 mm. The density of temper was about 25 to 30 per cent aplastic by volume. Bodysherd thickness at the shoulder ranged from 5.4 mm to 8.2 mm with a mean thickness of 6.0 mm. Rim thickness, measured from one to three centimeters below the lip, ranged from 5.0 mm to 6.4 mm with a mean of 5.1 mm. Thickness at the lip ranged from 4.6 mm to 7.2 mm with a mean of 5.5 mm for vessels with slightly thinned everted to recurved vertical rims (Fig. 11, *a*, *b*) and from 5.4 mm to 6.3 mm with a mean of 6.0 mm for the single vessel with a recurved vertical

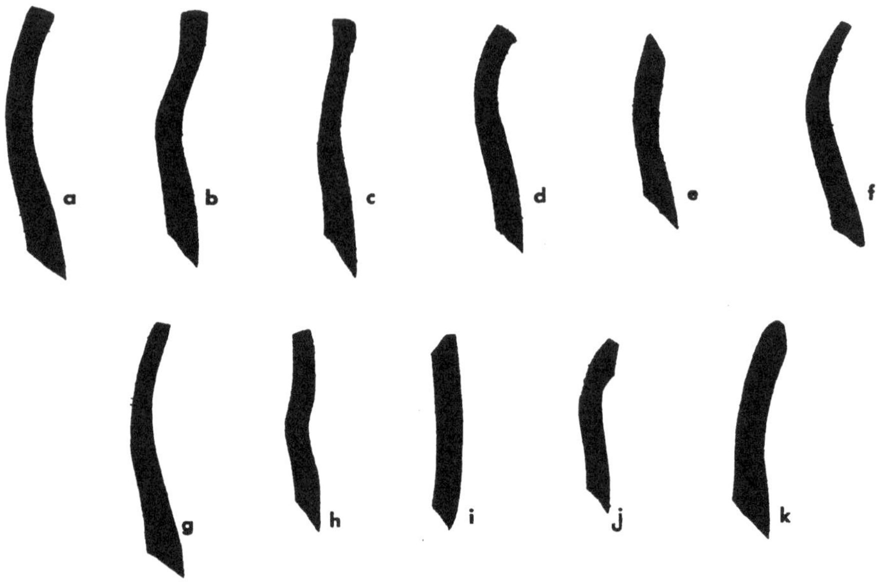

FIG. 11. Rim profiles of Middle Woodland ceramics.

rim having a slightly folded exterior collar (Fig. 11, *c*). All vessels in this group curved abruptly below the shoulder, probably to a conical base. Rim diameter ranged from 29.0 to 37.3 cm with a mean rim diameter of 32.9 cm. Vessel height was unknown, but the recurve below the shoulder was about 21 cm below the lip. Lips on all vessels were plain and flattened, although the collared vessel tended to greater roundness. Exterior lip decoration on eight vessels consisted of a single horizontal row of vertical to slightly oblique plain tool impressions. These stamps begin at the lip and extend downward 3.0 mm to 10.2 mm. They are 0.8 mm to 3.0 mm wide, 0.2 mm to 1.3 mm deep, and about 3.0 mm apart. Twelve vessels had no exterior lip decoration, while the "collared" vessel had a double row of vertical lip decoration. The upper row extends 6.0 mm down from the lip, the next row begins 2.5 mm below the upper and extends downward 7.8 mm. One uncollared vessel had two such doubled rows below the lip.

Interior lip decoration on five vessels consisted of a single horizontal row of vertical plain tool impressions 2.0 mm to 3.5 mm long extending down the interior surface. Sixteen vessels, including the "collared" vessel, had no interior lip decoration.

There was no significant association between interior and exterior lip treatment.

Exterior body decoration consists of from five to eight parallel horizontal rows of oblique discrete rectanguloid plain tool impressions. These stamps are generally all oriented the same way, although there are three vessels with two to four vertical rows over four to six oblique rows (Pl. V, *a*).

The rows of stamps are from 0.4 mm to 5.4 mm apart with a mean distance of 3.0 mm. On fourteen vessels the uppermost row is from 2.0 mm to 4.8 mm below the exterior lip edge. On the remaining seven vessels they commence at the lip. The design elements, or stamps, within each row may be as far apart as 6.3 mm or as close as 1.5 mm in the case of the more vertical elements. The oblique elements may often overlie each other, but along any one margin they are as much as 4.6 mm apart. The stamps are short (3.4 mm to 4.0 mm) and relatively wide (1.3 mm to 1.9 mm) on five vessels, and relatively long (7.6 mm to 14.0 mm) and narrow (0.6 mm to 1.4 mm) on sixteen vessels. The more vertically oriented impressions tend to be the longer and narrower ones.

All tool impressions that are oblique appear to have been applied from the upper right. Those three vessels with impressions that are more vertical appear to have been decorated by level application from the right. The punctating tool in either case has been applied with variable pressure and the depth of punctation ranges from 0.3 mm to 1.4 mm (with a mean depth of 1.0 mm) often on a single sherd. The angle of tool application varies from perpendicular to about 45 degrees and seems to be fairly consistant on a single vessel. The punctating tool itself seems to have been the smoothed edge of either a broken shell or splinter of bone or wood.

Similar ceramics have been recovered from other Upper Peninsula sites. The Naomikong Point site has yielded such ceramics as a minor type of the Middle Woodland occupation (Donald Janzen: personal communication). At the Ekdahl-Goudreau site the lower occupational stratum produced at least one sherd of this type (Prahl and Brose, n.d.).

Ceramics similar in decoration to this group have been reported from Minnesota as Laurel Linear Stamp (Stoltman, 1962: 47-50, Pl. 5) or simply as stamped band Laurel focus pottery (Wilford, 1952: 6). Further to the North MacNeish has included such ceramics within his broad Nutimik Oblique type (1958: 150-51, Pl. XV, no. 6).

Mason (1966: 93, 106-9) has described ceramics of this group from the Mero site as both unclassified (Pl. XII, Fig. 2, lower row) and as Becker Punctate (Pl. XVI, Fig. 2*a*) and a single rimsherd (Pl. XII, Fig. 2, lower right) is illustrated in both categories. Mason illustrates virtually identical ceramics from the Porte des Morts site as North Bay Linear Stamped (1967: 291-93, Pl. 6). A sherd of what Mason has called Simple Stab-and-Drag (1967, Pl. 9, Fig. *a*, no. 1) would also fall into my present ceramic group.

James V. Wright describes similar ceramics from numerous Ontario Laurel sites only as punctate (1967: 18) although many of the sherds he illustrates as linear punctate at Heron Bay (Pl. I, Fig. 8, 9) and at Pelican Falls (Pl. VII, Fig. 8), seem closer to discrete punctate than his own definition would indicate (J. Wright, 1967: 13-14). Wright also illustrates several sherds of Laurel ceramics from the Donaldson site (Wright and Anderson, 1963: Pl. XVI, Fig. 4-8; Pl. XIX, Fig. 4, 6) where they were associated with Saugeen Focus ceramics.

From further east in Canada similar ceramics have been reported from the Swan Lake site (Kenyon, 1961: 14-15; Pl. IX, no. 3) and from excavations near the Sheguiandah site on Manitoulin Island (Lee, 1965: 20-24, Fig. 4, no. 6). At this longitude such ceramics are referred to as Point Peninsula. The Point Peninsula type Wickham Punctate, Variant A (Ritchie, 1946: 14, Pl. 8, Fig. 26; Ritchie and MacNeish, 1949: 104) seems to correspond quite closely to this group of ceramics from Summer Island.

Ceramic affinities for this group can also be found to the south in some Illinois Hopewellian ceramic types. To some degree it corresponds to Griffin's late model of Sister Creeks Punctated, variation 1 (1952: 100-01) although Sister Creeks would be expected to considerably antedate the Upper Peninsula Banked Punctate. The vague resemblance to Illinoian types, such as Naples, Stamped, Plain (Griffin, 1952: 110, Pl. XXXIII, Fig. *g*), is certainly less evident than is the similarity to later Hopewellian types such as Montezuma Punctated (Griffin, 1952: 119, Pl. XXXIII, Fig. *j*, *l*) or some examples of Steuben Punctated (Morse, 1963: Pl. III, Fig. 2, upper right).

Upper Peninsula Banked Stamp; *Narrow tool variety [vertical group]* (Pl. VI) consisted of 14 vessels represented by 22 rimsherds and 51 decorated bodysherds from the Middle Woodland levels. An additional forty-seven sherds were recovered from subsequent deposits. Paste texture tended to be laminar, although coil breaks were observed. Temper consisted of very angular crushed crystalline granitic grit with quartz and plagioclase felspars predominating. Tempering particle size ranged from 1.3 mm to 4.5 mm, with a mean of 1.9 mm. Tempering was fairly dense and made up about 30 per cent aplastic by volume. Bodysherd thickness at the shoulder ranged from 4.9 mm to 5.6 mm, with a mean of 5.5 mm. Thickness of rimsherds, 1 to 3 cm below the lip, ranged from 5.0 mm to 7.1 mm, with a mean of 5.2 mm. Thickness at the lip ranged from 5.0 mm to 7.1 mm, with a mean of 5.3 mm. Vessels in this group all displayed a slightly everted rim, and had a moderately constricted neck and a rather gradual recurve below the shoulder to a conical base. Rim diameter ranged from 20.3 to 32.2 cm, with a mean diameter of 25.3 cm. Vessel height is unknown but the maximum vessel diameter at the shoulder occurred about 50 to 55 cm below a plain flattened lip (Fig. 11, *a*), or one slightly rolled to the outside (Fig. 11, *d*). Nine of the fourteen vessels have a single horizontal row of narrow (0.5 mm to 1.0 mm) vertical stamp impressions on the exterior lip edge. These are 2.7 mm to 8.2 mm long, with a mean length of 3.8 mm. They begin at the lip although the subsequent lip flattening occasionally has extruded a slight bit of obliterating clay. Six of these vessels have the same motif repeated on the interior lip. Rim decoration on twelve vessels consists of four to six parallel horizontal rows of oblique narrow linear stamp impressions beginning just below the lip where it is undecorated (five vessels) or 3.0 to 5.0 mm below the lip decoration (seven vessels). These horizontal rows are 3.5 mm to 8.0 mm apart. The impressions have a mean length of 7.0 mm. These stamps occasionally overlie their neighbor but along any one margin their mean distance is 3.5 mm apart (Pl. VI, *c*). Two of the four vessels with the more rolled lip (Pl. VI, *a*, *o*) have lip punctates underlain by a band of parallel oblique rows of narrow horizontal stamped impressions. These bands are about 35.0 to 40.0 mm high and the rows within them are 6.2 mm to 4.5 mm apart. The punctates are similar to those previously described for this group. Below this oblique band are two or three horizontal rows of oblique narrow punctate. On all vessels the decoration stops at the shoulder (Pl. IV, *g*).

The Naomikong Point site has also produced sherds similar to this group (Donald Janzen: personal communication) and at least two vessels are represented by sherds from the lowest levels of Ekdahl-Goudreau (Prahl and Brose, n.d.). Similar ceramics have also been reported from Isle Royale (Quimby, n.d.;

Bastian, 1963) and the Middle Woodland levels of the Wycamp Creek site in Emmet County, Michigan (Charles Cleland: personal communication).

This group of ceramics is not reported for any of the Laurel sites in Minnesota, although it seems to have been included in the Laurel Linear Stamped variety (James Stoltman: personal communication). MacNeish has illustrated sherds of his Nutimik Oblique from Manitoba which I would call Narrow Banked Stamp (1958: 150-51, Pl. XV, Fig. 8).

From Wisconsin, Mason has illustrated sherds from the Mero site (1966: Pl. XVI, Fig. 2, third row) and from the Porte des Morts site (1967: Pl. 6, upper right) called both Becker Punctate and North Bay Linear Stamped which are similar to this group.

In Ontario, Wright has illustrated a "fingernail impressed" sherd from the McLaren site (1967: PL. IX, Fig. 18), although this is described as vertical linear stamp (1967: 73), which seems to fall within the Narrow Banked Punctate variety. He also reports a "Saugeen" sherd from his Laurel Heron Bay site (Pl. III, Fig. 11) which is similar. The Saugeen focus Donaldson site has yielded a number of similar ceramics (Wright and Anderson, 1963: Pl. XV, Figs. 1, 3; J. Wright, 1967: Pl. XIV, Fig. 5), although these are sometimes described as incised (1963: 27). A number of similar sherds have been recovered from Point Peninsula deposits on the Bruce Peninsula, Ontario, at Inverhuron (Kenyon, 1957: 5, 17-18, Pl. VII, Figs. 1, 2), at the Swan Lake site (Kenyon, 1961: 14-15, Pl. IX, Figs. 4, 9), at Sheguiandah (Lee, 1964: 22-24, Fig. 4, no. 22), and at the Malcolm site (Dailey and Wright, 1955).

Farther east in Ontario, and in Upper New York State, the type Wickham Incised, variant B (Ritchie, 1946: 14; Ritchie and MacNeish, 1949: 103-4) would include this ceramic group. In Illinois the Naples Plain Stamped (Griffin, 1952: 110) or Montezuma Punctate (ibid.: 119-20, Pl. XXXIII, Fig. I) are close. Although close resemblances are uncommon they do occur, almost always in late Havanna contexts (see Lippincott and Herold, 1965: Pl. 56, *b*; McGregor, 1958: 40-42, Fig. 14, F, M; Morse, 1963: Pl. IV, Fig. 2, upper row, No. 4).

Bay de Noc Plain; *Unbossed variety [notched lip group]* (Pl. VII, *a*-*d*). Thirteen vessels of this group are represented by eighty-nine in situ rimsherds and an additional thirty sherds from subsequent levels. The paste tends to be quite compact with numerous coil breaks evident. Tempering consists of crushed granitic and occasionally dolomite or limestone grit, with particle size ranging from 2.1 mm to 9.3 mm with a mean diameter of 2.9 mm. Temper is extremely dense making up about 30 to 45 per cent aplastic by volume. Vessel thickness ranges from 3.9 mm to 9.5 mm for body and rimsherds with a mean bor both of 6.5 mm. Thickness at the lip ranges from 3.8 mm to 7.2 mm for nine vessels with slightly everted or recurved flattened lips (Fig. 11, *a*, *b*). For four vessels lip thickness ranges from 4.2 mm to 0.6 mm with a slightly everted flattened, exterior-thinned lip (Fig. 11, *e*). Rim diameters range from 24.5 to 35.2 cm with a mean rim diameter of 30.3 cm. Vessel height is unknown but maximum diameter at the shoulder occurs about 52 cm below the lip. The only decoration on these vessels consists of a single encircling row of oblique notches along the junction of the exterior surface and lip. These notches are 1.9 mm to 3.0 mm wide, 0.5 mm to 0.8 mm deep, 3.0 mm to 5.5 mm apart, and 3.0 mm to 8.3 mm apart. On one vessel (Pl. VII, *a*) with a thinned lip there is a row of wedge-shaped punctates along this beveled edge. Only three vessels bear this same lip notching along the interior lip junction. One of these sherds seems to show some evidence of smoothed-over cord-marking or smoothed vertical brushing (Pl. VII, *c*).

In general the plain ceramics from Naomikong Point show a very different style, with more rounded incurved lips and an almost universal row of circular punctates or bosses at the shoulder or area of maximum diameter. It is this "half-coconut shape" which also characterizes those few plain sherds from the lower levels of Ekdahl-Goudreau (Prahl and Brose, n.d.).

This is also the characteristic shape of the Laurel Plain reported by Wilford for the Rainy River Aspect (1952: 6) although Stoltman has illustrated flattened and everted lips for this type (1962: 41, Pl. IV) from Minnesota. MacNeish has illustrated both the everted and recurved rim Lockport plain type from southeast Manitoba which seem to correspond to the Upper Peninsula Plain, notched lip group (1958: 150, Pl. XIV, 6, 7, 9).

The closest ceramics, both geographically and typologically, seem to be the North Bay I and II Plain illustrated by Mason from Mero (1966: 78-80, 91-92, Pl. XII, Figs. 1 and 2, top and middle row) and from the Porte des Morts site (1967: 293-94, Pl. 2).

Several very moderately outflaring vessels of Au Sable Plain from the Goodwin-Gresham site on the west shore of Lake Huron are similar to these North Bay Plain, although they have the more rounded Laurel lip (Brose, n.d. *a*).

From Ontario James Wright has reported similar ceramics from the Pelican Falls site (1967: 42, 45), the Eaka site (1967: 80) and the Hungry Hall site (1967: 87). At many more Ontario Laurel sites the Laurel Bossed variety exists as well as, or in place of the plain notched variant. Wright has also reported similar ceramics from the Donaldson site (Wright and Anderson, 1963: 28, Pl. XVII, Fig. 2), although there is a far thicker lip on these ceramics as well as a tendency to dentate rather than to notch the lip. Further east in Ontario Johnston has recovered ceramics similar to the U.P. Plain which he designates Point Peninsula Plain (1968: Pl. 67, Fig. 1, 2, 3), and Lee has recovered similar sherds from Sheguiandah (1965: 23, Fig. 4, no. 2). This type, Point Peninsula Plain, with its outsloping rim and incised flattened lip is closer to the Summer Island ceramics than is the incurved Laurel Plain (Ritchie and MacNeish, 1949: 103, Fig. 37, 2, 3). Due to the very general nature of this group it is both easy and difficult to point to Illinoian parallels: easy because plain Hopewell ceramics occur at all time levels from early through late Middle Woodland (Griffin, 1952: 104, 119, 121) and difficult to be much more precise than this without being misleading. It is interesting, however, that only the middle Hopewell wares exhibit any degree of completely plain vessels, with types such as Naples Plain Stamped when confined to the lip (Griffin, 1952: Pl. XXXIII, Fig. D) or Hopewell Plain (Pl. XXXV, Fig. P), or it is the very late Middle and Late Woodland types such as Weaver Plain (Pl. XXXVI, Fig. D-F).

Summer Island Banked Stamp; *Dentate tool variety, [oblique group]* (Pl. VII, *e-t*) consists of thirteen vessels represented by twenty-eight rimsherds and eighty-seven decorated bodysherds from the Middle Woodland levels. An additional twenty-eight sherds were recovered from subsequent levels. Paste texture can be characterized as somewhat laminar although clear coil breaks were evident. Temper consists of crushed granitic grit with some preference being shown for dark angular minerals such as biotite, hornblende, and epidote. Temper particle size ranges from 0.7 mm to 4.5 mm with a mean diameter of 2.1 mm. Tempering is rather low in density representing only about 20 to 25 per cent aplastic by volume. Vessel thickness at the shoulder ranges from 4.9 mm to 11.0 mm with a mean of 6.5 mm. Rim thickness, 1.0 to 3.0 cm below the lip, ranges from 4.9 mm to 7.7 mm with a mean of 6.3 mm. All vessels had a somewhat constricted neck with a moderately everted rim having a flattened lip (Fig. 11, *a*) 5.5 mm to 7.8 mm thick with a mean of 6.3 mm.

Rim diameters range from 22.1 cm to 33.1 cm with a mean of 26.3 cm. Maximum diameter occurs at the shoulder about 60 cm below the lip. Vessel height is unknown. No interior lip decoration was noted on any rimsherds. There was a slight extrusion of clay to the outside due to the lip-flattening process. One vessel (Pl. VII, *e*) showed an exterior lip decoration consisting of a single horizontal row of vertical dentate-stamped punctates 0.7 mm to 3.5 mm apart, extending from the lip juncture to 3.2 mm to 5.0 mm below the lip. These punctates consisted, in whole or in part, of three rectangular elements, end to end, each being 2.2 mm long and 1.1 mm wide, separated by a band of clay (or in the positive by a notch in the tool) 1.0 mm high. The punctates were from 0.7 mm to 1.2 mm deep and appeared to have been put in from the right at a slight angle from perpendicular to the surface of the clay. All vessels had rim and upper shoulder decoration consisting of two to five parallel horizontal rows of oblique dentate stamps. The rows were as far apart as 7.0 mm in some cases but often overlapped. Within each horizontal row the dentate impressions were 2.4 mm to 3.5 mm apart. Eleven vessels showed similar dentate tools each about 10.5 mm long consisting of four rectangular elements end to end, each about 2.2 mm to 2.4 mm long, 1.1 mm wide, and separated by a band of clay (or notch in the tool) 0.5 mm wide. All these stamps seem to have been put in from the right at an angle of about fifteen degrees from perpendicular to the surface of the clay. There seems to have been no deviation from a horizontal plane of application. One vessel (Pl. VII, *g*) has a similar motif but the impressing tool was put in at a forty-five degree angle and seems to have been lifted out of the plastic clay with a movement to the left thus obliterating this margin of the dentate impression and creating a distinctly pseudo-scallop shell effect. One vessel (Pl. VII, *f*) has a single horizontal row of oblique dentate impressions just below the exterior lip and four to five horizontal rows of pseudo-dentate impressions done with a very wide, poorly notched tool. These impressions are ovoid in shape and are about 3.2 mm to 4.0 mm long and 3.0 mm to 3.8 mm wide. The notching, or dentate impressions are nearly obliterated but the tool appears to have two irregular notches, each about one-third way from the end, across the center.

There are several problems involved in the comparison of this ceramic group with material from other sites. Variations in angle of application of the dentate tool and of its withdrawal from the plastic clay can create quite dissimilar impressions.

The pseudo-scallop shell effect noted above is only one of many possible results. Had the tool been shallowly impressed into the clay at any angle between 30 and 60 degrees, a similar pseudo-scallop shell impression could have been attained. Experimental studies carried out by Donald Janzen and myself have convinced me that much of what in the past has been called pseudo-scallop shell impressed, is actually created with the edge of a normally dentate-notched tool. This is not meant to imply that true pseudo-scallop shell impressions do not occur as the result of impression with an alternate-edge notched tool. Such decoration, however, has not been recovered from Summer Island.

Several sherds from the lower levels of the Ekdahl-Goudreau site display a banked stamp, dentate tool decoration virtually indistinguishable from those on vessels from Summer Island (see Pl. VII, *h, i*) (Prahl and Brose, n.d.). The Naomikong Point site has yielded over 62 vessels of this ceramic group (Donald Janzen: personal communication). While the majority of such ceramics from this site are either clean dentate or true alternate-edge notched pseudo-scallop shell, a large number of the sherds also show banked dentate grading into what could be designated as quasi-pseudo-scallop shell resulting from sloppy dentate impressions. Bastian (1963: Pl. 7, *b*) has also illustrated several sherds of this ceramic group from various sites on Isle Royale, Michigan. He has described them as Linear Punctate, Laurel Dentate, and Pseudo-Scallop Shell Stamped. From the Arrowhead Drive "Ossuary" (actually a group burial) two vessels of this group represented by fourteen sherds were reported (Bettarel and Harrison, 1962: 39).

Wilford (1952: 6) has reported such dentated sherds from Minnesota Laurel as Dentate Stamped, but Stoltman (1962: 43-45) distinguishes these from single dentate stamping as "Linear Stamping." Many of these sherds within the Laurel complex are quite close to those from Summer Island. MacNeish has illustrated sherds of Nutmik Oblique from Manitoba which bears close resemblances as well (1958: Pl. XV, Figs. 4, 7).

Mason illustrates sherds of North Bay Dentate Stamped from the Mero site (1966: Pl. XIII, Figs. 1, 2) and from the Porte des Morts site (1967: 284, Pl. 3, upper left, third row, third column) which are similar to this group. Mason also illustrates several other sherds, which seem not the least bit different, as North Bay Linear Stamped (1967: Pl. 6, second row, second column; third row, third column) or as North Bay Scallop (1967: 287, Pl. 4, lower left).

James Wright, in his survey of Laurel sites in Ontario does not report the presence of this ceramic group although he has illustrated sherds, from Herron Bay and Pelican Falls, called Linear Punctate (1967: Pl. I, Fig. 8; Pl. III, Fig. 1) and Dragged Stamp (1967: Pl. II, Fig. 16; Pl. VII, Fig. 1) which appear to be rather a Banked Punctate, Dentate tool. He illustrates similar ceramics from the Donaldson site (Wright and Anderson, 1963: 77, Pl. XIX, Fig. 4, 6) and from the Malcolm site (Dailey and Wright, 1955), as "miscellaneous." Similar dentate sherds have been illustrated by Mitchell as pseudo-scallop shell (1966: 17, Pl. I, Fig. 8) at the Deep River site in Ontario.

Thomas Lee (1965: 22-25, Fig. 4, nos. 6, 10-12) has illustrated similar ceramics from near the Sheguiandah site on Manitoulin Island, in the Georgian Bay region. Further south on Lake Huron the Goodwin-Gresham site has produced a single vessel of Au Sable Dentate Stamped which bears some resemblance to the Upper Peninsula Banked Punctate Dentate tool ceramic group (Brose, n.d. *a*).

Ritchie has illustrated similar ceramics from East Sugar Island in Ontario (1949: 17, Fig. 4, *n*, *ff*) and from sites in Upstate New York (1946: 43, Pl. 8, Fig. 10). While the definition for Vinette Dentate (Ritchie and MacNeish, 1949: 100-2) could include the U.P. Banked Punctate, Dentate tool variety, the closest Point Peninsula type would seem to be Jacks Reef Dentate (ibid.: p. 105, Fig. 38, O), although the Jacks Reef Corded Punctate is extremely similar.

The Naples Dentate Stamped ceramics of Illinois are clearly related to these Summer Island ceramics (Griffin, 1952: 107-10). This is best seen in variants such as Pool Vertical Dentate Stamped (McGregor, 1958: 33, Fig. 8, *d*). At best this relationship is distant.

Upper Peninsula Dragged Stamp; *Dentate tool [oblique]*, (Pl. VIII) consists of 12 minimal vessels represented by 156 decorated bodysherds and 42 rimsherds from the Middle Woodland levels of the site. An additional 40 sherds were recovered from subsequent deposits. The paste tended to be somewhat sandy and compact. Temper consisted of crushed granitic grit, with some preference for angular quartz and quartzlike minerals, with small amounts of crushed dolomite or calcitic limestone. Tempering particle size ranged from 0.8 mm to 5.5 mm with a mean of 1.8 mm. Temper was rather scarce amounting to about 20 per cent aplastic by volume. Coil breaks were clearly seen on many sherds. Vessel thickness on bodysherds ranged from 6.5 mm to

10.1 mm with a mean of 7.0 mm. Shoulder thickness at the maximum vessel diameter 40 cm below the lip, ranged from 7.0 mm to 8.5 mm with a mean of 7.5 mm. Rim thickness at 2 cm below the lip ranged from 5.8 mm to 7.3 mm with a mean of 6.8 mm. Rims were slightly everted with a diameter of from 25.0 cm to 34.1 cm with a mean vessel rim diameter of 32.0 cm. Lips on three vessels were slightly thinned to the interior (Fig. 11, *f*) and were from 3.3 mm to 6.4 mm with a mean thickness of 4.0 mm. The other nine vessels had parallel-wall flattened lips (Fig. 11, *a*) and were 5.2 mm to 6.4 mm with a mean thickness of 5.6 mm. Interior decoration occurred on the unthinned lips only and consisted of a single horizontal row of parallel notches 5.0 mm to 7.5 mm apart, 1.3 mm to 2.5 mm wide, 1.5 mm deep angled slightly obliquely across the inner portion of the rim. These notches appear to have been made with the edge of a squared tool applied from the upper right. This lip treatment was repeated on the exterior of all nine of these vessels. The three vessels with thinned lips had no interior decoration and their exterior lip decoration consisted of a single horizontal row of dragged vertical stamps of the same type as used in decorating the body. The rim and upper shoulder of all vessels had four to seven horizontal rows of dragged dentate stamp encircling the vessel. The upper row was always close to vertical, with subsequent rows either vertical or slightly oblique. In all cases the dentate tool was placed in the plastic clay and dragged a short distance to the right with a gradual decrease in pressure before being put deeply into the clay again. Each horizontal row is separated from the one below by 3.0 mm to 6.2 mm of undecorated surface. The discrete high-pressure dentate impressions occur from 1.5 mm to 5.0 mm apart along the row with a mean distance of 3.0 mm. Several different dentate tools were used on these different vessels but in all cases only a single tool seems to have been employed on any one vessel although several vessels have impressions from the same stamp. The dentate tools appear to have been 5.5 mm, 6.3 mm, 7.5 mm, or 9.4 mm long respectively. They were composed of three, four, four, and three teeth, respectively, each respective tool having teeth 1.4 mm, 1.5 mm, 1.4 mm, and 2.4 mm wide. All the stamps seem to have been 1.5 mm to 2.3 mm wide, but this is extremely difficult to determine due to the technique employed. The angle at which the high-pressure, deeper impression within the row was made varies considerably between vessels and to a lesser extent displays some variation on a single vessel. In some cases the implement was held almost perpendicular to the vessel surface. In other cases the angle was decreased to less than forty-five degrees. The amount of pressure applied in each part of the operation is another variable factor: in some examples the whole row appears deeply channeled into the vessel surface, while in others even the high-pressure stamping is less than 0.8 mm deep.

Several sherds, representing at least two vessels of this group, were recovered from the Naomikong Point site (Donald Janzen: personal communication). Bastian illustrates sherds of this group as both Complex Dentate and Laurel Push-Pull (1963: Pl. IX, X, Figs. *a-c*). From the Ekdahl-Goudreau site only a single sherd of Dragged Dentate Stamped was recovered during the 1965 excavations (Prahl and Brose, n.d.). Bettarel and Harrison have illustrated a single sherd from Arrowhead Drive which clearly belongs to this group (1962: Pl. I, upper right), and I have further identified seven rim and decorated bodysherds representing two minimal vessels from The University of Michigan, Museum of Anthropology collections from this site.

Wilford has reported similar if not virtually identical ceramics from several Minnesota Laurel sites and has designated them as Laurel Complex Push-and-Pull (1952: 6, 8). Stoltman has more recently defined the Laurel Push-Pull type (1962: 54-56). He has also shown that there is a very strong positive correlation between this rim decoration and a decorated lip (Table 16, p. 81), and a strong negative correlation between Push-Pull and bossing. These observations would seem to be borne out by the Upper Peninsula Dragged Stamp ceramic types from Summer Island although the emphasis here appears to be reversed. MacNeish does not describe any ceramics from Manitoba that fit the Dragged Stamp definition although some sherds illustrated as Nutimik Oblique clearly display this technique (1958: 149, Pl. XV, Fig. 4).

Mason apparently did not recognize this group at the Mero site where it was included with miscellaneous North Bay Stamped sherds (1966: 237, Pl. XII, Fig. 2, lower left). From the subsequent excavations at the Porte des Morts site three vessels of "Complex Stab-and-Drag" were recovered (Mason, 1967: 296-97; Pl. 9, Fig. *b*). These are indistinguishable from the Summer Island Dragged Dentate ceramics.

From northern Ontario Wright reports numerous Laurel sites along the Lake Superior drainage system all of which have yielded some ceramics of this type called Dragged Stamp (1967: 12-13, 121, Pl. I, II, VII, IX, X). Wright has also reported similar ceramics as Malcolm Push-Pull from the Malcolm site (Dailey and Wright, 1955: 13), and as Laurel Push-Pull from the Donaldson site (Wright and Anderson, 1963: 30, Pl. XVI, 7, 8, 11) where they are presumed to be exotic although in good association with the native Saugeen ceramics (ibid.: 30). Similar pottery is illustrated as Vinette Complex Dentate from the Serpent Mound (Ontario) site where it was fairly common (Johnston, 1968: 53, Pl. 62, 63). In addition some of the ceramics included under the supertype Rice Lake Banded are also Dragged Dentate Stamp (ibid.: 54, 57, Pl. 68, Fig. 2; Pl. 69, Fig. 3).

The Point Peninsula Vinette Complex Dentate (Ritchie and MacNeish, 1949: 102, Fig. 37,*f*) in some varieties, is clearly related to the Upper Peninsula Dragged Stamp Dentate tool ceramics. Although initially considered to be Early to Middle Woodland, it has been found consistantly only on Middle Woodland sites in eastern Ontario and Upper New York State (ibid.).

There do not seem to be any good southern analogies to this ceramic group although Griffin has illustrated a bodysherd of Hopewell Zoned Stamped, rocked dentate variety from Illinois which looks quite similar to a Dragged Dentate Stamp (1952: 117, Pl. XXXV, I).

Upper Peninsula Dragged Stamp; *Plain tool [oblique]* (Pl. IV, IX) consisted of 11 vessels represented by 87 rimsherds and 342 decorated bodysherds from the Middle Woodland levels. An additional 19 sherds from later levels were assigned to this type. Paste and temper characteristics are identical to the previously described Dragged Stamp Dentate tool variety. The Plain tool variety while having virtually the same range for vessel thickness, tended to be somewhat finer and smaller with a mean bodysherd thickness at the shoulder of 5.5 mm, at the rim 6.0 mm, and, at a somewhat thinned, flattened, and moderately everted lip, 5.2 mm. Rim diameter ranged from 20.2 cm to 28.7 cm with a mean vessel rim diameter of 25.3 cm. The reconstructed vessel (Pl. III, *c*) has a mean rim diameter of 24.8 cm and a vessel height of 36.8 cm for an approximate capacity of six liters, or a little over two and one-half gallons (with volume estimated as for an elliptic paraboloid [Burlington, 1956: 36]).

Eight vessels had no interior decoration while three displayed a single row of vertical tool impressions encircling the interior surface-lip junction. These impressions were 1.0 mm to 2.5 mm wide, 3.0 mm to 5.0 mm long, 0.5 mm to 1.3 mm deep, and 2.2 mm to 3.1 mm apart. All vessels displayed a similar encircling row of vertical exterior lip decoration although these impressions tended to be somewhat longer (mean length, 7.5 mm). Immediately below the vertical lip decoration, vessel exteriors were decorated with twelve to twenty-four parallel, horizontal rows of plain tool dragged stamp. All the technical qualifications described for the previous variety, Dragged Stamp, Dentate tool, are applicable here. The plain tool dragged stamp rows are considerably closer to each other than are the dentate stamped rows, being about 2.0 mm apart and about 4.5 mm long. The tool impressions were oriented obliquely with only a single exception (Pl. IX, *a*) which seemed to show vertical rows of horizontally oriented impressions. The Dragged Stamp Plain tool impressions are uniformly deeper than those of the Dentate tool variety, with high-pressure impressions as deep as 1.8 mm and low-pressure dragging from 0.6 mm to 1.2 mm deep. On two of those vessels some punctation occurs. On one (Pl. IX, *b*) this takes the form of circular punctates about 2.0 mm in diameter, 5.2 mm apart, 1.2 mm deep, forming a single horizontal row about 18.0 mm below the lip of the vessel. On the other vessel (Pl. IV, IX, *c*) there is a horizontal row of vertical narrow plain tool-stamped impressions about 26 mm below the lip, 4.0 mm apart, 0.7 mm wide, 7.0 mm long, and 0.4 mm deep. This row is intermittently overlapped by a horizontal row of oblique narrow plain tool punctates about 29 mm below the lip. All of these rows of punctates were applied over a single or double dragged stamp row while the vessel was still somewhat plastic. On the latter vessel the lower row of dragged stamping along the maximum shoulder diameter, 85 mm below the lip, is bounded by a similar superimposed row of vertical plain narrow tool punctates. There is also a single roughly triangular area on this vessel which has been partly smoothed and filled with parallel horizontal rows of this same vertical punctate. This zone is 52.3 mm below the lip and is 24.5 mm wide at the top with the apex 24.5 mm below. This would seem to represent the area where horizontal rows of dragged stamp impressions failed to meet after encircling the vessel. This same solution to mismatched rows resulting from sloppy execution of the stamping has been noted on several vessels from Summer Island.

Several sherds representing at least two vessels of this group from Isle Royale are illustrated by Bastian as Linear Punctate (1963: Pl. XIX) and he further indicates that some of his Complex Dentate may be considered in this group (1963: 88-104). A single sherd of this group was also found in the 1965 surface collections from the Ekdahl-Goudreau site. There are at least 62 vessels of this type represented by over 460 sherds at the Naomikong Point site, 120 miles to the northeast on Whitefish Bay, Lake Superior (Donald Janzen: personal communication). Several fitted sherds from this site (Pl. IX, *s*) were so similar to the reconstructed vessel from Summer Island (Pl. IV) that if broken sherds from both sites had been filed flat they could have been glued together with no observable discontinuity. Neither Janzen nor myself were able to note any significant differences between these sherds. The potters (if not identical) must have been highly cognizant of the prevailing ceramic styles.

This ceramic group is reported from many Minnesota Laurel sites where it has been called Simple Push-Pull bands (Wilford, 1952: 6) or merely described as a plain variant of Push-Pull (Stoltman, 1962: 43-44, 54-56). Similar ceramics occur at Malmo focus sites (Wilford, 1955: 134). MacNeish has illustrated similar Manitoba ceramics as Lockport Linear (1958: 145; Pl. XIV, no. 3), although the definition of Nutimik Oblique does not seem to exclude them (1958: 150).

The Mero site has produced ceramics of this group which Mason has described as Stab-and-Drag (1966: 109) although some of the illustrations raise some doubts about the banked punctate nature of several sherds (1966: 247, Pl. XVII, Fig. 2, *b*). Mason also has reported Simple Stab-and-Drag ceramics from the Porte des Morts site where they represent a larger percentage of vessels (1967: 295-96, Pl. 9, *a*).

From northern Ontario James Wright has reported these ceramics from a number of Laurel sites. He has described this group as Linear Punctate (1967: 13), although the illustrations indicate that much of what I have called Banked Punctate, Plain tool, oblique has been included in his "type" (1967: 143, Pl. I, Fig. 8, 9; Pl. III, Figs. 1, 2; Pl. VIII, Fig. 2; Pl. X, Figs. 13, 14). Similar ceramics have been reported from the Parker site (Leechman and de Laguna, 1949) in southern Ontario, but the decoration of this ceramic group does not appear to extend to the east for any great distance. Johnston has illustrated sherds of Rice Lake Banded from the shell midden associated with the Serpent Mound which seem to show a horizontal Dragged Plain Stamp much like the unique vessel from Summer Island (1968: 139, Pl. 69, Fig. 6). Ritchie has also shown ceramics from East Sugar Island which seem close to the Dragged Stamp, Plain Tool [oblique] (1949: 17, Fig. 4, *nn*). These are untyped by Ritchie, and none of the well-defined Point Peninsula types are similar (Ritchie and MacNeish, 1949), although some examples of the Wickham site linear, corded-stick-impressed design do show remarkable similarities (Ritchie, 1946: Pl. 43, Figs. 2, 7). I have seen no materials of Hopewellian affinity from Illinois that displayed even a reasonable resemblance to these ceramics.

Upper Peninsula Banked Punctate; *Fingernail variety* (Pl. X) consists of eleven vessels represented by seven rimsherds and twenty-six decorated bodysherds from the Middle Woodland levels, and ten sherds from subsequent levels at the site. Paste texture could be characterized as friable. Coil breaks were evident on many of these sherds. Temper was rather plentiful (30 to 40 per cent aplastic by volume) and consisted of crushed granitic grit 0.5 mm to 6.9 mm in diameter and with a mean of 2.5 mm. Bodysherd thickness ranged from 7.3 mm to 9.8 mm with a mean of 8.0 mm, thinning somewhat at the shoulder to range from 6.5 mm to 7.9 mm with a mean of 6.9 mm. Rims were either vertical (Fig. 11, *i*) or recurved to vertical above a very slightly constricted neck (Fig. 11, *h*). At 2 cm below the lip they were 5.3 mm to 6.9 mm with a mean thickness of 6.2 mm. The lips were from 3.4 mm (with an interior bevel) to 7.1 mm with a mean thickness of 6.0 mm. Rim diameter was 20.0 cm to 26.2 cm with a mean vessel rim diameter of 21.6 cm. All lips were plain and flattened with only the single beveled-lip vessel showing any exterior decoration. This consisted of an encircling series of parallel notches 3.0 to 5.1 mm apart, cut into the clay extruded by flattening the lip. This vessel (Pl. X, *a*) was also the only one with interior decoration, consisting of a single horizontal row of oblique large ovoid-shaped dentate stamps on the beveled portion of the lip. This dentate impression looks quite like a three-pronged version of Naples Ovoid Barred Stamp (Griffin, 1952: 113, Pl. XXXIV, A-E), and was placed into the clay from the upper left. Extending from the lip, or just below, all vessels are decorated with four to six parallel horizontal rows of oblique fingernail impressions. These rows are 0.8 mm to 6.9 mm apart. The impressions within each row are 3.2 mm to 8.7 mm apart and of quite variable width. Some impressions show only the fingernail (Pl. X, *b*-*g*) while others show the indentation caused by the tip of the finger (Pl. X, *h*-*l*). On some impressions the finger was twisted slightly as it was withdrawn (Pl. X, *m*-*q*). In general the technique is quite sloppy.

The only other Middle Woodland site in Michigan to produce similar ceramics has been the Goodwin-Gresham site, where several vessels of Au Sable and Iosco Fingernail punctated were noted. In neither case however, were these impressions arranged in banks as were the Summer Island ceramics (Brose, n.d. *a*).

From the Laurel sites of Minnesota, Wilford has described Rainey River Aspect sherds decorated with horizontal rows of shallow fingernail impressions (1952: 10). Stoltman has illustrated sherds of Laurel Linear Stamp which show some indication of being fingernail produced (1962: 44-54, Pl. III) although they are not specified as such. Some of the non-pseudo-scallop shell Nutimik Oblique from Manitoba seems also to be fingernail incised (MacNeish, 1958: 150; Stoltman: personal communication) but this decorative technqiue at best is rare at any distance to the west of the Great Lakes.

Mason has illustrated and described several vessels similar to Banked Punctate, Fingernail variety, from both the Mero site (1966: 106-8, Pl. XVI, Fig. 2, *a*, *b* upper right) and the Porte des Morts site (1967: 299; Pl. 10, *c* [wrong orientation]) where they are classified as Becker Punctated (1966), Becker Punctate (1967), or miscellaneous punctate (1966).

No similar ceramics have been reported by James Wright (1967) in his survey of northern Ontario Laurel sites. While some of the incised sherds from the Donaldson site look like incising over fingernail impressions (Wright and Anderson, 1963: 69, Pl. XV, 3) they are not described as such. Lee has described Banked Punctate fingernail-impressed ceramics from Manitoulin Island (1965: 23, Fig. 4, nos. 13, 22), and this may be the easternmost representation of this group.

Within the Illinoian Middle Woodland ceramic complex some similarity can be found with types such as Hummel Plain Stamped (Griffin, 1952: 111) or even with earlier types such as the finger pinched variety of Sister Creeks Punctated in its later phases (Griffin, 1952: 100-1; Pl. XXX, *j*). Mason (1966: 107) refers to the close similarities of some of the fingernail decorated Becker Punctated from Mero to the "pinched" Montezuma Punctated from Illinois. While this correlation is more realistic chronologically, the particular resemblances cited seem to be far closer to Banked Punctate, Plain tool [oblique] than to fingernail impressions.

Upper Peninsula Linear Stamped; *Braided cord variety*, (Pl. XI) consists of eight vessels represented by fifteen rimsherds and thirty-seven decorated bodysherds in situ, and an additional thirteen sherds from subsequent deposits. The paste is somewhat more sandy than the other ceramics from this component. It is somewhat friable and laminar although one clear coil break was observed. Temper was rather plentiful (about 35 per cent aplastic by volume) and consisted of crushed granitic grit with a definite preference shown for angular dark minerals such as olivine, biotite, and hornblende. Temper particle size ranged from 1.5 mm to 3.7 mm with a mean diameter of 2.3 mm. At the shoulder sherd thickness ranged from 6.4 mm to 7.5 mm with a mean of 6.7 mm. At the moderately constricted neck, thickness was from 6.2 mm to 7.4 mm with a mean of 7.0 mm. The lips on all sherds were flattened and plain with two vessels displaying a slight collar (Fig. 11, *j*) and the other six somewhat thinner with a negligible rolled exterior lip extrusion (Fig. 11, *d*). Thickness on all lips ranged from 5.5 mm to 6.3 mm with a mean of 5.6 mm. The rim diameter of this variety ranged from 25.2 cm to 34.7 cm with a mean vessel rim diameter of 33.1 cm. This was the only ceramic variety from the Summer Island Middle Woodland component that showed evidence of having a smoothed-over cordmarked body surface on several vessels. The two vessels with the thickened rim (Pl. XI, *a*, *c*) both had exterior lip decoration consisting of a single horizontal row of oblique from vertical twisted $^{Z}_{Z}S$ cord impressions 2.4 mm wide, 9.0 mm long, 1.2 mm deep, and 3.7 mm apart. Below this was the thickened lips' maximum width and below this was another offset horizontal row of $^{Z}_{Z}S$ looped cord-end oblique impressions, 4.5 mm to 5.1 mm long, 3.1 mm wide, and 2.0 mm deep. Below the lip decoration the same cord had been impressed lightly into the smooth body surface for varying lengths (21.0 to 29.1 mm) as far as the upper shoulder were it fades out.

The other six vessels of this variety have an exterior lip decoration consisting of a single, encircling row of vertical looped cord-end impressions extending from 7.9 mm to 9.1 mm ($\bar{X}$ = 8.3 mm) down the vessel. The lip covers the upper portion of these impressions with the extruded clay indicating that the lip flattening occurred subsequent to the cord impressing. These impressions were made with a $^{Z}_{Z}S$ twisted cord, each element of which was about 1.3 mm wide. The total impression is 3.4 mm wide and 0.9 mm deep.

On three of these vessels this same vertical cord-loop has been turned horizontally and brought down the vessel from below the lip decoration to the shoulder in a series of roughly parallel vertical rows (Pl. XI, *b*, *d-f*). These rows are about 8.0 mm apart and the horizontal corded elements composing them are 3.0 mm to 5.7 mm apart ($\bar{X}$ = 4.8 mm). At the shoulder this motif is terminated by a double horizontal band of this same corded element, once again turned vertically.

The other three vessels show a series of roughly parallel slightly curved bands extending from 12.6 cm below the lip down to just past the shoulder (about 8 cm). These bands are about 7 mm apart, 3.9 mm to 4.2 mm ($\bar{X}$ = 4.0 mm) wide and 0.9 mm deep. These impressed bands result from laying a corded element consisting of a four-strand braided cord upon the plastic

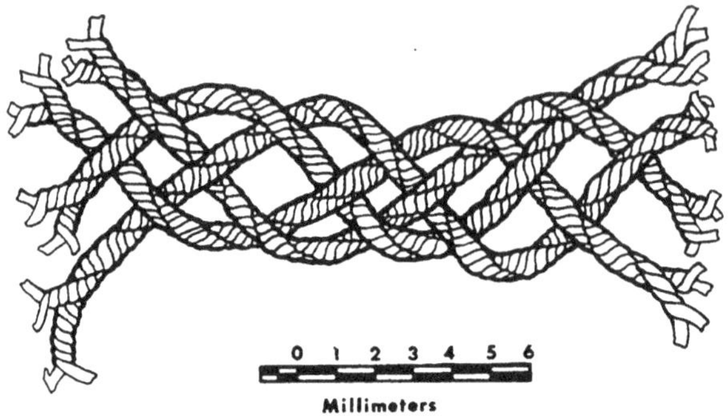

FIG. 12. Reconstruction of braided cord.

surface of the clay. Each element of this braid is composed of two ${}^{Z}_{Z}S$ twisted cords to form a $\begin{matrix} {}^{Z}_{Z}S \\ {}^{Z}_{Z}S \end{matrix} Z$ strand. The braiding of these cords (Fig. 12) was discerned by Volney Jones, Lewis Larson, and myself, using a low-powered binocular microscope with an oblique light source. Larson and I eventually succeeded in duplicating in plasticene the impressions seen on these ceramics. Braided cordage similar to this has been recovered from the B-95 cave at Burnt Bluff on the Garden Peninsula which is associated with charcoal radiocarbon-dated to A.D. 375±130 (M-1795) (Jones, 1968: 95).

Similar ceramic decoration is not reported for any other Middle Woodland site in the State of Michigan. At Naomikong Point, Ekdahl-Goudreau, Isle Royale, and Bois Blanc Island the corded impressed sherds were all typologically or stratigraphically assignable to the Late Woodland Occupations.

No ceramics of this type are reported from the Laurel sites of Minnesota (Stoltman, 1962; 1968; personal communication) although Wilford has illustrated sherds somewhat similar to the loop-end corded group as coming from Howard Lake (1951: 11-12; 1955: 131-32). MacNeish has illustrated sherds of Lockport Cordwrapped Stick from Manitoba, which are also similar to the corded-end Summer Island ceramics (1958: 155, Pl. XVI, Figs. 6, 7, 9). The chronological placement of these is given as associated with the Laurel-like Nutimik focus (MacNeish, 1958) but Stoltman (1962: 92) has expressed doubts about this. Neither Minnesota nor Manitoba have yielded ceramics similar to the braided cord impressed vessels from Summer Island.

The five corded stamped vessels from Summer Island are quite like the North Bay Corded-Stamped reported from the unstratified areas of the Mero site (Mason, 1966: 104, Pl. XVII, Fig. 2, *a*). They are even closer to what Mason has called Corded Stamped (Pseudo Dentate) from Porte des Morts (1967: 295, Pl. 8). Neither of these sites have produced ceramics similar to the Braided Cord-Impressed vessels, however.

None of the Laurel sites James Wright has reported in northern Ontario show any use of cordmaking as a decorative technique (1967: 120, Table 36, 123). Further to the southeast in Ontario the Malcolm site produced ceramics similar to the loop-end corded stamped Upper Peninsula vessels from Summer Island (Dailey and Wright, 1955: 14), but nothing comparable to the Braided Cord Impressed vessels. The Donaldson site produced a single Cord-Wrapped Stick Impressed rim (Wright and Anderson, 1963: 29, Pl. XVII, 7) but this was unlike any of the Summer Island ceramics.

It is in the eastern Ontario and upper New York State Point Peninsula sites that the closest affinites to the Upper Peninsula Linear Impressed Corded ceramics exist. From the East Sugar Island site Ritchie has illustrated sherds of Point Peninsula Corded, Jacks Reef Corded Punctate, and Wickham Corded Punctate that show relationships to the corded loop-end sherds from Summer Island (1949: 12-13, Fig. 3, *t*, *k*, *nn*). From the Wickham site, sherds of Vinette 2 Linear Corded-stick Impressed are also similar (Ritchie, 1946: Pl. 8, Fig. 7). The Summer Island Corded ceramics seem to show a combination of Point Peninsula Corded technique with Vinette Complex Dentate motifs (Ritchie and MacNeish, 1949: 102, Fig. 37, *f-j*, *m*). The single eastern site that comes closest to displaying the same range of corded decoration as the Summer Island site is the Serpent Mound site on Rice Lake, Ontario. Here Johnston has recovered sherds he calls Rice Lake Banded which account for over 25 per cent of all ceramics recovered from the habitation areas of the site (1968: 56-57). Several of the sherds Johnston illustrates are quite similar to the Summer Island Braided Cord ceramics (1968: Pl. 68, Figs. 1, 3, 4; Pl. 69, Fig. 2). Johnston has stated that the decoration on several of these sherds, ". . . superficially resembled cording but . . . evidently [were] made with a tool (About 4 mm. in width) held at approximately a 45° angle to the long axis of the lines so as to leave a series of oblique impressions when employed in an interrupted linear fashion. The technique . . . effected distinct decorative results" (Johnston, 1968: 58-59). While most of these exhibited a dragged dentate stamp technique, Johnston was able to identify a small percentage as cord impressed (ibid.).

The Illinoian affinities of the Upper Peninsula Linear Impressed, Corded vessels are seen in the unbossed Naples Stamp, cord-wrapped stick variety (Griffin, 1952: 112; Pl. XXXIII, A-C), although in terms of decorative motif illustrations of Naples Ovoid Stamped, cross-barred variety seem to be closer (ibid.: p. 112, Pl. XXXIV, C).

Upper Peninsula Banked Punctate; Plain tool [chevron] (Pl. XII, *a-i*) consists of six vessels represented by seven rimsherds and twenty-six bodysherds in situ with eight additional sherds from later levels of the site. Paste, temper, vessel thickness and rim diameter are the same as for Banked Punctate, Plain tool [oblique] (p. 55). All lips are parellel-sided, plain, and flattened (Fig. 11, *a*). Interior lip decoration occurs on two vessels only and consists of a single encircling row of short notches across the interior lip edge 3.8 mm apart, 1.5 mm wide, 1.5 mm to 2.5 mm long, and 0.7 mm deep. One of these vessels also displays a similar exterior lip decoration (Pl. XII, *a*). Rim decoration extends from just below the lip to the upper shoulder. It consists of four to ten parallel horizontal bands of oblique plain tool punctates. On three vessels two contiguous rows have the oblique punctate elements oriented in the same direction while the next two contiguous rows are opposed by sixty to ninety degrees. This motif is repeated from two to five times (Pl. XII, *a-d*). On the other three vessels the oblique elements within each horizontal row are opposed to those above or below it (Pl. XII, *e-i*). These oblique punctates are 5.2 mm to 11.3 mm long, 0.7 mm to 1.6 mm wide, 0.3 mm to 0.9 mm deep, and 2.3 mm to 6.1 mm apart. The horizontal rows occasionally overlap, or are as far as 5.8 mm apart.

Sherds of this ceramic group have been reported from Isle Royale where they are designated Linear Punctate (Bastian, 1963: Pl. XIX, Fig. a-e). Several sherds, representing possibly only a single vessel, were recovered from Naomikong Point (Donald Janzen: personal communication). From the 1965 surface collections from Ekdahl-Goudreau a single sherd of this group was found.

Ceramics resembling this group have not been reported from Minnesota or Manitoba. Mason has illustrated several similar sherds from the Mero site as Becker Punctated (1966: 245, Pl. XVI, Fig. 2, *a*, center), but these are not duplicated in the ceramics from the Porte des Morts site (Mason, 1967).

None of the northern Ontario Laurel sites yields ceramics of this group, and the closest resemblances in Ontario seem to be some of the pseudo-scallop shell and dentate chevron rimsherds from the Donaldson site (Wright and Anderson, 1963: 61, Pl. XI, Fig. 5, 6; Pl. XIII, Fig. 8). Ritchie has illustrated a single sherd of Vinette Dentate from the East Sugar Island site which also utilizes a chevron motif (1949: 11, Fig. 3, *g*). This is not uncommon for Vinette Dentate (Ritchie and MacNeish, 1949: 100-2) but the dentated stamp is certainly different than the Upper Peninsula Banked Punctate. Ritchie has also illustrated a rim of Wickham Punctate type B which seems to correspond quite closely to the Summer Island group (Ritchie, 1946: 14, 42-43; Pl. 8, Fig. 34). The Wickham Punctate types are quite loosely defined however (Ritchie and MacNeish, 1949), and many regional variations can find a place within their boundaries.

There are striking, albeit improbable, relationships between some sherds of this ceramic group from Summer Island and decorative techniques characteristic of early Illinois types such as Morton Incised (Griffin, 1952: 100; Pl. XXIX, F-L) or Fettle Incised (Griffin, 1952: 105; Pl. XXIX, K, Pl. XXXVIII, B). Some interpretation of these similarities will be offered in the chapter dealing with the chronology and external relationships of the Middle Woodland component at Summer Island.

Upper Peninsula Linear Stamped; Dentate tool variety (Pl. XII, *j-p*) consists of five vessels represented by eight rimsherds and fourteen decorated bodysherds from the Middle Woodland levels, with ten additional sherds from subsequent deposits. The paste was poorly fired, quite friable, and rather soft. Temper was sparse (about 20 to 25 per cent aplastic by volume) and consisted of crushed granitic grit with muscovite, quartz, and plagioclase felspar predominating. Temper particle size ranged from 0.9 mm to 7.0 mm with a mean diameter of 2.8 mm. Bodysherds were 7.3 mm to 8.9 mm thick with a mean of 7.5 mm. At the upper shoulder the range was 7.0 mm to 9.0 mm with a mean thickness of 7.2 mm. Two distinct rim profiles were noted on these vessels. Two vessels (Pl. XII, *i, l*) displayed almost no neck constriction and had a slightly everted rounded thick lip (Fig. 11, *k*). At 2 cm below the lip, rim thickness on these vessels was 7.8 mm to 10.5 mm with a mean of 9.5 mm. The rounded lip was from 5.0 mm to 5.8 mm with a mean of 5.3 mm thick. The other three vessels of this group (Pl. XII, *j, k-p*) displayed a slight neck constriction and a thinned rim with a flat, exterior beveled lip (Fig. 11, *e*). The rimsherds were from 5.8 mm to 6.8 mm with a mean thickness of 6.1 mm. The lip itself was 5.6 mm to 6.0 mm with a mean thickness of 4.9 mm. Rim diameter ranged from 17.3 cm to 24.8 cm with a mean vessel rim diameter of 20 cm. Only one vessel with a beveled flat lip bears any exterior lip decoration and this has a single encircling row of vertical plain tool punctates 3.0 mm apart, 1.8 mm wide, and 5.5 mm long. Subsequently the rim was smoothed over obliterating the upper margin of these impressions. All the flattened beveled lip vessels have interior lip decoration consisting of a single encircling row of vertical dentate impressions, 6.8 mm to 9.5 mm apart, 9.2 mm long, 2.1 mm wide, originating 1.2 mm to 2.0 mm below the lip edge.

All vessels have exterior rim decoration consisting of dentate stamping beginning at the lip. These dentate stamp impressions are as long as 33.0 mm. The stamp is 1.6 mm wide with rectangular teeth 2.6 mm to 3.3 mm long separated by a ridge of clay (notch on the tool) 0.5 mm to 0.9 mm wide. The teeth are impressed 0.7 mm to 1.3 mm into the clay and the notch on the tool seems to be about 0.3 mm deep. On both rounded lip vessels there is a band 8 mm wide originating 3.5 to 5.5 mm below the lip where the dentate impressions have been subsequently smoothed and more or less obliterated. The dentate stamping on these vessels extends down to the upper shoulder in parallel vertical or slightly oblique rows 3.2 mm to 4.9 mm apart. On two of the other vessels the dentate stamping begins at the lip and extends downward to the upper shoulder in five to ten parallel horizontal rows 4.1 mm to 6.7 mm apart (Pl. XII *k, p, o*). The remaining vessels in this group (Pl. XII, *j, m, n*) are decorated with parallel vertical rows of dentate stamping 3.6 mm to 4.7 mm apart beginning at the lip and extending downward to the neck area 3.7 mm below. This dentating has been somewhat obliterated along its upper margin but this was probably accidental during the lip smoothing. Below the vertical dentate rows is a band of 5 to 7 horizontal rows of end-to-end dentate stamp impressions 4.2 mm to 6.3 mm apart extending down to the maximum vessel diameter at the shoulder.

Similar dentate stamped ceramics have been recovered from the lower levels of the Ekdahl-Goudreau site where at least two vessels are represented (Prahl and Brose, n.d.). Bastian has reported several vessels of this group from Isle Royale (1963: Pl. X). From Naomikong Point 297 sherds representing 62 minimal vessels were recovered. While these vessels are somewhat finer in execution than those from Summer Island, very similar ceramics have also been described as Goodwin-Gresham Dentate from farther south in the state (Brose, n.d. *a*).

Wilford (1952: 6; 1955: 134) has described similar dentate stamped ceramics for the Laurel focus of Minnesota, and Stoltman (1962: 43, 81, Pl. IV) has further illustrated and defined the type Laurel Linear Dentate which corresponds to the Upper Peninsula Linear Impressed, Dentate tool ceramics from Summer Island. From southeast Manitoba, MacNeish has described the rounded lip group as Laurel Dentate (1958: 144, Pl. XIV, Nos. 4, 5) while the flattened lip decoration occurs on his Lockport Linear type (1958: 145-50, Pl. XIV, Nos. 1-3).

Mason has reported similar ceramics as North Bay Dentate from both Mero and Porte des Morts in Wisconsin (1967: 284-87, Pl. 3). A sherd from Porte des Morts which Mason describes as North Bay Scallop (1967: 287-88, Pl. 4, lower left) is also a good example of the Upper Peninsula Linear Dentate Stamped decoration as seen on the flattened lip vessels.

Wright has described dentate stamped ceramics as a minority type from nearly all of the northern Ontario Laurel sites (1967: 15, 121-22). Many of these ceramics show quite close resemblances to those from Summer Island (1967: Pl. I, Fig. 11; Pl. III, Fig. 3). Wright has also reported dentate stamped ceramics as one of the major decorations for the Saugeen Focus Donaldson site (Wright and Anderson, 1963: 25-26; Pl. XIII). The vertical over horizontal motif accounts for 24.9 per cent of all sherds using this technique of decoration. Similar ceramics have also been recovered from the Inverhuron site (Kenyon, 1957: 17-23, Pl. VII, Figs. 12-14, 16) and the Burley site (Jury and Jury, 1952: 65-70; 72; Pl. IV).

From the Point Peninsula sites in eastern Ontario and New York State, ceramics quite similar to the Upper Peninsula Linear Dentate Stamped have been reported as "Kant Rectangular Dentate" from the Kant Site (Emerson, 1955: 37-41, 58-59; Pl. IX, Figs. 12-15); "Inverhuron Dentate" from both the Inverhuron site (Kenyon, 1957: 20) and the Serpent Mounds site (Johnston, 1968: Pl. 29, Fig. 3); as "Saugeen Focus Dentate Stamped" from the Plum Point site (J. Wright, 1967: 113-14); "Dentated" from the Malcolm site (Dailey and Wright, 1955); as "Vinette Dentate" from the Ault Park site (Emerson, cited in Wright, 1967: 114); and "Untyped" from East Sugar Island (Ritchie, 1949: 10; Fig. 3, *r*). These ceramics have also been reported from the Wickham site (Ritchie, 1946: Pl. 8, Fig. 11) and often included as Vinette Dentate in early components and as Jacks Reef Dentate in later ones (Ritchie and MacNeish, 1949: 100-2).

While these ceramics show the same technique as Naples Stamped, Dentate Variety (Griffin, 1952: 110), the motif is quite different and relationships in the Illinois area are not clear.

Upper Peninsula Banked Stamp; *Narrow tool*, *[horizontal]* (Pl. XIII, *a-j*) consists of five vessels represented by twelve rimsherds and fifty-two decorated bodysherds from the Middle Woodland levels. An additional ten sherds of this group were recovered from subsequent levels. Paste, temper, and vessel thickness are the same as those described for Upper Peninsula Banked Stamp, Narrow tool variety [vertical]. Rim diameter for the present group ranged from 17.8 cm to 27 cm with a mean vessel rim diameter of 23 cm. All vessels displayed a moderately everted flattened rim (Fig. 11, *d*) with a plain interior and a slightly rolled exterior lip (due to the extrusion of plastic clay in the flattening process). Subsequent to the lip flattening, three of these vessels received an exterior lip decoration of a single encircling row of vertical to slightly oblique notches 2.0 to 5.0 mm apart, 3.0 mm to 5.0 mm long, 0.2 to 0.7 mm wide, and 0.6 mm deep (Pl. XIII, *a-c*). Below this rim, decoration consists of three to six horizontal rows of very closely banked linear stamp impressions or controlled incisions. These elements are often overlapping and are nearly horizontal, rarely being oblique at more than 20 degrees from horizontal. The width of each row is 1.5 mm to 4.3 mm and the rows are 7.2 mm to 9.4 mm apart.

This group seems to be an extreme variation of the previously described Narrow Banked Stamp, and its ceramic affinities are to be found with those of that group and of the group described next.

Upper Peninsula Linear Incised; *Interrupted variety* (Pl. XIII, *k-p*) consists of four vessels represented by thirteen rimsherds and seventeen decorated bodysherds in situ with five sherds from subsequent levels. The paste was rather sandy and quite compact. Temper, excluding the sand, was rather scarce (about 20 to 25 per cent aplastic by volume) and consisted of crushed granitic grit, 1.0 mm to 4.2 mm in diameter ($\overline{X}$ = 2.3 mm) with some preference shown for darker minerals such as olivine, biotite and augite. Vessel thickness ranged from 6.5 mm to 9.2 mm below the shoulder ($\overline{X}$ = 7.5 mm), and 8.9 mm to 9.2 mm ($\overline{X}$ = 9.0) at the shoulder itself. Three vessels displayed a moderately everted parallel-sided flattened lip (Fig. 11, *a*) with a rim thickness of 6.9 mm to 9.3 mm with a mean of 8.7 mm, and a lip thickness 6.0 mm to 7.2 mm with a mean thickness of 6.5 mm. The other vessel shows a vertical rim (7.5 mm thick) with a flattened lip having an interior bevel (Fig. 11, *i*). This lip ranged from 4.2 mm to 5.0 mm with a mean thickness of 4.5 mm. Rim diameter ranged from 17.2 cm to 25 cm with a mean vessel rim diameter of 20 cm.

The single vessel having the beveled lip had an exterior lip decoration consisting of a single row of incised vertical chevrons 1.2 mm deep, and 2.0-3.1 mm apart each leg of which was 9.0 mm long (Pl. XIII, *k*). Below this were a series of opposed triangular plats composed of parallel interrupted incised lines. Within the center of each triangular plat the surface was blank and a random series of dentate stamps occasionally occurred. These stamps were created by a rectangular three-toothed dentate tool, 1.0 mm wide, 3.5 mm long, each tooth of which was about 1.0 mm long and separated by a narrow notch in the tool about 0.2 mm wide and 0.3 mm deep.

The other three vessels displayed exterior lip decoration consisting of a single encircling row of vertical rectangular four-toothed dentate stamps, 11.4 to 12.0 mm long, 1.8 mm wide, each tooth of which was 2.1 mm long and separated by a ridge of clay 0.3 mm wide. Pottery which James Wright has illustrated as pseudo-scallop shell has a striking resemblance to the punctated interrupted linear incised sherds from Summer Island (1967: Pl. II, Figs. 4, 6, 8, 9; Pl. VII, Fig. 2).

Similar ceramics are not reported from any of the Saugeen Focus components in Ontario.

While there are clear motif similarities to some examples of Vinette Dentate (Ritchie and MacNeish, 1949: Fig. 37, *c*, *d*) the differences in technique seem to overshadow these. Much the same statement can be made for Point Peninsula Corded (Ritchie and MacNeish, 1949: 102; Fig. 37, *h-g*, *m*). The closest ceramics to those from Summer Island do, however, come from Point Peninsula components in eastern Ontario. From East Sugar Island Ritchie has recovered untyped sherds of several vessels which bear strong resemblances to the Summer Island Interrupted Linear Incised (1949: 16-17; Fig. 4, *o*, *s*, *t*, *ee*). From the nearby Serpent Mound site Johnston has recovered sherds of Rice Lake Banded (1968: Pl. 69, Fig. 3; Pl. 70, Fig. 1, 2); Point Peninsula Corded (1968: Pl. 64, Fig. 1); and "Aberant" Vinette 2 (1968: Pl. 29, Fig. 1) which are remarkably similar in all respects to the vessels from Summer Island.

In terms of decorative motif alone, these ceramics do seem to show some broad similarities to the early incised wares from central Illinois (e.g., Black Sand Incised [Griffin, 1952: 98, Pl. XXVIII]). The significance of these relationships is clearly minor.

Upper Peninsula Linear Incised; *Uniform variety*, *[crisscross]* (Pl. XIV, *a*, *b*) consists of three vessels represented by two rimsherds and thirty-two decorated bodysherds in situ, and five additional bodysherds from subsequent levels. Paste is compact with rather abundant crushed granitic grit tempering (about 40 per cent aplastic) 0.9 mm to 6.0 mm in diameter ($\overline{X}$ = 2.0 mm). Bodysherds range in thickness at the shoulder from 5.0 to 6.1 mm with a mean of 5.8 mm. All vessels have a parallel-sided slightly everted rim (4.5 mm to 6.5 mm; $\overline{X}$ = 5.2 mm) with a flattened lip (Fig. 11, *a*) ranging in thickness from 4.8 mm to 6.2 mm with a mean of 5.3 mm. Rim diameters range from 24 cm to 31 cm with a mean vessel rim diameter of 27 cm. All vessels display interior lip decoration consisting of a single horizontal row of vertical lip notches 0.5 mm deep, 2.5 mm wide at the surface, 5.5 mm long, and 5.5 mm apart. Exterior decoration on all vessels consist of a band of two opposed oblique uniformly incised lines below the exterior lip. These lines cross each other at thirty to ninety degree angles to form a double row of incised crisscross designs. On one vessel (Pl. XIV, *a*) these incised lines are 4.0 mm to 7.0 mm high, 0.8 mm to 1.1 mm wide, and 1.5 mm deep. Lines oriented in the same direction are 4.0 mm apart. On the other vessels (Pl. XIV, *b*) the incised lines are 20 to 30 mm high, 0.5 to 0.8 wide, and 0.5 mm deep. Lines with the same orientation are 9.5 mm to 15.0 mm apart.

Similar ceramics have been reported as Laurel Linear Incised from several sites on Isle Royale (Bastian, 1963: Pl. XI, *f*, *g*). A single sherd of this type was also excavated from the Naomikong Point site (Donald Janzen: personal communication). Over fifty sherds representing two vessels of this group were recovered from the burial at the Arrowhead Drive site (Bettarel and Harrison, 1962: 38-39, Pl. I, left).

Both Wilford (1952, 1955) and Stoltman (1962: 43) report these ceramics as a minor but ubiquitous variant of Laurel Incised Line, present at all Minnesota Laurel sites. MacNeish has described "cross-hatched rims" for Cemetery Point Incised ceramics from Manitoba (1958: 151) although these are not illustrated.

While Mason did not recover any similar ceramics at the Mero site, he illustrates a sherd from Porte des Morts which seems identical to vessels from Summer Island (1967: 300; Pl. 10, *d*).

No similar ceramics seem to have been recovered from the northern Ontario Laurel sites (J. Wright, 1967: 122). The Donaldson site has produced sherds with roughly the same motif (Wright and Anderson, 1963: Pl. XV, Fig. 2) but execution and vessel shape are quite different. It is in eastern Ontario and upper New York State that these ceramics find close affinities, most strongly in the Wickham Incised (Ritchie, 1946; Ritchie and MacNeish, 1949: 103-4; Fig. 38, *a*, *b*) and to a lesser extent with the later Kipp Island Criss-cross (Ritchie and MacNeish, 1949: 104-6; Fig. 38, *h*).

That these ceramics bear certain resemblances to the Hopewell Cross-hatched Rim (Griffin, 1952: 116) is clear. The northern ceramics are considerably cruder however, and much sloppier execution is evident. If the relationship is real it must be with the later degenerate Hopewell manifestations such as Baehr (Griffin, 1952: 119-20), or Weaver Plain with "Short thin gashes" on the upper rim (1952: 121).

Upper Peninsula Miscellaneous Punctate (Pl. XIII, *c*-*k*) is not really an acceptable type, but rather a category in which to place the vessels represented by twelve rimsherds and thirty punctated bodysherds from the Middle Woodland levels of the Summer Island site. While all of these sherds have the paste and tempering characteristic of the other Upper Peninsula Ware ceramics at the site, very little else is common. All extant rimsherds show a plain flattened lip, but no vessel had enough rim present to measure rim diameter. In general these ceramics seem most closely related to the Upper Peninsula Banked Punctate type, but as they all display different tool impressions it was considered inadvisable to set up an additional nine varieties on the basis of twelve sherds. All vessels seem to have one to five horizontal rows of dentate, or corded-stamp, or tool impressions on the exterior rim. None have any interior decoration. Among the varied elements creating these impressions are the following: one vessel (Pl. XIII, *f*) shows rows of stamping that look as if the end of a miniature steel girder or "I-beam" had been pushed into the clay. This stamp is 4.5 mm high, 3.0 mm wide, and 0.9 mm deep. The stamps are approximately 5.5 mm apart. One sherd (Pl. XIII, *e*) bears a row of rectangular dentate stamping above (or below) a plain smooth area which has three alternate-notched pseudo-scallop shell impressions 3.0 mm apart. This is the only possible true pseudo-scallop shell impressing at the site, and the identification offered here is only tentative. One sherd (Pl. XIII, *d*) bears a double row of "cuneiform" impressions 7.8 mm high, 2 mm wide at their base and 2.5 mm deep at the base. This sherd is quite similar to the design on a vessel of Goodwin-Gresham Punctate from Iosco County, Michigan (Brose, n.d. *a*). Other sherds bear crescentic, rectangular, corded (Pl. XII, *k*) and annular punctates. Miscellaneous punctated potsherds are reported from virtually every Middle Woodland site in the Great Lakes area, and a search for ceramic affinities would be as lengthy as it would be inconclusive.

Three additional vessels are represented by twenty-one bodysherds from the Middle Woodland levels of the site. These sherds were either exfoliated or sand-blasted to such a degree that accurate interpretation of their decorative technique was impossible and they are listed in the tables as Indeterminate.

DISCUSSION

While the external relationships of the Middle Woodland ceramic component from Summer Island have been discussed in detail in the previous section some general comments do not seem out of place here. As an integrated ceramic assemblage the Upper Peninsula pottery from Summer Island is somewhat unusual. In terms of paste, temper, vessel shape and thickness, and rim profile the Upper Peninsula ware has a clearly intermediate position between the more northern Middle Woodland complexes of Laurel-Point Peninsula and the thicker North Bay-Au Sable-Saugeen ceramics immediately to the south. In terms of the ceramic decoration as seen in frequency of each type, this intermediacy is expressed quite differently. Pseudo-scallop shell impressions are seen as a major decorative element in all Laurel components (and from the Saugeen and to some degree, the Point Peninsula sites) in Ontario. They are weakly represented in the North Bay ceramics in Wisconsin, and absent from Summer Island with the exception of a single questionable sherd. The Banked Stamp varieties which account for nearly 53 per cent of all the vessels represented in the Middle Woodland component at Summer Island, account for less than 20 per cent of the North Bay ceramics (Mason, 1966: 113, Table II) and less than 5 per cent of Laurel or Saugeen ceramics (Wilford, 1955: J. Wright, 1967: 120, Table 36). They have quite a low frequency in Point Peninsula sites (J. Wright, 1967; Ritchie, 1965: 203-12). The Dragged Stamp vessels which make up 17.5 per cent of the ceramics from the Summer Island component represent less than 10 per cent of the vessels from the North Bay component at Porte des Morts. Dragged stamp is one of the dominant decorations in the Minnesota Laurel sites (James Stoltman: personal communication), and accounts for decoration on about 30 per cent of the vessels in all Ontario Point Peninsula and Laurel sites

(J. Wright, 1967), but only about 10 per cent of the ceramics from New York Point Peninsula components (Ritchie, 1965: 212-13), and seem to be totally absent from Saugeen components (J. Wright, 1967). Cord decoration of any kind seems to exist only in the Manitoba Laurel components (MacNeish, 1958) in any amount. It is totally absent from the Minnesota and Ontario Laurel sites (Stoltman, personal communication; J. Wright, 1967) but accounts for at least 30 per cent of the ceramic decoration from all Point Peninsula components (J. Wright, 1967) and nearly 40 per cent of the North Bay component ceramics at Porte des Morts (Mason, 1967: 304, Table 3). It is represented on less than 4 per cent of the vessels from Summer Island.

In general, while the Laurel-North Bay-Saugeen-Point Peninsula ceramics share most of their decorative attributes, they express these in radically different frequencies. Mason has stated (1967: 341) that most of these shifts in relative frequencies are probably more representative of geographical clines than of chronological changes. To a great extent this does represent an economical explanation for the available data. In this respect, however, the Upper Peninsula ceramics from Summer Island represent an anomaly. If a theory of gradual geographic clines is acceptable the ceramics from Summer Island should fit between the North Bay and the Ontario Laurel ceramic complexes in terms of north to south frequency changes, and between the Point Peninsula and the Minnesota Laurel complex in terms of an east-west cline. This could be indicated schematically by a generalized listing of the various frequencies reported in the literature for different ceramic attributes by areas, with the components arranged in the following manner:

Minnesota Laurel		Ontario Laurel	Ontario Point Peninsula
	Summer Island		
	North Bay		New York Point Peninsula

The schema for the percentages of major ceramic attributes would then be as follows:

Pseudo-Scallop Shell:

>25		25	<20
	0		
	<10		<10

		Banked Stamp:	
>10		<5	10
	>50		
	20		15
		Plain:	
>20		15	>5
	10		
	5		<5
		Dragged Stamp:	
>30		30	25
	<20		
	10		10
		Corded Impressions:	
0		0	0
	<5		
	>40		>35
		Punctates or Bossing:	
>25		>50	10
	0		
	<5		<20
		Linear Dentate Stamping:	
>5		10	15
	<5		
	20		20
		Rocker Stamping:	
0		0	<5
	0		
	<5		30
		Cordmarked Surface:	
0		0	>5
	0		
	<40		>25

Granted the validity of this model one could postulate a number of regional "style-zones" showing differential preferences for different attributes from a ceramic repertoire whose contents were known throughout the entire area. While a stylistic epicenter may not be definable, certain regions could be expected to show the greatest similarities in frequency of any particular attribute with their closest neighbors. Indeed this is merely a restatement of the culture-area concept. In this model a strong preference for dentate stamping, rocker stamping, and corded decoration, as well as a preference for (or at least no selection against) cord-marked surfaces could be predicted to occur to the south of this area. Pseudo-scallop shell impressions as well as plain rims seem to be confined to the northern portion of this area and appear more frequently in the west than in the east. The dragged-stamp technique also seems more northern in its occurrence, but is stronger in the west-central part of that area. The banked stamping seems to be strongest in the south-central region and similar frequencies of this motif could be predicted further to the south. The only major decorative element that does not neatly fit the model is the incidence of a single row of punctates or bosses encircling the vessel just below the rim. No clear distribution can be found in the literature for this attribute, and within our area it would seem to be most common in the north-central region. The model outlined above could be tested by examining the ceramic attributes it predicts for the areas lying to the south.

Certain of the most commonly reported attributes of the Illinois Hopewell ceramics correspond quite closely to what would be expected on the basis of the model described. Dentate stamping, rocker stamping, and cordmarked vessel surfaces are all characteristic of the Middle Woodland Havana complex (Griffin, 1952). Of further interest is the high incidence of bossing and rim-encircling punctates which are seen in these ceramics, indicating a possible south-central correlation with the same decorative element seen in the northern area of the model.

Before this synchronic model is accepted, however, it is essential to know just what time period it purports to represent. This culture-area model, is, in fact, quite static and it is essential that all the components from which it derives data be of the same age. If significant temporal differences exist between these components the model must be revised to account for chronological changes as well as geographic ones. The relative chronological position of the integral components should not be determined by reference to similar components of known age which lie within or just outside the area of the model. To do this would be accepting the premise that within a given area ceramics of similar appearance are of similar age. This would entail assumptions concerning the diffusion of ceramic attributes, assumptions that the model was designed to test. The model will thus be valid only to the extent that the chronology of components within the area can independently be shown to exhibit relative harmony.

In terms of relative chronology, all the stratified components occur above Archaic, and below either Late Woodland, Upper Mississippian, or a mixture of the latter two components. The absolute chronology as seen in the available C^{14} dates also falls within these expected limits. If one includes the Saugeen and Au Sable components the following list of dates can be compiled:

669 ± 220 B.C.	Burley Site	(S-119)
530 ± 60 B.C.	Donaldson Site	(C-192)
290 ± 80 B.C.	McGillvary Mound	(Gak-1278)
A.D. 20 ± 200	McGillvary Mound	(Gak-1492)
A.D. 50 ± 120	Arrowhead Drive Burials	(M-1392)
A.D. 58 ± 200	Serpent Mound	(M-850)
A.D. 70 ± 280	Summer Island	(M-2073)
A.D. 128 ± 150	Serpent Mound	(M-1104)
A.D. 140 ± 150	Heron Bay	(GSC-686)
A.D. 160 ± 80	Lewiston Mound	(Y-1276)
A.D. 160 ± 130	Summer Island	(M-2074)
A.D. 160 ± 100	Porte des Morts	(I-888)
A.D. 240 ± 80	O'Neil 3	(Y-1277)
A.D. 250 ± 100	Summer Island	(M-1985)
A.D. 302 ± 150	Serpent Mound	(M-1105)
A.D. 310 ± 100	Kipp Island 2	(Y-1378)
A.D. 320 ± 100	Sand River	(M-1507)
A.D. 410 ± 160	Heron Bay	(GSC-445)
A.D. 610 ± 100	Goodwin-Gresham	(M-1625)
A.D. 610 ± 170	Heron Bay	(GSC-208)
A.D. 630 ± 100	Kipp Island 3	(Y-1379)
A.D. 700 ± 100	Tufano	(Y-1382)
A.D. 700 ± 60	Heron Bay	(S-171)
A.D. 740 ± 100	Wickham 2	(Y-1172)
A.D. 790 ± 130	Heron Bay	(GSC-449)

Within this series there is some doubt concerning just what is being dated at the Burley and Donaldson sites (see Griffin, 1965*a*: 665-65; Mason, 1967: 337). The earlier date on the McGillvary Mound is from materials below the Laurel-like mound itself (K. C. A. Dawson: personal communication). At the other end of the series, the Kipp Island 3, Tufano, and Wickham 2 dates should indicate the end of the Point Peninsula tradition and the beginning of the Hunter's Home phase which is transitional Middle-Late Woodland in Ritchie's opinion (1965: Fig. 1; p. 228, 253). The range of dates for the Heron Bay site are quite acceptable, although not all should pertain to the Laurel occupation (J. Wright, 1967: 6-8). Given the variable nature of the materials submitted for dating with the possibility of deviations produced by isotopic fractionation (Hall, 1967: 171-80), the possibility (probability?) of deviations between true ages and radiocarbon ages from 250 B.C. to A.D. 1000 (Stuiver and Suess, 1966: Table 1), and the fact that the standard deviation range accompanying each date is a statistic indicating a 67 per cent probability exists that the computed radiocarbon age is correct, all indicate that the series of dates listed above are quite compatible with each other. If two standard deviations are allowed (giving a 98 per cent probability that the true radiocarbon age has been counted) all the dates except Burley, Donaldson, the early McGillvary Mound date, Kipp Island 3, Tufano, and Wickham 2 are seen to overlap in the period A.D. 110 to A.D. 420.

Accepting this 300-year period as the most conservative estimate for the Laurel-North Bay-Au Sable-Saugeen-Point Peninsula components would agree with the dates accepted for those components to the south of the model area which show the strongest ceramic relationships. Problems still exist in that there are no available dates for the Manitoba or Minnesota components and the only dates for the Saugeen focus components are best understood as *terminus post quem* dates rather than as actually dating the Saugeen occupations. Another problem is that there are at least three centuries in which temporal changes surely took place within the model area. The question then becomes, do the changes in relative frequencies of different ceramic decorations represent temporal differences within a stylistically homogeneous area or do they represent regional preferences existing throughout a stylistically conservative period of time?

To some extent both alternatives are probably operative, and therein lie several further problems. The use of ceramic seriations to order the components temporally must assume a relatively large area wherein similar styles come into popularity and go out of favor at the same time. This method does not account for regional variations in style frequencies. On the other hand, to interpret the intercomponent variation as a simple expression of style-zones does great injustice to any understanding of possible ceramic development in what Fitting (1965*a*) has called the "Lake Forest Middle Woodland." If any conclusion can be drawn from this discussion it may be that, given the present state of knowledge, no analytical model can be constructed for these components which will not display logical inconsistencies. While the "culture-area" type of model seems to display some predictive capability this is true only when grossly oversimplified data are used as input for deriving extraareal comparisons. The model cannot be refined to adequately cope with interregional variations until the integral components consist primarily of tightly dated single occupations. Ideally these components will also be functionally equivalent and of approximately equal size. In this respect some consideration must be given to sample size. Even aside from the very real problems of statistically measurable sampling error due to the discrepancy in the size of the populations involved, two sites displaying similar frequencies of ceramic decoration will not mean the same thing if at one site only three or four vessels are represented while at the other site several dozen were recovered. The reasoning behind this is not immediately obvious, and traditionally percentages have been used to express these differences. This often results in assigning the same weight to five rimsherds as to five hundred. Nonetheless, pots are made by people and one would not expect a single potter to utilize all the currently acceptable decorative elements available to the entire cultural group, be that a family, band, or a tribal confederation (see Bunzel, 1929: 62-63). This would be the ceramic equivalent to the "founder effect" seen in genetics.

While concepts of functionally differing ceramic decoration are not generally utilized in this area of North America, some distinction can be made between ceremonial and utilitarian ceramic decorations in the Middle Woodland of Ohio, Illinois and adjacent areas (Griffin, 1965*b*: 107-9). This fact should be kept in mind when comparing ceramics from a Minnesota burial mound to those recovered from a Michigan fishing village. Even within a single component of a nonceremonial site variations in the uses of vessels may correlate with differing decorative elements. At the Late Woodland Spring Creek site in Muskegon County, Michigan, Fitting (1968*a*: 22-29) has noted a highly significant association between rim type and rim diameter. This may be merely a mechanical relationship due to the need for a thicker rim on larger vessels to prevent collapse during drying. In the Middle Woodland component at Summer Island where there is also a very significant association of certain decorations with vessels having a certain rim diameter (Table 7) no such mechanical explanation can be invoked. Since the ratio of vessel height to rim diameter seems relatively constant and all vessels display a similar shape, three distinct size groupings for these vessels can be proposed. Using the volumetric formula for an eliptic paraboloid (Burlington, 1956) and the rim: height ratio observed on the reconstructed vessel (Pl. III, *c*), vessels having a rim diameter of about 20 cm will have a capacity of about 3.1 liters; vessels with a rim diameter of 25 cm will have a capacity of about 6 liters; and vessels with a rim diameter of 33 cm will have a capacity of just under 12 liters. If these three sizes of vessels represent functionally different uses of pottery, and as the designs applied to each different size group seem not to be random but rather culturally determined, functionally different sites occupied by the same group during the course of a single seasonal cycle could be expected to show quite different frequencies of the various ceramic decorations. It is also quite possible that different areas within single component sites would show radically different frequencies of ceramic decorations depending on the function of that area of the site. This is just what Fitting (1968*a*) found at Spring Creek where the frequency of vessels with collared rims (and larger rim diameters) was inversely proportional to the distance from the creek itself. At Summer Island too, variations in ceramic design can be correlated with different areas of the site but not so simply as at Spring Creek. This will be explored in more detail in the following discussion of areal distributions. At that point some attention will also be paid to the influence social structure may exert on ceramic decoration (to the extent that archaeological evidence will allow such inferences to be made).

It would be tempting to close the chapter on this promissory note, but some reference must be made to the origins of the ceramic complex under analysis. It should be obvious (in my opinion) that ceramic seriation charts may indicate temporal differences, geographical differences, functional differences, sample size differences (with the intendent "founder effect"), sampling error, or a combination of any of these. If they are purported to represent the first of these the rest must, a priori, be assumed nonsignificant. Even more important is the assumption that ceramic styles will always exhibit a uniform rate of gradual change. This should be one of the basic questions of archaeology, not basic dogma. Having made these disclaimers the ceramic complex represented by Laurel-North Bay-Saugeen-Point Peninsula must now be attacked as it has traditionally been. That is, I will assume that this "Lake Forest" represents a relatively homogeneous style-conservative culture area during an imprecisely defined Middle Woodland period. All sites will be assumed to have been functionally equivalent insofar as ceramics are concerned. Variations in sample size will be ignored, and social structure will not be considered to affect ceramic design.

It is obvious that even under these restrictive conditions which deviate considerably from any ethnographically reported, there are difficulties involved in applying a scheme of ceramic seriation to determine the earliest components. While certain ceramic attributes do tend to show higher frequencies in one region than another, some attributes appear quite randomly distributed throughout the entire area (eg., incising). The choice of which attributes are to be considered temporally significant is up to the individual archaeologist. Needless to say, a different choice of attributes may well produce different seriation of components. Even if some list of chronologically valid attributes were determined and a seriation of components based on these were created there would be no intrinsic way to determine which end of the series was earlier. Indeed, if most of the components were stratified with clearly differing frequencies of the different ceramic attributes in each stratum, this difficulty would be considerably reduced. Unfortunately this has been the rare occurrence within the area under discussion, and all such sites have been Point Peninsula components. Even in these sites, the sequent occupations have been so separated in time that little is known of the ceramic changes taking place within the A.D. 100 to A.D. 400 period (see Ritchie, 1965: 203-53).

In lieu of adequate stratification the tendency on the part of some who have felt impelled to derive the Lake Forest Middle Woodland from earlier ceramic complexes has been to select those ceramic attributes that find their earliest occurrence in areas the investigator feels contribute most significantly to the total material culture assemblage. Thus both MacNeish (1958, 1962) and James Wright (1967) have looked to the north and brought Laurel out of Asia. While some of the Asian ceramics do bear striking resemblances to some of the Lake Forest Middle Woodland ceramic decorations, the Asian ceramics seem to predate 1000 B.C. while the Laurel ceramics seem to antedate A.D. 100. This 1100-year gap is unexplained. Also unexplained is the 2000-mile gap separating the most tenuous Laurel-like ceramics (Brown, 1962) from the Asian ceramics. No similar ceramics exist anywhere in the North American Arctic (Griffin, 1962: 161). Having chosen an early Arctic source for Laurel, James Wright thus is committed to a rather early date for this complex in the Lake Forest zone despite the available radiocarbon dates (1967: 95). Having precluded any southern source of origin, Wright chooses boss-producing punctating or bossing, and cordwrapped decoration as late attributes within the Laurel sequence as these occur on the post-Laurel Blackduck ceramics (1967: 99-102). That they also occur in a fair amount on the Siberian ceramics in the Arctic (Griffin, 1962: 160-62) is ignored. Also ignored, since the source for the Laurel complex has been already chosen as northern, is the fact that in the closely related North Bay and Point Peninsula complexes cordwrapping can be seen as an early attribute, in the latter at least, clearly derived from the resident Early Woodland groups. In fact, both bossing and punctating associated with cordwrapped surfaces and corded decoration, are quite characteristic of the Havana ceramic complex which clearly can be derived from the earlier Morton focus ceramics which also display these attributes (Griffin, 1952). There is also excellent evidence that this Illinois Hopewell complex of ceramics was geographically quite expansive for several hundred years beginning just before the birth of Christ (Griffin, 1964; 1967: 180-85; Flanders, n.d.). If one is not committed to finding progenitors for the Laurel-North Bay-Au Sable-Saugeen-Point Peninsula ceramics in the distant northwest, a much more economical source can be found for their major decorative traditions in Illinois at a more reasonable date.

I would reject the seriation proposed by J. Wright (1967) for Laurel ceramics, just as I would reject the resultant inferences that both the Saugeen focus of Ontario and the little known Malmo focus of Minnesota (Wilford, 1955) represent a fusion of late Laurel and early Hopewell. In this same negative vein I would also reject the hypothesis that the "Laurel Tradition" represents a major population movement into the Lake Forest from the northwest. The relative homogeneity of the ceramics in this area are best interpreted as the adoption and adaptation of ceramic styles (which reached their greatest elaboration in the Illinoian areas where the best developmental sequence for them can also be found) by people whose ecological adaptation to the area imposed the need for great mobility over large distances on their culture. The confinement of these "Northern Tier Middle Woodland" styles (Mason, 1967: 340-41) to the Lake Forest formation biotome (as Fitting [1965*a*] noted) reinforces this theory.

In summary, the frequencies of different ceramic attributes seen in the Summer Island Middle Woodland component display the same range as do most of the Laurel to Point Peninsula ceramic complexes. This indicates the participation of the Summer Island inhabitants in a cultural expression widespread throughout an ecological zone characterized by mixed hardwood-conifer forests bordering a lacustrine-riverine system extending from Lake Winnipeg to the Saint Lawrence estuary and existing from at least A.D. 100 to at least A.D. 400. Within any part of this region intercomponent variations in the percentages of each particular decorative attribute might broadly characterized as geographic clines with most well-defined attributes showing an increase toward the south-central area. This is taken to indicate the most probable direction from which to derive the ceramic styles which have influenced the Laurel to Point Peninsula continuum. The more realistic and detailed analysis of ceramic variations must also consider sample size, site size, site function, and functional area of the site in attempting to assay the importance of these frequency variations. The high frequency of Banked Stamp ceramics from Summer Island is thus assumed to represent more of a "founder effect" due to limited-function occupation by a small familial group, than to be an expression of temporal difference or extraareal intrusion.

Given the nature of most components and the present paucity of thoroughly excavated and internally dated sites, continental schemes of culture history hinging upon ceramic seriations involving small, mixed components from this region are indeed, "a reconstruction . . . speculative to the point of fantasy" (J. Wright, 1967: 126).

VI

CHIPPED STONE

SAMPLE

FROM the 134 5 by 5 foot excavation units at the site yielding in situ Middle Woodland material, 33,718 pieces of chipped stone with a total weight of 64,205 grams were recovered. With the exception of eight corner-notched projectile points, it was considered prejudicial to assign typologically similar materials from later deposits to this component. This must mean that later components will be biased by introduction of some earlier materials. Unlike the ceramic assemblage, there is no possible way to apply any corrective factor to these later complexes other than to test them for sampling error. Necessarily, then, conclusions concerning ratios of chipped stone categories will be more tentative as the distance to the surface of the site decreases. Nonetheless, the earliest Middle Woodland component of the Summer Island site should be relatively free from mixture with other components, and the strongest hypothesis can thus be formed in its interpretation.

METHODS OF ANALYSIS

The entire chipped stone sample from the Middle Woodland levels of the site was analyzed by 5 by 5 foot units or by features within units. A listing of the chipped stone breakdown is first given with detailed discussion to follow. The material from each unit was first segregated into four rather broad classes: flakes, cores, unifacial tools, and bifacial tools. Within the first class, flakes, a further breakdown was made into four categories and three subcategories: primary or decortication flakes, secondary or block flakes, and tertiary, or flat flakes. Within this last category three distinct subcategories would occasionally be recognized: hard-hammer flakes, soft-hammer flakes, and flakes of bifacial retouch. A fourth category of flakes, those which exhibited signs of usage, was also set up. Within the class of cores three categories were recognized: pebble cores, block cores, and bipolar cores. The bifacial tool class was divided into four categories: bifacial scrapers or choppers, bifacial blades, bifacial blanks or preforms, and projectile points. The unifacial tool class was divided into four categories: end scrapers, side scrapers, notched scrapers, and bladelets.

Each of the enumerated subcategories was further divided into three groups on the basis of raw materials. The largest group (Type B) consisted of light tannish gray to dark bluish gray chert with a good amount of crystalline quartz or white fossiliferous inclusions. This chert has a fairly smooth texture with a moderately good conchoidal fracture where no inclusions occur. Some traces of banding can be seen but these are quite faint. This chert is opaque, and displays little or no luster in some cases while some examples are rather waxy. This seems to be the same chert referred to by Cleland and Peske (1968: 46) as their Type 2 and Type 3. Harrison (1963) has referred to a similar chert from the Juntunen site as local Bois Blanc chert. In all cases this would seem to be chert weathering out of the Silurian Manistique Dolomite which forms much of the Niagara escarpment from Point Detour to Drummond Island, and which underlies the brecciated Devonian Mackinac Limestone which outcrops on Bois Blanc Island and is devoid of chert or silicaeous inclusions (Martin, 1936).

The second group of raw materials (Type A) distinguished an olive drab to dark brown to black chert. Cortical sections tend to lighter colors and to a grainier texture with the centers of nodules being quite black, almost translucent, and with a very good conchoidal fracture. This is similar to the chert Cleland and Peske (1968) have described as Type 1 at Spider Cave, and to the major variety of Harrison's "Other" category (1963). No source is known for these cherts.

The third group of raw materials from Summer Island (Type C) consists of all remaining chipped stone. Within this broad group are several pieces of translucent waxy yellow to white flint, as well as several pieces of taconite, agate, jasper, quartzite, and a single fragment of a red and bluish-green block core of highly lustrous translucent flint which bears some resemblance to Flint Ridge, Ohio specimens. The source of these cherts and quartzites is presumed to be glacially deposited gravels.

A further subdivision was made within the nearly sixty groupings previously outlined. All pieces were checked for fire-popping, variable areas of darkening, exfoliation, or other characteristics of heat-treatment (Fitting, Devisscher and Wahla, 1966: 19, 34-36). It was soon evident that only an extremely small number of chipped stone pieces displayed "heat-treatment" of any type (0.28 per cent), that these pieces were randomly distributed by classes of chipped stone, and that the same "heat-treatment" criteria could be used to infer frost action. This dichotomy was therefore abandoned as nonsignificant if not misleading.

The categorization by raw material, while not inherently nugatory, also produced relatively nonsignificant results (Table 8). This is clearly a result of the low frequency of group II and III cherts within the sample. There is one divergence from a random distribution however, which is seen in the relatively high frequency of bladelets occurring on nonlocal chert. The explanation for this is mechanical rather than cultural as will be made clear in the detailed discussion of these artifacts below. The distribution of chipped stone categories by number and weight is presented for the entire component in Table 8.

DESCRIPTION OF ARTIFACTS

Primary or decortication flakes were those flakes removed from the exterior of small chert nodules. The external face consists of unmodified cortex. Internal faces lack clearly defined bulbs of percussion and are often characterized by a disjointed block, or irregular angular appearance following old planes of structural weakness within the nodule. While many of these flakes exhibited a concave-convex longitudinal section (Binford and Quimby, 1963: 286-87) most internal faces were too irregular to be so easily classified. Striking platforms were occasionally observed on these flakes (see Wobst, 1968: 201) but probably represent the nodular surface left by removal of a previous decortication flake. Faceted or prepared platforms were not observed on any of these flakes. While some of these flakes may represent chert fragments derived by natural agency as Wobst has suggested (1968), in most cases the location of such flakes within the midden, unassociated with nodules from which to have been so derived, argues against this hypothesis as a generally acceptable explanation. I would agree with Binford and Quimby (1963) that this material represents the debitage resulting from the initial modification of the raw material by heaty percussion. This definition of decortication flakes is in accord with that of Fitting (1966; 1968*b*), McPherron (1967: 131, 134-35), Binford and Quimby, (1963: 286-87), and would be part of Wobst's Category A (1968: 201).

TABLE 8

CHIPPED STONE FROM 134 MIDDLE WOODLAND EXCAVATION UNITS
(Weight in Grams)

Category	No.	Percentage No.	Weight	Percentage Wt.	$\overline{X}$ Wt.	$\overline{X}$ N Per Unit	$\overline{X}$ Wt. Per Unit	σ N Per Unit	σ Wt. Per Unit	Percentage Group I Chert
Flakes:										
Decortication	5179	15.4	17300	26.95	3.4	386	129.1	543	213.3	99.5
Block	9837	29.1	14419	22.25	1.5	735	107.6	619	173.2	99.3
Flat	17682	52.4	15556	24.12	0.9	1318	86.2	2504	166.7	98.7
Utilized	223	0.66	922	1.44	4.1	1.68	6.8	4.25	14.7	99.3
Bladelets	88	0.26	89.2	0.13	1.1	.62	.61	1.47	1.5	75.0
Chert nodules	16	0.045	105.2	0.16	65.7	.12	0.8	2.17	14.3	94.7
Cores:										
Pebble	129	0.38	6707	9.55	52.3	.96	50.1	.89	119.7	98.1
Block	190	0.56	4966	7.75	26.1	1.4	37.1	2.0	107.0	98.1
Bipolar	259	0.77	2597	4.05	10.0	1.9	19.4	2.7	46.3	99.3
Bifaces:										
Scrapers	12	0.036	210	0.33	17.5	.09	1.57	.56	4.6	100
Blades	15	0.044	348	0.54	16.5	.11	2.59	.80	13.8	100
Blanks	12	0.036	256	0.40	21.3	.09	1.92	2.31	8.9	100
Points	22	0.06	522	0.81	23.7	.45	3.89	.25	7.5	95.5
Unifaces:										
End scraper	33	0.09	327	0.51	9.9	.25	2.44	.63	6.9	93.9
Side scraper	17	0.05	172	0.27	10.1	.13	1.28	.41	.4	100
Notched scraper	4	0.012	39	0.06	9.8	.03	0.29	.17	1.9	100
TOTAL	33718	100	64205	100	1.9	2506.83	451.70	4670.13	1136.5	

Secondary or Block Flakes are those flakes derived from the rough trimming of that portion of the nodule from which the cortex has been removed. These flakes are characterized by an unprepared striking platform having an angle of about 90 degrees with the inner face. The flakes are rather massive and irregular in longitudinal section. In cross-section these flakes are characteristically rectangular or square and display all the criteria of the "ridged flakes" from Eastport (Binford and Papworth, *in:* White, Binford and Papworth, 1963: 84-86) except for cortical surfaces. This flake category also includes some amount of secondary shatter due to natural agency (Fitting, 1968*b*; Wobst, 1968: 201) but primarily due to rather freely applied direct percussion, and to breakage. This is the flake type that White calles "tabular flakes: (*in* White, Binford and Papworth, 1963: 13-14) and which McPherron referred to as "irregular thick wedges, evidently the result of trimming cores to shape" (1967: 131). Wobst has included these flakes within his Category B (1968: 201). Binford and Quimby have noted the presence of these flakes from the upper levels of the Summer Island site as both "secondary shatter" and "expanding flakes" (1963: 298-99) where they are purported to indicate a block core technology.

Tertiary or Flat Flakes were sorted into three subcategories. Hard-hammer flakes were thin flat flakes with a well-defined striking platform with a prominent bulb of percussion, no lip on the interior surface striking platform junction, heavy ripple marks on the interior surface with occasional radial shatter lines extending downward from the bulb of percussion, and crushing and shatter scars at the point of impact on the striking platform (Fitting, 1966: 21; n.d., 1-2). In plan view these flakes showed expanding (60 per cent) or parallel (40 per cent) edges (White, *in* White, Binford and Papworth, 1963: 9) and would seem to have been struck from prepared cores (ibid.: 14-15). Soft-hammer flakes were thin flat flakes having a well-defined striking platform with a distinct overhanging lip on its junction with the interior face. Crushing and shatter at the point of impact were absent as were ripple scars and radial shatter lines on the interior face. The bulb of percussion was much less prominent than on hard-hammer flakes although it tended to be somewhat larger. In plan view these flakes showed expanding (30 per cent) parallel (35 per cent) or contracting (35 per cent) edges (White, ibid.: 9, Fig. 6) and may also have been struck from prepared cores. Flakes of bifacial retouch are similar to the soft-hammer flakes described above but have an acute angle between the striking platform and the exterior surface of the flake (Fitting, 1966: 21-23; Fig. 4). These flakes are presumed to be derived from retouching or final shaping of bifacially worked blanks or tools, although as Wobst has mentioned, flakes struck from highly acute-angled cores would be indistinguishable (1968: 201).

Within this flat flake category all flakes from which the striking platform has been broken could not be assigned to one of the three subcategories. There was no reason to assign them to the bifacial retouch group and they were described simply as flat flakes. As the lithic analysis proceeded, it became evident that over 65 per cent of all flat flakes could not be further categorized. An investigation of the chippage recovered from flotation samples of the features and some midden areas revealed that standard and fine screen sieving were missing large amounts of very small soft-hammer and bifacial retouch flakes. These flat flakes were generally under one-eighth of an inch in maximum dimension and represented scraper retouch and bifacial tool resharpening. Because these flat flake categories were very definitely smaller than all the hard-hammer and many of the soft-hammer flakes, and because only selected areas of the Middle Woodland occupation were subjected to flotation, any correlations between these flat flake subcategories and other material from the site would be highly skewed to the hard-hammer flakes. To avoid this bias all flat flakes were considered as a single category in such comparisons. In the subsequent discussions of areal distribution of materials at the site, special mention will be made of those areas where subcategories of flat flakes can be distinguished without introducing this bias. Of the 17,682 flat flakes recovered by all methods, 11,606 (66 per cent) were distinguishable only as flat flakes; 3,059 (17 per cent) as hard-hammer; 1,227 (7.5 per cent) as soft-hammer; and 1,790 (9.5 per cent) as flakes of bifacial retouch.

Utilized Flakes were defined as any flake of any previously described category showing evidence of purposeful retouch or flaking, polishing, crushing, or striation as a result of use. From the Middle Woodland levels the 223 utilized flakes were further analyzed to determine if any significant relationship could be determined between original flake category and usage. As Table 9 indicates, there is a very strong, significant relationship that would be expected by chance alone less than one time in a thousand. This distribution indicates a definite avoidance of block flakes for subsequent usage and a rather strong preference for decortication flakes. In the latter case all the decortication

TABLE 9

PERCENTAGE OF UTILIZED FLAKES BY FLAKE TYPES
MIDDLE WOODLAND COMPONENT

Flake Type	Utilized	Non-Utilized	Total
Flat flakes O/E	48/51	54/51	102
Block flakes O/E	9/20	31/20	40
Decortication flakes O/E	43/29	15/29	58
TOTAL	100	100	200

χ^2 = 25.814
df = 2
p < .001
ϕ^2 = .1280

flakes selected for use were thin, well-formed, and had a rather smooth interior face which met the distal cortex surface at an angle of between 30 and 60 degrees. The block flakes selected for utilization were invariably those having two adjacent faces meeting at the utilized edge in an angle of about 60 degrees. It would seem that in these cases the angle of working edge was the desideratum. Edge wear on both types of flakes were primarily determined using a binocular microscope at low power (45x) with oblique lighting. The principal wear pattern seemed to be characterized by minute pressure flaking, verging on crushing, removing a small series of step-flakes along one surface of the edge of the blade, with numerous overlapping longitudinal striae along the opposite surface of the edge. These striations were quite pronounced although not too deep. This is somewhat similar to wear patterns observed on flint saws by Semenov (1964: 71-73) although these flakes were not chipped to produce a serrated edge. They were apparently drawn through or across a rather unyielding material while held at a slight angle, and with a fair degree of pressure to produce this "crushed" opposite surface.

The utilized flat flakes were all somewhat contracting-edged flakes. Of the 110 utilized flat flakes, 93 displayed a single cutting edge with two surfaces meeting at an angle of about 15 to 25 degrees. There were a few very small pressure-chipped flakes removed from each of these flakes along the working edge which also exhibited one or two superimposed longitudinal striae on each surface. There was a suggestion of a very slight polish on both surfaces as well. I would interpret these wear patterns as evidence that these flakes were used to cut meat, skins, or some similar substance (see Semenov, 1964: 101-7). As these utilized flakes were not subjected to detailed staining or high-power microscopic analysis these functional interpretations should be taken as tentative only.

Pebble Cores were simply defined as small chert or flint nodules from which two or more flakes had been struck off so that, while most of the core retained the cortex, it was not possible to determine the original shape of the nodule. In general these cores were from 40 to 50 mm long, 30 to 50 mm wide, and about 20 to 30 mm thick. These seem to have been raw nodules from which flakes were struck and which were discarded when better material was available or when impurities were discovered. On most such cores several flake scars show hinging in or out at crystalline quartz inclusions or on fossiliferous inclusions.

Block Cores were generally about one-third the volume of pebble cores. They retained no cortex and were quite irregularly angular although there was a definite tendency toward a rectangular shape. These cores were clearly the final waste product of that technique which had initially modified raw nodules into pebble cores. The suitable pebble cores seem to have been further reduced by the removal of flakes utilizing previous flake scars as striking platforms (Binford and Papworth, *in*: White, Binford and Papworth, 1963: 83; Fitting, 1965 : 53-55; Wobst, 1968: 211). On this interpretation the resultant cores, which show no evidence of use, were merely byproducts in the production of flakes. Since the block cores are quite small the final flakes struck from them must also have been quite small. The longest flake scar on any block core from this component is 37 mm. While earlier struck flakes were clearly larger the later flakes were also quite narrow and could not have undergone much alteration without a severe reduction in strength.

Bipolar Cores were defined with references to the six types of bipolar cores described from northern Lake Michigan sites by Binford and Quimby (1963: 287-96). These cores all show clear evidence of having been produced by a technique which involved placing a pebble or tabular (block) core on an anvil and applying heavy percussion directly to the top of the core with little or no angle away from vertical. The resulting core is characterized by diametrically opposed zones of percussion resulting from the initial application of force by the hammer, and either the rebound of the core on the anvil or the reflection and refraction of the shock waves at the base of the core where it rested upon the anvil. Binford and Quimby (with a sample of 114) were able to distinguish six varieties of bipolar cores depending on the final shape taken by the percussion zones at either pole of the core (1963: 300, Table 2). McPherron, working with the collection of 744 bipolar cores from the Juntunen site, was able to distinguish only two varieties (1967: 135). The varieties distinguished by McPherron (ibid.) represent the extremes of the varieties Binford and Quimby have segregated as opposed ridge, ridge-area, right-angled ridges (really area-area), point-area, point-ridge, and opposed point (1963: 291-96). While Binford and Quimby have confined most of their discussion to the methods of production, they have noted the possibility that such cores may have been utilized as tools (1963: 288-89). They have not indicated how much of the characteristic resolved flaking of the polar areas may have been due to such subsequent utilization. McPherron has stated his belief that many if not most of the opposed point cores are actually production mistakes better classified as "shatter" (1967: 126-27). McPherron also implies that the opposed ridge bipolar cores (the only other variety that he recognizes) are created to be used like a wood gouge which will produce a characteristic gouged-end artifact (1967: 137-42). McPherron has not, however, mentioned how many of the opposed-ridge bipolar cores from Juntunen actually exhibit this distinctive pattern of wear, and, in fact, has only analyzed fifty-seven cores "selected (subjectively) as 'typical'" from the entire sample (1967: 133) basing all subsequent discussion of bipolar cores on this biased 7.6 per cent of the population.

The 259 bipolar cores from the Middle Woodland component at Summer Island included not a single example of Binford and Quimby's right-angled bipolar cores. With this exception there was a complete continuum from opposed point to opposed ridge, and the boundaries of each group were drawn quite arbitrarily. Thirty-three were defined as opposed point bipolar cores (Pl. XV, *a-e*), twenty-two were defined as point-ridge (Pl. XV, *f-j*), nineteen as point-area (Pl. XV, *k-m*), twenty-three as ridge-area (Pl. XV, *n-q*) and one hundred sixty-two as opposed ridge bipolar cores (Pl. XVI). This last variety displayed the greatest variability in all dimensions, but this may merely be a function of greater sample size. The metric attributes of the five varieties of bipolar cores from this component are presented in Table 10 of the opposed ridge variety of bipolar cores, thirty-eight (23.4 per cent) displayed the dished area of multiple hinge-fractures characteristic of McPherron's "gouged-end" artifacts (Pl. XVI,

TABLE 10

METRIC ATTRIBUTES OF BIPOLAR CORES FROM MIDDLE WOODLAND COMPONENT
(Measurements In Millimeters)

Attributes	Opposed point	Point-ridge	Point-area	Ridge-area	Opposed ridge
Length $\overline{X}$	30.6	32.1	34.5	36.2	34.3
σ	6.0	8.0	9.0	7.2	9.9
Width $\overline{X}$	17.9	25.6	30.0	29.7	30.0
σ	5.8	9.9	7.2	8.3	11.2
Thickness $\overline{X}$	14.5	21.4	22.7	27.8	13.9
σ	6.3	5.4	5.9	6.2	2.7
Sample Size	33	22	19	23	162

a-h). Several of these cores showed subsequent retouching which modified the artifact into a different formal and functional class. The traces of production as an opposed ridge bipolar core were still quite evident and these artifacts are discussed here for that reason. Two cores, both with cortex along one side, were retouched along the opposite side and along the base to form what seems to be a bifacial blade (Pl. XVII, *i*). Three cores with cortex along one side were bifacially retouched along the opposite side and along both ends to form what seems to be a functional equivalent to a chopper (Pl. XVII, *j*). Two cores have been modified by scraper retouch along one side (Pl. XVII, *k*, *l*). Two cores appear to have been turned on edge and again subjected to direct percussion on an anvil thus producing what could be called a tetrapolar core, looking rather like an angular disc core (Pl. XVII, *m*, *n*).

Time was not available to subject all bipolar cores to detailed microscopic examination. A random selection of fifty opposed ridge cores, and seven of each of the other varieties were examined, unstained, under a low-power binocular microscope for signs of use. None of the point-area or ridge-area bipolar cores showed any evidence of wear indicative of deliberate use. Three of the seven point-ridge bipolar cores showed some slight gloss on the ridges of the ridge end and definite crushing of the point area. The slight gloss on the high ridges is probably attributable to being held in the hand while these cores were employed (Semenov, 1964: 14). The crushing of the point end could as easily be due to the technique of manufacture as to the use to which it was subsequently put. Two of the opposed point bipolar cores showed parallel longitudinal striations along the axis of the core from one end for about one-third of the distance along the axis. No polishing existed on these specimens. This may indicate onetime use as an awl or punch (Semenov, 1964: 101) but this hypothesis is put forward with trepedation. Of the fifty opposed ridge cores examined, twelve, including two gouged-end cores, exhibited crushing and very small pressure flakes driven off from the concave face along one "ridge." The other face of the same ridge bore faint longitudinal striae extending about one-quarter of the distance down this face of the core. Four of these cores exhibited a slight gloss along one or two high ridge facets on this "outside" face. There seemed to be some evidence of transverse striae on the end of this ridge, but the heavily battered condition resulting from the manufacturing technique obscures most signs of wear along this edge. One such specimen was stained with a thin solution of methyl violet and, after drying, wiped with a chamois. Transverse striae were visible with oblique light on this specimen and it is assumed that similar treatment would also reveal them on the other specimens. The interpretation of these wear patterns is not immediately evident. The concave side of the artifact bears a pattern similar to a burin which has not been subjected to much pressure (Semenov, 1964: Fig. 38-6) while the edge and convex side shows patterns somewhat similar to an end scraper or "meat knife" (ibid.: 88, Fig. 31-1; 92, Fig. 35-5; 101-4). I would suggest that these artifacts were used to scrape bone to which some flesh or tendon still adhered, but alternative functions are clearly possible. Three opposed ridge bipolar cores showed a slight gloss on both faces of one edge for about one-quarter of the distance along the longitudinal axis of the core. On two of these cores transverse striae were noted across this edge of the artifact and several striations on both faces extended one-quarter to one-third of the distance, parallel to the longitudinal axis. Semenov (1964: 106-7) has reported similar wear on blades from Crimea. He interprets this wear as the result of scaling fish. There are no ethnographic accounts of fish-scaling for the Great Lakes region (see Rostlund, 1952). Four opposed ridge cores showed longitudinal striae parallel to the long axis of the core on both faces, but only along one side of the artifact. No gloss was evident on these artifacts and transverse striae on the edge were looked for in vain. The side of the core which exhibited the striation seemed to show heavier battering and a greater amount of hinge-fracture flake removal than the other side, but this is a subjective judgment. These artifacts may have been used as wedges for splitting bone or wood although the evidence for this is rather slight. No signs of use were noted on the remaining thirty-one opposed ridge bipolar cores, one of which was a "gouged-end" artifact. It is quite possible that these artifacts were employed as wedges or scrapers for a very short time and that such usage was not sufficient to be recognized with the heavily battered ridge edges resulting from the bipolar technique.

Fourteen *Bifacial scrapers and choppers* were discovered in situ within this component at the site. Two large roughly trimmed artifacts manufactured from a nodule of local chert were designated as "choppers" for comparative purposes only, as they bear a formal resemblance to similar artifacts from the Porte des Morts site which Mason has called choppers (1967: 315-17). The first specimen (Pl. XVII, *o*) is roughly ovate with the assumed proximal end unmodified and still showing the nodular cortex. This chopper is 62 mm long, 37 mm wide, and 23 mm thick. The bifacially chipped portion comes down rather smoothly on one side to a rounded tip. On the other edge a beak or keel is evident a short distance from the butt, below which the edge curves smoothly to the tip. The rounded edge of this implement bears considerable areas of crushed or minute resolved-flaked fractures. Striae are visible on both faces parallel to the long axis of the edge. These striae often overlap and obliterate each other. There is no polish on this working portion of the tool but the proximal end bears clear evidence of hand holding in the form of gloss, on almost all the high ridges, extending about one-fifth of the way down the faces on one side of the artifact, and about halfway down the artifact on the opposite face. This implement would seem to have been held in the hand and used to cut through a rather hard resistant material. The second "chopper" (Pl. XVII, *p*) is considerably larger being 73 mm long, 65 mm wide, and 38 mm thick at the butt or proximal end. This artifact is quite rectangular in shape with three edges displaying some degree of bifacial retouch. The distal edge shows a great deal of battering and crushing and short striae perpendicular to this edge extend about 3.0 mm up either face. Polish is non-existant on this edge but blunted ridges with faint gloss can be seen on the proximal end and a faint gloss exists on several high ridges on either face on the upper third of the artifact. It would appear that this implement was in fact a hand-held chopper which never penetrated more than 5.0 mm into whatever material upon which it was employed. It is difficult to imagine anyone attempting to chop down a tree using this implement, and dismemberment of a mammal carcass should have produced considerable gloss on the working faces as well as much longer striations.

Twelve bifacial scrapers (Pl. XVIII, *a-d*) were recovered from the Middle Woodland levels of the site. These fall into two distinct classes. Four of these scrapers (Pl. XVIII, *a*) are trapezoidal in shape and may originally have been opposed ridge bipolar cores although subsequent scraper retouch has obliterated definite indications of this. These scrapers average 40 mm long, 30 mm wide, and 11 mm thick, with a rather straight scraping edge showing such minimal scraper retouch that it may have occurred as a result of use, rather than as preparation for use. The remaining eight bifacial scrapers (Pl. XVIII, *b-d*) could all be classified as elongated end scrapers. All of these were made on decortication flakes and large amounts of cortex are present on all. On one of these scrapers the cortex completely covers one face, but on the others cortex is more closely confined to nonbifacially retouched portions of the artifact. These scrapers averaged 58 mm long and 20 mm thick with a maximum width of 28 mm. The retouch on these implements consisted of very steep bifacial retouch on one or more edge, producing a rather broad beveled edge. Transverse striae characteristic of scraper wear were not observed on any of these artifacts and their functional designation is merely assumed.

Bifacial Blades (Pl. XVIII, *e-j*). Fifteen bifacially chipped triangular to ovate artifacts, functionally equivalent to knives although formally equivalent to unfinished bifacial blanks, were recovered in situ from Middle Woodland levels. Five of these artifacts are pointed ovates with convex lateral edges having the greatest width ($\overline{X}$ = 32 mm) about one-quarter of the distance from the flattened to slightly concave base. In length they range from 53 mm to 71 mm ($\overline{X}$ = 63 mm) and in thickness from 6 mm to 16 mm ($\overline{X}$ = 8.5 mm). In cross-section all are diamond-shaped. Ten of these artifacts (Pl. XVIII, *g-j*) are triangular in shape with straight to slightly convex lateral edges, and have their maximum width ($\overline{X}$ = 32 mm) at, or just above, the straight to slightly convex base. These range in length from 85 mm to 62 mm ($\overline{X}$ = 72 mm) and in thickness from 5 mm to 11 mm ($\overline{X}$ = 7.1 mm). In cross-section these bifaces are elongated lenticular-shaped. One of these bifaces (Pl. XVIII, *g*) was made on a somewhat grainy dark brown taconite. All others were made of local chert.

No evidence of hafting was observed on any of these artifacts. Although all of them could have been hafted in a cleft stick, as seen by the thinned bases, there is no lateral edge grinding present on any of them.

With a single exception (Pl. XVIII, *j*) all bifacial baldes had one lateral edge which displayed crushing, very small resolved flake scars, and striae roughly parallel to this edge on both faces. From this edge faint polish on the surfaces extending as far as the center of the blade was observed. The opposite edge showed no evidence of either blunting or use. These would seem to have been employed as "meat knives" (Semenov, 1964) but were probably neither hand held nor used as a backed blade. If they were hafted some resinous substance may have been used to hold them seated: without some lateral grinding lashings would have been useless.

The only remaining example (Pl. XVIII, *j*) exhibits a fairly uniform high gloss on the ridges of both faces although no dulling of the edge was noted. It may have been used for some different purpose than those blades just described, but no traces of that use which can be deciphered are evident on the specimen.

Bifacial Blanks, or Preforms (Pl. XVIII, *h-l*). Twelve roughly finished bifaces were recovered from the Middle Woodland levels of the site. All of these had been roughly trimmed into triangular to ovate pointed shape by percussion flaking. These bifaces form a continuum, having at one end crudely blocked-out bifaces which are clearly the initial blanks from which tools were to be produced. These blanks are quite thick in cross-section with irregular profiles due to protuberances on one face which have not been trimmed (Pl. XVIII, *l*). Often such an eminence results from impurities in the chert producing hinge-out fractures (Pl. XVIII, *k*).

Some of these blanks have been further processed to a stage where they are thinner and more uniform in shape and thickness. Some degree of marginal retouch has been carried out on this end of the "blank" spectrum. Often this thinning and further shaping has uncovered structural defects in the blank and processing was abandoned (Pl. XVIII, *j*). If not the blank might be thinned to a final shape and so resemble an ovate bifacial blade, or unnotched projectile point. When processing had been carried to this degree the blanks are formally similar to the ovate bifacial blades. None of these blanks exhibit any indications of use, which functionally distinguishes them from the blades. Whether these bifacial blanks were being reserved for some different future use or were lost before they could be used as blades cannot be known. Some were too crude to have functioned efficiently as knives but most would have been quite serviceable.

Projectile Points (Pl. XIX, *a-t*). Fourteen projectile points were recovered in situ from the Middle Woodland levels of the excavation. An additional eight projectile points from subsequent levels were assigned to this component on the basis of typological similarity. This is a generally unreliable method of dealing with aboriginal artifactual material. Indeed it is often begging the question, for to do so one must assume a priori certain concepts of artifact-style change through time that excavation is designed to test. Nonetheless, these eight points were all recovered from disturbed areas of the site at levels where the major component was clearly historic, and to discuss them with their associated materials would only add confusion to the picture of the material culture of an 1860 fishing settlement. These points were well within the range of variation for similar in situ projectile points from the Middle Woodland component. They were quite unlike in situ projectile points from late aboriginal occupations. For these reasons these twenty-two projectile points are here discussed as a single group, although in Table 11 the metric data is presented by the provenience where they were recovered.

Mason (1967: 304-10), describing the North Bay projectile points from the Porte des Morts site, has stated that they form a continuous series from side-notched to stemmed. His discussion makes it clear that his assignation of points to one of his seven arbitrary classes is quite subjective. He has noted that two categories, corner-notched and stemmed, account for half of the points. In fact, clearly side-notched points account for only 5 per cent of all points from the site. Mason has interpreted the lack of tight attribute clusters in the Porte des Morts points to the knappers lack of fastidiousness in making the final artifact conform to the "ideal." Cleland and Peske (1968), describing a much larger sample of similar projectile points from the Spider Cave at Burnt Bluff, were able to distinguish nine different varieties on the basis of shape alone. Five of these projectile point varieties would seem to find counterparts among the points from Summer Island.

The twenty-two projectile points from Summer Island have been described under three, rather loose headings. The three side-notched points (Pl. XIX, *a-c*) in all dimensions are the smallest group from the entire component. Within this group are points like those Cleland and Peske have classified as Bay de Noc Side Notched (1968: Table 3, Fig. 8). These latter, with a mean length of 4.62 cm and mean width of 2.42 cm are somewhat larger points than the side-notched points from Summer Island. This may be due to the small sample size from the

TABLE 11

MIDDLE WOODLAND PROJECTILE POINTS

Catalog Number	Length	Width	Thickness	Shoulder Width	Haft Width	Base Width
In Situ—Corner Notched Points						
74657	4.11	2.78	0.65	2.78	1.18	1.19
74649	4.00	2.41	0.79	2.41	1.21	1.37
74567	5.39	2.43	0.85	2.43	1.42	1.59
74014	5.21	2.42	0.91	2.42	1.24	1.63
74375	5.16	2.23	1.02	2.23	1.38	1.67
75134	. . .	2.87	0.73	2.87	1.57	. . .
74184	3.98	. . .	0.70	. . .	1.43	1.63
74170	3.15	. . .	0.61	. . .	1.09	. . .
Surface—Corner Notched Points						
75177	6.69	. . .	1.20	. . .	1.02	. . .
74984	3.97	2.73	0.70	2.73	1.30	1.61
75304	. . .	1.60	0.76	1.56	1.19	1.67
74857	5.42	2.52	0.97	2.52	1.39	2.06
74170	. . .	. . .	0.87	3.10	1.58	1.93
75187	. . .	. . .	. . .	. . .	1.52	2.14
MEAN	4.71	2.44	0.83	2.51	1.32	1.68
σ	0.644	0.23	0.11	0.28	0.09	0.16
Side Notched Points						
75137	. . .	2.25	0.74	2.25	1.34	2.01
74586	3.75	2.29	0.72	2.29	1.62	1.96
74858	2.62	1 08	0.41	1.08	0.89	1.12
MEAN	3.19	1.87	0.62	1.87	1.29	1.70
σ	0.102	0.21	0.02	0.07	0.01	0.05
Stemmed Points						
74301	4.40	2.42	1.05	2.29	1.23	1.99
75146	5.27	2.73	1.33	2.73	1.21	1.46
75257	5.08	2.06	1.30	2.06	1.26	1.49
74140	. . .	2.06	0.80	2.06	1.47	1.57
75131	. . .	2.56	0.74	2.56	1.31	1.90
MEAN	4.92	2.36	1.04	2.36	1.30	1.68
σ	0.16	0.12	0.11	0.12	0.04	0.10

island. Although Mason does describe such side-notched points from the Porte des Morts site as side-notched, and presumably also as "intermediate intergradiation 1.5" (1966: 308), he does not illustrate these points. He has illustrated points from Mero which would clearly fall into these groups (1966: Pl. IX, Fig. 1, center, Fig. 2, upper row, Nos. 2, 3).

The fourteen corner-notched points from Summer Island (Pl. XIX, *d-n*) range from what Mason calls North Bay Point "intergrade 1.5" through "intergrade 2.5" at the Porte des Morts site. Cleland and Peske have illustrated quite similar points as Lang Corner-Notched (1968: 35-38, Figs. 12, 13). Three of the Summer Island corner-notched points (Pl. XIX, *g*, *k*, *l*) are equivalent to the Lang Corner-Notched Variety 1, two are quite similar to the Lang Corner-Notched Variety 2 (Pl. XIX, *j*, *n*), while the rest fall between in both shape and metric attributes. In general all the corner-notched points from Summer Island are somewhat thinner and narrower than the Spider Cave points, and considerably smaller in all dimensions than the North Bay points from either Mero or Porte des Morts. Some of the points Cleland and Peske have classified as Burnt Bluff Expanding Stem (1968: 22-24, Fig. 6) are also quite close to these corner-notched points from Summer Island.

The five stemmed points from the site (Pl. XIX, *o-r*), are all rather strictly defined to include only those points where width at the shoulder divided by basal width equalled 1.5 or less. While this was an arbitrary point, it seemed to correspond with the visual dichotomy seen in the small sample from the Summer Island site. Its application to other sites or to larger samples from the same site, is not expected to prove equally useful. These stemmed points are quite close to what Cleland and Peske have called Garden Stemmed, Variety 3 (1968: 32-34, Fig. 11) although the stemmed points from Summer Island tend to be thicker and narrower on the whole. These would correspond to Mason's (1967: 308-9) "stemmed" categories 3.5 to 4. I am unable to distinguish corner-removed from expanded stemmed and so have included both as a variant of corner notching.

While all the projectile points from Summer Island displayed a fair amount of variation in most metrical attributes, width of hafting element, was remarkably consistant with a mean variance of only 0.3 mm between the three series and a within-series mean standard deviation of less than 0.5 mm. This must indicate that while most attributes were rather loosely clustered and often displayed considerable ranges, there was a rather strict requirement for a hafting element width of 13.05 mm (see Table 11). This in turn would indicate that the shaft to which these projectile points was affixed was approximately one-half inch in diameter at its distal end. Since none of these points had any lateral grinding the shaft could not have been less than this without the point cutting its own lashings.

In general all the points appear to have been primarily finished by percussion chipping which removed most of the primary flake scar ridges although some of these do remain on the centers of some point faces. There is some marginal retouch along most point edges which have removed short thin expanding flakes. While these flakes of bifacial retouch may have been removed by pressure flaking, they may also have been removed by indirect percussion. I know of no valid method for determining which of the two methods was employed. In overall appearance the entire projectile point assemblage seems to agree quite well with the Middle Woodland date suggested by the ceramics. Several of the side-notched points seem to resemble early Middle Woodland (or earlier) types such as Raddatz Side-notched (Wittry, 1959*a:* 44-46, Fig. 3) which occur in central Wisconsin. The stemmed points also seem to show resemblances to central Wisconsin Middle Woodland types such as Durst Stemmed (Wittry, 1959*b*: 179-80) or the untyped "straight-stemmed" points from the upper zones at Durst (ibid.: 180; Fig. 11, *k'-p'*). They also resemble MacNeish's "Lockport Stemmed" from Manitoba (1958: 102, Pl. VI, 4, 5). The corner-notched and "corner-removed" or expanding-stemmed points also have clear parallels with types such as Jacks Reef Corner-Notched (Ritchie, 1961: 26-27) to the east, and Snyder's Corner-Notched from Illinois and southern Michigan Hopewell sites (Flanders, n.d.). From the southeast Manitoba sites of this time period the Larter Tanged and Anderson Corner-Notched are similar (MacNeish, 1958: 100-2). From Laurel sites in northern Ontario, Wright has illustrated a number of such projectile points grading between side-notched and expanding-stemmed (1967: Pl. IV, Figs. 1-6; Pl. VIII, Fig. 4; Pl. IX, Fig. 2). These also are quite similar to the projectile points recovered from the Middle Woodland component at Naomikong Point (Donald Janzen: personal communication).

Unifacial End Scrapers (Pl. XX). The term "scraper" as used here, will include those tools deliberately prepared for scraping use by steep unifacial retouch flaking on one or more edges. These scrapers have a working edge that lies predominantly along the edge perpendicular to the main axis of the flake and generally opposite the striking platform. The thirty-three end scrapers from the Middle Woodland levels were generally the smallest in size of any scraper category at the site. The means for metric attributes are presented in Table 12. Although cortex is present on five of these scrapers (Pl. XX, *a-e*) there is no regularity as to its distribution on the surface of the scraper (except that it occurs, by definition, on the dorsal surface), nor does the presence of cortex correlate with any other attributes. The end scrapers appear generally trapezoidal in plan view, and distinctly so in transverse cross-section. These scrapers appear quite heavy in comparison to similar artifacts from some nearby sites (e.g., McPherron, 1967: 156-58), although in shape and size ranges they do not differ greatly from scrapers from North Bay sites to the south (Mason, 1966: 62-63; 1967: 317-19).

Ten of these end scrapers were selected at random for study under a low-powered microscope. Six of them displayed faintly the transverse striae along the edge characteristic of end scraper use (Semenov, 1964: 88, Fig. 31). Of the remaining four end scrapers one was broken but all displayed battered and crushed edges as if they had been resharpened or used for heavy scraping activity. This type of usage would have obliterated any traces of skin-scraping striae had they existed.

Unifacial Side Scrapers (Pl. XXI) includes both standard straight or convex scrapers whose working edge parallels the long main axis of the flake (Pl. XXI, *a-k*), as well as the scrapers whose similarly located axis is concave (Pl. XXI, *e-o*). In Table 12 the latter are represented by negative degrees of arc, thus indicating the extent to which the working scraper edge is "hollow," or spokeshave-like. These have been designated *Unifacial Notched Scrapers* in Table 9, although they are not so segregated in Table 13.

Three rather straight side scrapers were analyzed under a low-powered microscope. These all bore very faint transverse striae, thus confirming the formal identification as being a functional one also. The one notched scraper analyzed displayed small resolved flake scars and crushing, consistent with its inferred use as a "spokeshave." No striations were observed on this piece which is difficult to explain. All scrapers bore slight polish on the unchipped surfaces indicating that they may have been hand held.

With relatively few exceptions, all scrapers were made of the local chert. There seems to have been no feeling that edges were too weak to be serviceable (cf. McPherron, 1967: 124-29). The lack of any evidence for long usage of scrapers in this component may indicate that it was more economical to make a scraper of any flake exhibiting the proper shape regardless of the type of material, than to work a large number of nodules hoping for one of "quality" material to yield the preferred flake.

TABLE 12

MIDDLE WOODLAND SCRAPERS
(Measurements In Centimeters)

UMMA Catalog Number	Maximum Length	Maximum Width	Thickness at Scraping Edge	Length of Scraping Edge	Degree of Arc on Working Edge	Cortex Present	Flint Type
74844	3.67	2.68	0.91	2.00	0	No	B
74983	2.00	1.86	0.40	1.86	65	Yes	B
75308	1.87	1.88	0.55	1.87	0	No	B
75308	2.57	1.50	0.40	1.40	10	No	B
74630	2.85	1.71	0.72	2.10	75	Yes	B
74630	2.24	2.52	0.55	2.62	91	Yes	B
74623	2.58	1.96	0.52	1.97	0	No	B
74623	2.57	1.70	0.50	1.81	80	No	B
74986	2.37	1.62	0.44	2.41	75	Yes	B
74953	2.85	2.97	0.80	1.47	40	No	B
74401	4.08	2.73	0.36	2.73	-25	No	B
74586	3.70	2.04	0.50	1.86	0	No	B
74554	4.19	1.71	0.55	3.92	0	No	B
74491	2.55	2.58	0.50	2.66	60	Yes	C
74453	3.06	3.14	0.66	3.14	70	No	A
74168	2.12	2.09	0.71	2.09	65	Yes	B
74069	3.08	3.62	0.58	2.81	55	Yes	B
74318	1.82	1.70	0.34	1.60	65	No	B
74290	3.03	2.32	0.43	1.87	-35	No	B
74200	2.68	1.60	0.34	1.95	-20	Yes	B
74298	2.31	1.97	0.57	1.97	60	No	C
74252	2.77	3.32	0.42	1.54	30	No	B

74273	. . .	2.32	. . .	2.32	60	No	B
75142	3.07	2.00	0.62	2.23	60	No	A
75150	2.08	2.27	0.76	2.27	50	No	B
75184	2.34	3.16	0.78	3.06	100	No	A
75151	. . .	2.35	0.91	2.34	80	Yes	B
75191	1.69	2.07	0.50	1.44	0	No	B
75298	. . .	1.73	0.44	1.67	70	No	B
MEAN	2.77	2.26	0.55	2.22	64		
σ	.59	.40	.10	.32	23		

If this is a correct assumption, there was no selection for raw material exhibited in the manufacture of scrapers at the site. The high frequency of scrapers made on group I chert merely reflects its greater availability.

Bladelets (Pl. XXII) are simply parallel-sided flat flakes whose length is greater than twice its width. Most bladelets display multiple, more or less parallel flake scars on their dorsal surface with a smooth, relatively flat to slightly convex ventral surface. Eighty-eight such bladelets were recovered from the Middle Woodland levels at the site. These had a mean length of 24.71 mm (σ = 5.515 mm), a mean width of 9.60 mm (σ = 2.748 mm), and a mean maximum thickness of 2.25 mm (σ = 1.698 mm). While some of these flakes were undoubtedly struct from bipolar cores (e.g., Pl. XXII, top row) there seems no way to determine from which type of core most of these bladelets were produced. To refer all such flakes to a bipolar core technique, as do McPherron (1967: 142-43) and Binford and Quimby (1963: 297-98), is unjustified. Most of these bladelets are probably the result of a particularly flawless section of some core, or a rather better-than-average control of the angle at which the percussion occurred. There is no indication that they were a deliberately created artifact or phase of production of artifacts such as Cahokia drills. There seems no way to either prove or disprove the deliberateness of their production. While striking-platform alteration is evident on most of these bladelets, this fact only indicates that some sort of core preparation occurred, but whether as an attempt to achieve a more symmetrical core (as in some nearby block-core techniques [Binford and Papworth, 1963]), or in an attempt to produce uniform blades (*viz*, Sanger, cited in Wright, 1967: 31*n*) like the Arctic microblade tradition, or even as the result of carelessly overlapping flake scars from the previously removed flakes (as would result in a bipolar technique), cannot be assumed and often cannot be determined.

While only ten of these bladelets were subjected to microscopic examination the results of these analyses were applied to the remaining seventy-eight bladelets which exhibited similar microscopic traces of usage. Twenty bladelets exhibited crushing and resolved flakes removed from one surface only along one edge Thirteen bladelets exhibited faint overlapping to parallel transverse striae extending from the edge to the midline along one or both faces. Seven bladelets had similar striations on both faces paralleling one of the edges of the artifact and extending from that edge about one-half the distance to the midline ridge. Thirteen bladelets exhibited some degree of gloss or polish on both faces. This was especially noticeable on the higher ridges of flake scars.

The thirteen bladelets which exhibited nibbling flake removal as the only sign of use (Pl. XXII, top and second rows) were interpreted as having been employed as wood scrapers or planes for a short time, or used with heavy pressure to cut across a rather unyielding object (Semenov, 1964). The seven bladelets that exhibited this nibbled edge as well as having faint transverse (perpendicular to the line of the edge) striations (Pl. XXII, third row) are interpreted as having been used to cut into some tough material, or having been used to scrap wood or bone (Semenov, 1964). The six bladelets having such striations and exhibiting a gloss or polish on the high ridges (Pl. XXII, fourth row) are interpreted as having been hand held while performing as a whittling knife (ibid.: 107-13). The seven bladelets exhibiting faint striae parallel to the edge of the blade and polishing on both surfaces (Pl. XXII, row 5) seem to display the same traces as knives used to cut into meat (ibid.) and a similar function is inferred for these bladelets. The remaining fifty-five bladelets from this level displayed no recognized signs of use.

In general the bladelets displayed only scalar vector differences from other flat flakes found in this component. That is, they are longer, narrower, somewhat thinner, display a significantly higher frequency of usage, and are more often found on nonlocal cherts. As indicated previously (p. 97) these are not independent factors. There seems to be a direct mechanical relationship between the nonlocal cherts, with their relative freedom from impurities, more compact texture, and more predictable fracture, and the ability to produce long narrow flat flakes. Such flakes, once struck, would be less likely to break into several pieces when subjected to pressure—principally due to fewer internal cleavage planes and finer texture. It should be noted here that any bladelet broken transversely into two, three, or more sections, would be classified under the present taxonomy as several flat flakes, only one of which could be further subcategorized. These factors, taken together, may explain why although there may be some cultural significance to the frequency of utilized exotic bladelets from this component, a simple statistical test, such as Chi-square, would be misleading with its indication of significant attribute clusterings.

DISCUSSION

As in most chipped stone industries, the projectile points are the most diagnostic artifact for assigning the complex to a temporal position. As has already been indicated the projectile points from Summer Island show the closest resemblance to the nearby North Bay complex. Marked similarities also exist with the entire Laurel to Point Peninsula continuum and with some of the late Illinoian Hopewell-derived styles further south. If earlier prototypes are needed from which to derive these styles the indigeneous Late Archaic populations of this same area have obligingly provided them. In the New York area it would be difficult to distinguish long Brewerton Side- or Corner-notched points which may be as early as 2500 B.C. (Ritchie, 1961: 16, 19, Pls. 4 and 7) from many of the less carefully made Middle Woodland types prevalent there. In Manitoba and Minnesota the Late Archaic types such as Larter Tanged (MacNeish, 1958: 100-1, Pl. VI, Figs. 9-11) and Parkdale Eared (ibid.: 100; Pl. VI, Figs. 6, 7) do not differ too much from the local Middle Woodland types like Anderson Corner-notched or Whiteshell Side-notched (MacNeish, 1958: 101-3; Pl. VI, Figs. 1-6; Pl. VII, Figs. 16-10).

Between these two areas there are a number of Late Archaic or Early Woodland projectile point types which, in size and shape, appear quite close to the later Middle Woodland projectile points. Such points have been reported from the Archaic stratum at the Inverhuron site (Kenyon, 1957: 12; Pl. IV, 5-11), from the Terminal Archaic level at the Butterfield site in northern Bay County, Michigan (Wobst, 1968: 223-31; Pl. VI, *a-g*, *o-r*; Pl. VII, *c*, *h*) at the Port Washington site, Door County, Wisconsin (Quimby, 1957), in several central Wisconsin rockshelters (Wittry, 1959*a*; 1959*b*) from the Archaic component of the Lamb site, Pierce County, Wisconsin (Brandon, 1968: 8-11, Fig. 6, *a*, *f*, *j-m*, *p*, *q*) and associated with the burials at the Riverside Cemetery, Menominee County, Michigan (Hruska, 1967: 198-99, 208-10, 217, Fig. 48, top row; 54, top left; 64). From further south similar points are reported from the Schmidt site, Saginaw County, Michigan (Harrison, 1966: 60; Pl. I), the Andrews site, Saginaw County, Michigan (Papworth, n.d.), and the Warner School site, in northern Genesee County, Michigan (Roosa, 1966: 28-30; Pl. II, *e-l*), all presumed to date to the period 3000 B.C. to 1000 B.C.

The bipolar core chipping technique does not have the same wide geographical range as do the projectile point styles noted.

This technique seems to have been a method for utilizing local chert nodules in northern Lake Michigan practiced from Late Archaic through Late Woodland times (Binford and Quimby, 1963; Fitting, 1967; McPherron, 1967). The only other purportedly diagnostic chipped stone artifacts, the end scrapers, have also been reported from numerous sites in this area from the Early Archaic through the Protohistoric period. While the proportions of the different end scraper varieties change from site to site these changes do not seem to have any demonstrable geographical significance. Throughout this entire area, at all horizons, end scrapers tend to outnumber other types. The variations in relative proportions that do occur are perhaps best understood as functional differences, implying different site utilization, rather than temporal change.

With the exception of a few sites in the northern Lake Huron area the local Archaic chipped stone complexes offer the most reasonable sources from which to derive the succeeding Middle Woodland industries. To seek parallels in the lithic assemblages of the Northwest Territories may be interesting insofar as a similar ecological adaptation seems to have been practiced in those complexes where such parallels appear (MacNeish, 1964: 461-64), but there is no necessity to seek out such distant areas in place of the local sources. The problems intendant upon using changing ratios of functionally dissimilar tools to infer temporal changes (e.g., Wright, 1967: 102-3) can only be resolved when a great deal more is known of the cultural ecology of these areas for the periods in question.

VII

ROUGH AND PECKED STONE

SAMPLE

FROM the Middle Woodland component at Summer Island fifty-six modified or altered pieces of ground and/or pecked stone were recovered. Not included in this number were seventeen small flat (mean thickness 5 mm) waterworn igneous pebbles. These were all more or less oval in shape, 2.5 mm to 3.9 mm long, and 1.5 mm to 2.2 mm wide. Five of these were basalt, two were granite, nine were gabbro, and one was diorite. No evidence of deliberate modification could be discerned on these pebbles. They are mentioned only because, while clearly glacially derived beach gravel in origin, no natural agency could have deposited them in their cultural matrix on an aeolian sand dune. No functional interpretation is offered beyond the suggestion that they may have been gaming pieces of some sort. Also deleted from the present discussion were the 1,231 pieces of fire-cracked rock (weight = 491.7 kilograms) recovered from the midden at these levels..

The fifty-six items of ground stone from this component consisted of hammerstones, anvils, mortars, pestles, abraders, net-sinkers, and manos. The rough stone consisted of fragments of specular and silicaceous hematite, ocherous limonite (J. Wright's "paintstone nodules" [1967: 34]), and cut and ground sheets of muscovite.

DESCRIPTION OF ARTIFACTS

The eleven hammerstones can be divided into two classes on the basis of shape. Seven hammerstones (Pl. XXIII, *a*) were roughly symmetrical being subrectangular in cross-section, and rather long. These were classed as elongated hammerstones. I identified three of these as gabbro or diabase, two each were basalt and felsite, and one was seyenite. It should be noted that these are all rather vague terms for the dark igneous rocks with a low silica content that are plentiful in the glacially derived gravels of this area. All seven were waterworn and could have been obtained from the beach less than one hundred yards away. These were all cobble-sized artifacts displaying no artificial modification other than the hammering facets on either end. These facets covered an area of roughly six to eight square centimeters, and were characterized by a crushed and battered surface which markedly flattened the ends of the implement. Quite often the hammering facets were slightly concave. In length these artifacts ranged from 126 mm to 188 mm with a mean of 151 mm. Maximum width ranged from 79 mm to 105 mm with a mean of 93 mm. Of four circular hammerstones (Pl. XXIII, *b*), two were composed of diorite and two were diabase or gabbro. These were waterworn cobbles displaying the shape of a short cylinder. The shape is clearly a result of artificial modification with a number of flattened hammering facets along the circumference. In central thickness these ranged from 35 mm to 59 mm with a mean of 49 mm—the lower end of the range is due to a pecked surface on one circular face of the implement as if it had been used for an anvil at some time.

Six anvils were identified from the sample of ground stone artifacts. As a class these stones were rather amorphous being generally flat or at any rate having the two largest surfaces relatively parallel to one another. All of these artifacts were characterized by one or more concave areas of crushing or pecking on at least one of these surfaces. These worked facets were quite irregular in shape but were generally 3 cm to 4 cm in maximum dimension, with a mean area of about 6 cm. Several of these facets were as deep as 8 mm but the mean depth was 4.5 mm for the fifteen worked areas noted. In size these artifacts were quite variable with maximum length ranging from 18.5 cm to 27.0 cm, maximum width from 13.2 cm to 17.3 cm, and maximum thickness from 4.1 cm to 9.6 cm. Three of the anvils were a fine-grained gabbro or diabase, and one each were composed of basalt, felsite, and diorite, all of which are abundant in the local glacially derived beach gravels.

Fourteen complete "net-sinkers" were recovered from this component of the site (Pl. XXIII, *e-i*). All specimens consist of waterworn flat cobbles rather irregularly oval in shape. Three of these were made on cobbles of granitic gneiss, four on light tan to gray sandstone, and seven on what can be identified as Engadine Dolomite. In all cases the only modification consisted of roughly diametrically opposed notches chipped or pecked into the edges of the artifact. The weight and metrical attributes of these fourteen "net-sinkers" are presented in Table 13.

TABLE 13

NOTCHED STONES ("NETSINKERS") FROM MIDDLE WOODLAND COMPONENT
(In Centimeters)

Maximum Length	Maximum Width	Maximum Thickness	Weight (Grams)	Length Between Notches	Mean Width of Notches	Mean Depth of Notches	Volume (cc)
7.55	5.70	1.25	90	5.50	0.80	1.00	53.4
7.05	6.30	1.70	91	6.60	1.25	0.25	74.9
7.60	6.10	1.11	80	5.40	1.00	1.10	51.1
8.15	5.80	1.15	94	6.20	0 90	0.95	54.1
6.90	4.80	1 60	108	4.95	0.90	1.02	52.9
6.35	6.25	1.81	84	5.90	1.40	0 30	71.5
7.90	6.40	1.40	108	7.40	1.70	0.30	70.8
7.50	5.00	1.45	117	5.45	1.00	1 02	52.5
7.90	5.90	1.20	100	6.00	1.10	0.95	55.9
8.60	6.00	1.15	120	6.85	1.15	0.90	56.9
6.05	5.00	1.25	107	4.85	0 85	0.95	53.0
7.05	5.80	1.55	111	5.50	1.05	1.00	55.0
7.25	6.15	1.40	95	6.25	1.05	0.95	70.0
7.75	6.35	1.35	116	7.10	1.55	0.40	70.5

Notched stones similar to those recovered from Summer Island have been reported from numerous archaeological sites in eastern North America (Rostlund, 1952: 86-88, 158-59). While generally interpreted as net-sinkers (ibid.; Wright, 1967: 33; Mason, 1967: 67-68), some questions have been raised about their possible function as weights of unknown function (Johnson, 1961: 197) or as bolas weights (Coe, 1964: Fig. 70). In all cases, however, they occur in sites near some sizeable body of water. A good case can be made for considering these notched stones at Summer Island as net-sinkers not only because bolas are unreported ethnographically in this area (Driver and Massey, 1957: 359-61), but as the subsequent faunal analysis will indicate, the Middle Woodland component of the site was inhabited as a summer fishing site. While the copper and bone artifacts indicate that hook and line angling and fish-spearing were practiced, Rostlund clearly shows that fish-spearing was generally a winter practice in the Great Lakes, and of distinctly minor importance to those for whom fish was a staple (1952: 106-8). The fish-spearing seems to have been a rather specialized form of fishing in shallow water. It is also the case that sturgeon, lake herring or whitefish will rarely take a baited hook or gorge (Rostlund, 1952: 115-19). Rostlund has also noted of the Great Lakes area that, "here far more than in any other major region the fish net was the most commonly used implement in the fishery," (ibid.: 85). Nets are also the most effective and efficient method of lake fishing (ibid.: 81, 88-89, 115, 116-19). Indeed, if some archaeological evidence of net fishing had not been recovered from this component it would probably have been postulated anyway. A final quote from Rostlund indicates that, "if these [notched] stones are accepted as proof of fish nets, they *must* imply large seine or gill nets, for sinkers are not required on small hand nets, dip nets, scoop nets, or the like" [emphases in the original] (1952: 88). While seine nets may be exotic, there is no doubt that gill nets are aboriginal (ibid.: 83, 84).

As Figure 13A indicates, the distribution of the length of the stone between the notches closely approximates a normal curve. The mean length between notches is 5.99 cm, with a standard deviation of 6.3 mm. There is also a close correlation between the weight of the net-sinker and the distance between notches (Fig. 14B), with a mean weight around 100 grams for these artifacts. This is in contrast to the maximum length which varies considerably more than the length between notches. I would interpret this as indicating that weight was the principal desideratum in selecting beach pebbles to be used as net-sinkers. These

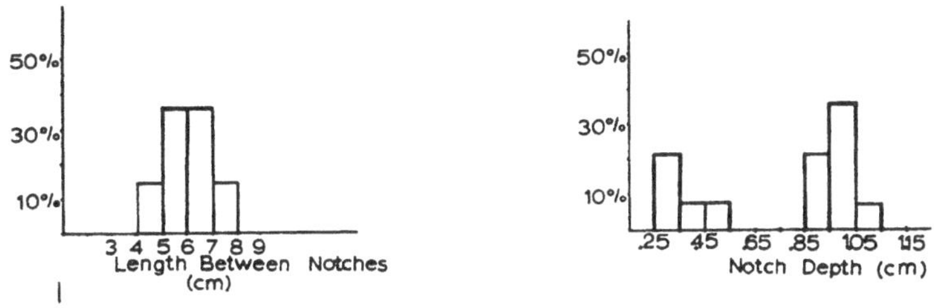

FIG. 13. Graph of notched stone metric attributes.

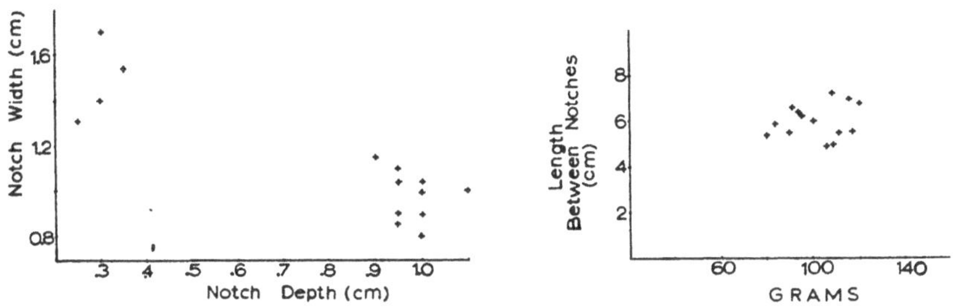

FIG. 14. Notched stone correlations.

stones were subsequently notched so that regardless of original length they had roughly the same length between notches. This must, of course, imply that longer cobbles had longer notches cut into them. It is thus surprising to note that the depth of notching does not follow a uniform curve but instead shows a distinctly bimodal distribution with one modal category having a mean depth of 3 mm, and one having a mean of 1 cm (Fig. 13B). This implies that notch depth was not simply determined by the desire to equalize the distance between notches. The added factor affecting this attribute seems to have been the width of the notches (Fig. 14A). This was not a simple mechanical relationship for the deepest notches are the narrowest. I would assume that this latter attribute, notch width, was in turn determined by the size of the cordage employed in securing these weights to the nets. If this assumption is correct, two modal categories of net-related cordage may be inferred from Figure 14A, one which a mean diameter of 16.0 mm, and one with a mean diameter of 9.2 mm. Why the smaller cords required deeper notching is not at all clear. It may be the case that two different sizes of nets are represented here, or that one type of net-sinker (the longer cobbles with the narrow deep notches) was used in shallower water where it rested on the bottom and thus received more disturbances requiring a more secure fastening. In any event it should be clear that these notched stones are not carelessly manufactured or randomly selected cobbles but represent an artifact whose final shape was conditioned by the cultural concepts of its makers as fully as were the shapes of the ceramics or the projectile points they employed.

Three abrading stones (Pl. XXIII, *c*) were recovered from this component. These were all rather fine-grained sandstone cobbles of irregular shape having at least one relatively flat surface. This surface displayed numerous long U-shaped grooves roughly paralleling the long axis of the artifact. These grooves were from 1.5 mm to 3.8 mm wide and had a maximum depth of 1.2 mm. The groves possibly are the result of using these stone abraders for smoothing and shaping cooper or bone artifacts, or perhaps for grinding chipped stone artifacts to blunt them.

Two "manos" were recovered consisting of rather rectangular flat slabs with clear evidence of grinding on both faces and at least one edge. One of these artifacts was made of a very sandy shale while the other was a compact sandstone quite close to quartzite in texture. These artifacts may be abraders shaped by use as J. Wright has suggested (1967: 34-35) although he offers no evidence to support this view. The use of these artifacts is not clearly understood. Microscopic analysis of the working surface added nothing to the understanding of their function. Wear patterns on the faces and edges consisted of faint parallel transverse striae indicating that they had been moved in one direction primarily, but to what effect could not be determined.

One mortar was recovered which was made on a flat subrectangular block of diorite. This artifact in all formal attributes was similar to an anvil with only one worked facet. This worked area was larger than those on any anvil, being 4.3 cm in maximum length and 3.6 cm in maximum width. This area was quite smoothed as if it had been ground after having been initially created by pecking and hammering. At its greatest depth this area was about 1.1 cm below the surrounding surface of the cobble. Traces of dark reddish brown pigment were noted within this depression.

A second mortar from this component was considerably more bowl-shaped (Pl. XXIII, *j*) being made on a concave-convex circular cobble of extremely hard, fine-grained dolomite about 7.5 cm in diameter. This artifact was about 3.3 cm thick around the "rim" but only 2.5 cm thick in the center. The central depression showed only slight evidence of pecking or crushing but bore numerous faint helical and circumscribed striations, many of which yielded evidence of dark reddish brown stains and flecks of black pigment. Associated with this mortar was a pestle (Pl. XXIII, *k*), 10.1 cm long and plano-convex in cross-section. This artifact was made of a waterworn pebble of diorite and was 3.1 cm wide at one end tapering to 2.0 cm wide for about two-thirds of its length. Both ends were spatulate. Evidence of grinding could be seen in the form of faint helical striae on both ends, and as very faint longitudinal striae along the flat surface. Traces of black and dark reddish brown pigment were noted on the broad end of this artifact. It is hypothesized that these mortars and the pestle were used to crush and mix some ferric or ferrous oxides (Pl. XXIII, *l*) into paint or pigment. The broad spatulate end of the pestle may also have been used to apply the resultant mixture.

There were nine amorphous fragments of ocherous limonite with a mean weight of 13 grams. Seven of these showed evidence of structural crystalline breakdown such as results from roasting or burning, being highly friable and quite streaky. The streaks from these fragments on a porcelain plate ranged from dark brown to ocherous yellow.

Also recovered were four fragments of specular hematite with a mean weight of 25.2 grams. These fragments are characteristic of the micaceous schistlike Mchigan hematite found in the Negaunee deposits of Delta, Schoolcraft, and Menominee counties. These fragments were considerably harder than the limonite, and streak tests showed a bright or dark red streak, thus distinguishing them from silicaceous hematite or magnetite. The weak magnetism that these fragments display evidences their having been heated or roasted.

Two fragments of very soft silicaceous hematite were also recovered from this component. These displayed a highly metallic luster and were extremely friable leaving a very metallic streak bright pinkish red to dark red in color. According to James Robertson of the Department of Mineralogy, The University of Michigan, these fragments have been subjected to roasting for quite some time (personal communication).

Three of the limonite fragments and all of the specular hematite fragments displayed flattened areas of grinding or abrading. The other fragments of limonite and the two fragments of silicaceous hematite were so soft and easily weathered that the absence of grinding facets should not be taken as evidence that they were not similarly employed.

The last two modified stone artifacts recovered from this component were two small sheets of yellowish-white to transparent muscovite (Pl. XXIII, *m*). These mica sheets were each about 6 cm long by 3.5 cm wide and about 1.5 mm to 2 mm thick. Both appeared to have been cut and/or ground along at least two edges. No functional interpretation is offered for these items and their employment is assumed to have been nontechnical in the strict sense of the term.

DISCUSSION

The assemblage of rough and ground stone artifacts recovered from the Middle Woodland component at Summer Island is not a highly distinctive one. In most respects it shows close relationships with quite similar industries from numerous components reported within the Canadian Biotic province (see Dice, 1938) from late Archaic (Wobst, 1968: 266-67; Taggert, 1967: 155; Hruska, 1967; MacNeish, 1958: 123-28; Ritchie, 1965) through Middle Woodland (Mason, 1966: 67-70; 1967: 320; Wright, 1967: 32-35; Ritchie, 1946) Upper Mississippian (Mason, 1966: 178), and Late Woodland (McPherron, 1967: 159-64; MacNeish, 1958). Of special interest, however, is the noticeable absence of any celt-like ground stone artifacts from this component at Summer Island, and a frequency of net-sinkers surpassed only by Naomikong Point (Donald Janzen: personal communication). This may indicate that extensive wood-working was not carried out at the Summer Island site. Another related explanation may be that there was no need for forest clearing to the practiced, hypothesis consistant with the geomorphological data. The net-sinker frequency, if these artifacts have been correctly interpreted, may indicate that net fishing was more important at Summer Island (and Naomikong Point) than at other sites in the area. This would agree with their locations on the shores of relatively deep still water in distinction to many of the other sites located along very shallow bays or rivers. These latter would be areas where, as Rostlund has indicated (1952: 88-89) dip-netting was often the easiest (although one of the least efficient) methods of fishing.

In general, this stone industry at Summer Island can be viewed as a continuation of those ecologically oriented tools whose use in this area seems to show little temporal variation for at least the last three or four thousand years (Quimby, 1960: 43-52; Griffin, 1964: 231).

VIII

COPPER

SAMPLE

SEVENTY pieces of native Lake Superior copper, weighing 179.7 grams were recovered in situ from the Middle Woodland levels of the site. Of these, twenty-nine were finished artifacts while the remainder (weighing 79.55 grams) were unaltered raw copper or copper scrap. Not included in these counts and weights were two fragments identified by Mr. James Robertson, Research Assistant for the Department of Mineralogy, The University of Michigan, as angular pieces of burned green epidote showing traces of copper adhering to Keweenaw Basalt. This is the matrix in which the Lake Superior copper is normally found. A metric analysis of the finished copper artifacts from this component is presented in Table 14. While most of the data is self-explanatory the measurements on the fish hooks and the rolled beads require some clarification. Length was not measured along the central axis of the completed bead, but rather refers to the length of the rectangular strip of copper from which the bead was rolled. Width and thickness also refer to this pre-rolled copper strip. The width thus expressed corresponds to the length of the finished bead measured along the central axis. External and internal diameters refer specifically to the finished rolled bead. Length and width for the copper hooks are given for the unbent copper strip from which the artifact was fashioned.

ANALYSIS OF ARTIFACTS

The thirteen rolled copper beads fall into two metrically distinct groups. Eleven (Pl. XXIV, *a-k*) were manufactured by rolling a rather thin ($\bar{X}$ = 1.1 mm) rectangular strip of copper so that the ends overlapped along one-quarter to one-third of the circumference. There has been some degree of hammering the exterior end so that it often feathered out, becoming quite thin and broken along its edges. Some dowel-like object must

TABLE 14

COPPER ARTIFACTS FROM THE MIDDLE WOODLAND COMPONENT*

Artifact	Length	Width	Thickness	External Diameter	Internal Diameter	Weight	Illustration Plate XXIV
Rolled bead	1.90	.94	.21	.72	.30	.60	Fig. *a*
"	1.60	.80	.09	.58	.41	.70	Fig. *b*
"	1.39	.72	.18	.82	.46	.60	Fig. *c*
"	1.38	.83	.14	.58	.30	.58	Fig. *d*
"	1.71	1.08	.15	.68	.39	1.20	Fig. *e*
"	1.32	.78	.08	.75	.59	.70	Fig. *f*
"	1.26	.96	.15	.65	.35	1.01	Fig. *g*
"	1.60	1.00	.13	.66	.40	.59	Fig. *h*
"	1.64	1.18	.18	.76	.40	.80	Fig. *i*
"	1.61	.99	.20	.65	.25	.61	Fig. *j*
"	1.74	1.08	.14	.69	.41	1.10	Fig. *k*
"	1.67	.67	.18	.73	.38	.60	Fig. *l*
Rolled bead	1.52	1.12	.23	.84	.38	2.40	Fig. *m*
Unfinished bead	1.71	.77	.09	...	...	.85	Fig. *n*
Fish hook	6.81	.19	.18	...	...	2.16	Fig. *o*
Fish hook	5.87	.32	.17	...	...	3.09	Fig. *p*
Fish gorge	4.55	1.18	.64	...	...	14.40	Fig. *q*
"	5.71	.65	.18	...	...	5.80	Fig. *r*
Fish gorge	7.77	.91	.27	...	...	7.40	Fig. *s*
Awl	11.63	.45	.33	...	...	10.20	Fig. *t*
"	9.10	.59	.32	...	...	8.71	Fig. *u*
"	9.31	.39	.32	...	...	6.94	Fig. *v*
Awl	1.75	.48	.45	...	...	3.01	Fig. *w*
Knife	5.70	.86	.31	...	...	2.90	Fig. *x*
Knife	14.10	.62	.27	...	...	12.12	Fig. *y*
Chisel	6.55	.42	.40	...	...	4.10	Fig. *z*
Chisel	5.22	1.24	.27	...	...	5.00	Fig. *aa*

Punch	2.17	.49	.39	. . .	. . .	1.40	Fig. *bb*
Effigy claw	1.44	.41	.22	. . .	. . .	.58	Fig. *cc*

*Measurements in centimeters, weights in grams

TABLE 15

MIDDLE WOODLAND COPPER HARDNESS BY TYPE OF ARTIFACT

Artifact	Highly Ductile	Somewhat Ductile	Brittle	Total
Finished tool				
O/E	1/3.8	10/4.6	4/3.8	15
Finished ornament				
O/E	2/3.5	4/4.4	8/3.5	14
Copper scrap				
O/E	30/19.9	6/12.9	5/10.9	41
TOTAL	33	20	17	70

$x^2 = 26.0584$
df = 4
p = <.001
$\Phi^2 = .37226$

have been inserted through the center of the bead to prevent it from being flattened at this stage of production. Subsequently several of the beads were turned on edge and hammered along their side resulting in a flattened edge of the joint where the ends overlapped, with slightly extruded flanges along the inside of the bead. Two of the beads (Pl. XXIV, *l-m*) exhibit this same basic manufacturing technique although initially constructed of a much heavier piece of copper. These latter beads are overlapped along one-half to two-thirds of their circumference further increasing their girth. There is no evidence of subsequent hammering on the external surface of the joint. The edges have been rather heavily hammered and abraded so that these beads can best be described as spherical whereas the former eleven are cylindrical.

The two hooks (Pl. XXIV, *o, p*) were each formed of a single lump of copper pounded into a long bar, more or less square in cross section. On both hooks the short leg has been rounded to a point while the opposite leg has been dorsally thinned by grinding or by hammering and trimming. While there is no evidence of any grooving, notching, or other hafting element both hooks resemble what have been traditionally called fishhooks (e.g., Mason, 1967: 322; Pl. 14, *d*) in this area. They could equally well have been used as a side barb on a small leister (see Steinbring, 1967).

The three "fish gorges" (Pl. XXIV, *q-s*) are relatively flat, lens-shaped, bipointed artifacts. All are symmetrical as far as can be determined, although only one is unbroken. One of these artifacts is clearly eccentrically notched on each edge to a depth of about 1.2 mm. Another such gorge appears to have shallow eccentric notches, while the third does not show any attempts at such notching. Whether these latter two artifacts were completed is impossible to say. None of the three shows any signs of use although one, and probably two are functionally quite employable.

The four copper awls (Pl. XXIV, *t-w*) or bodkins are square or rectangular in cross section with rounded points. All of these artifacts appear to have been constructed of several thinner sheets of copper folded on one another and hammered together. On the three unbroken awls one end is much sharper and more rounded than the other. This more pointed end displays overlapping circumscribed and longitudinal striations, indicating that it was employed both in a punchlike and drill-like manner. One of these implements is twisted and bent. This awl shows distinct gouges along one side and two edges as though it had been used to pry or lever some resistant material. This may be an early example of the modern tendency to use tools for functions other than those for which they were designed. In general the functional designation seems to be supported by the wear patterns found on one end of these awls. The other end would seem to have been hafted, probably by driving into a bone, wood, or antler handle like a modern awl or reamer.

The two copper knives (Pl. XXIV, *x*, *y*) are so designated because of their formal resemblance to the Old Copper "butter knives" (Wittry, 1957) although both display some variation from this Platonic Ideal. Both were apparently constructed from a single nugget of copper, and bear no traces of the fold-and-hammer technique seen in the awls. The larger of these two artifacts is quite uniform in thickness with no evidence that either edge of the blade was sharpened, or indeed even used. No striae are visible along either edge of these knife blades. Some hammer impressions are visible along both edges, however, and these appear to have deliberately blunted the edge indicating that the term "knife" may be purely a formal one with no functional correspondence. The rounded tang portion of the large "knife" was quite smooth and polished. It was encircled by a series of helical or circular overlapping to parallel striations. These data may indicate that this "knife" was badly corroded but seemed to have one edge blunted by hammering while the other "outer" edge had been flattened to a degree that approximated a modern knife blade. No grinding or striations indicating use were seen on this "knife" but the degree of oxidation is such that none would have been preserved had they originally existed. Both ends of this artifact are turned in the same direction--away from the blade. This artifact approaches the shape of the earlier Old Copper crescents or ulus reported from this area (Wittry, 1957). Whether this artifact is a badly bent "crescent" or a badly disintegrated "butter knife" cannot be determined by either functional analysis or by its areal associations which are consistant with either view.

The two chisels (Pl. XXIV, *z*, *aa*) were both manufactured by the fold-and-hammer technique used to manufacture the awls. Both implements were heavier than the awls although quite similar in shape. One end (probably hafted) was rounded and pointed while the other end had been squared off obliquely to produce a flat square-ended chisel. The cutting edge of both chisels show short transverse striations. These extend across the face of the oblique end of the tool thus lending a functional confirmation to this formal classification of artifacts.

One small elongated conical artifact (Pl. XXIV, *bb*) was designated as a punch. This artifact is quite evenly cylindrical to within 4.0 mm of one end where it gradually tapers to a point. No signs of use were noted on this part of the artifact. The other end was still an unmodified cylinder but the tip had been subjected to repeated heavy pressure leaving it distinctly burred and flattened with much scarring, gouging, and short striations. The assumption made here is that the pointed end was hafted by being driven into a bone or wood handle. The tool must have functioned as some sort of pressing or punching device. This artifact was located in an area of the site where final projectile point retouching was carried out, and was associated with numerous small flat flakes of bifacial retouch, thus suggesting that it functioned as a pressure flaker.

The last copper artifact recovered from the Middle Woodland component of the site has been termed an "effigy claw" (Pl. XXIV, *cc*). This artifact was apparently formed of a single lump of copper with no evidence of the fold-and-hammer technique. The artifact is round in cross section and tapers gradually to a rather sharp point. The entire artifact is curved to a degree so that it resembles a tooth or claw. No signs of use were noted on this artifact, nor can any functional interpretation be readily assigned to it. It is quite likely that this object served a ceremonial rather than a directly functional purpose. The "effigy claw" was quite well finished and was by far the least ductile copper artifact recovered at the site, indicating that its manufacture may have received more careful attention than that of many of the more functional implements.

MANUFACTURING TECHNIQUES

The forty-one unfinished pieces of copper from the Middle Woodland component provide clear evidence of the major techniques employed in the manufacture of copper artifacts. Copper is present in all stages of manufacture from finished artifacts to the two fragments still in their igneous rock matrix.

There is no evidence that any copper was reduced from ores at the site. Nor is there any indication of smelting or casting of copper. In terms of hardness the copper was occasionally found in a highly ductile ("dead soft") condition seen in many of the small waste flakes (which ranged from 0.5 grams to 8.0 grams) and in the copper lumps or bars formed by folding and hammering sheets of copper over on itself. This ductile condition is quickly lost by hammering and these fragments must have been reheated to restore their soft condition. Several fragments of copper, notably the finished artifacts and the two large copper bars formed by hammering folded sheets of copper together, were almost brittle and displayed very little ductility indicating that they had not been annealed after finishing. As Table 15 indicates, the ductility exhibited by the copper recovered from this component is not a random factor but seems to have been deliberately avoided in finished artifacts. The Middle Woodland inhabitants of the site were clearly aware of annealing and used it in manufacturing but left finished artifacts in a harder, somewhat more brittle state. Assuming that the "effigy claw" and rolled beads are ornaments rather than tools, a definite tendency toward harder tools can be seen.

The two basic manufacturing methods, hammering into the desired shape a single lump or nugget of copper, and folding several thin sheets over upon themselves and hammering the final lump into shape, do not show any clear correlation with either the size or function of the final artifact. The choice between the two techniques may have been determined by the size of the available raw material at the time some particular implement or ornament was fashioned.

With the exception of the two epidote-bonded fragments, no copper was recovered that displayed the distorted hackly masses without crystal forms, characteristic of the pure copper in a natural vein state. This is of some importance in ascertaining the source of these copper fragments. While the original source was clearly the Lake Superior deposits it is not possible to determine whether from Isle Royale or the Keweenaw Peninsula. No very large pieces of unworked copper were recovered from Summer Island although several of the finished artifacts pounded out of a single lump of copper are of good size. While it is possible that the source of this copper was the occasional nugget found in the glacial gravel, the amount of copper recovered from the site would make this doubtful. Also, the extensive amount of waste copper and the large unutilized fragments argue against the high premium such a method of collection would have placed on this mineral.

Little archaeological work has been done along the south shore of Lake Superior in those areas where native copper occurs. On Isle Royale, Bastian's survey (1963) has indicated the presence of several Middle Woodland occupations whose ceramic components are quite similar to that of Summer Island. While this cannot be taken to demonstrate that Isle Royale was *the* source for all or even part of the copper recovered from Summer Island, it certainly indicates one possible, if not probable, location.

Whatever the ultimate source, it is clear that the copper artifacts employed by the Middle Woodland inhabitants of Summer Island were fashioned on the site itself from raw native copper nuggets of variable sizes. There is no evidence to suggest that Summer Island represented a center of copper manufacture for trade, although this possibility does exist.

DISCUSSION

In general, the copper industry recovered from the Middle Woodland component at Summer Island is quite similar to many of the Laurel components excavated along the north shore of Lake Superior (J. Wright, 1967). Most, if not all of the copper artifacts from Summer Island can be duplicated by finds from sufficiently large sites such as Heron Bay (*ibid:* Pl. VI, Figs. 1-29) or from Naomikong Point, farther south (Donald Janzen: personal communication). Most of these copper artifacts have been reported from North Bay components in Wisconsin (Mason, 1966: 68-69; 1967: 320-23). From further west, the Minnesota Laurel components have also yielded copper artifacts but in much decreased frequency (Wilford, 1952; 1955). While copper artifacts do occur in the Point Peninsula components in southeastern Ontario and New York State, these are most often in the form of rolled copper beads and only occasionally a fishhook (Ritchie, 1965; Johnston, 1968). With the possible exception of copper celts found in Hopewell mounds in central Illinois and Ohio, the number of functional copper artifacts in Middle Woodland sites seems to be inversely proportional to the distance from Lake Superior.

In the earlier Archaic period this dichotomy between functional and ornamental appears to have been less significant although the declining frequency of copper artifacts with increased distance from Lake Superior sources is also evident (Fogel, 1963: 129-79). It is difficult to see the Middle Woodland copper industry exhibited at Summer Island as anything other than a continuation of the Archaic copper industry. While lacking many artifact types such as spuds or large socketed projectile points, the Laurel and North Bay components (and to some extent many of the Point Peninsula components as well) seem to have carried the major part of the copper artifact inventory seen in the Archaic "Old Copper Complex" (Wittry, 1957; Fogel, 1963). Many of the beads, awls, and knives from the Riverside Cemetery are indistinguishable from those of Summer Island or Heron Bay (Hruska, 1967).

IX

WORKED BONE

SAMPLE

FROM the Middle Woodland levels of the site eighty-four whole or fragmentary artifacts of worked bone were recovered. Twenty of these were so broken that it was not possible to say much more than that they bore signs of having been worked. In all cases these were short (8-20 mm) flat polished sections of bone showing longitudinal striations. These may have represented broken awls or netting needles, although this cannot be demonstrated. Since the remaining sixty-four tools were composed of both mammal and bird bone, a test by relative frequency of various bone artifact types was made (Table 16) but proved inconclusive. Although there seems to have been some preference for mammal bone for producing artifacts, their frequencies closely approximate the availability of the type of unworked bone present as refuse, and the differences can clearly be attributed to the greater size and strength of mammal bone. In fact even this functional "preference" is misleading and could probably be best expressed in terms of a table comparing size of available scrap

TABLE 16

PERCENTAGE OF WORKED BONE ARTIFACTS BY TYPE OF BONE IN MIDDLE WOODLAND COMPONENTS

Artifact	Mammal Bone	Bird Bone	Total
Worked bone O/E	90.6/91.05	9.4/8.95	100
Unworked bone O/E	91.5/91.05	8.5/8.95	100
TOTAL	182.1	17.9	200

x^2 = .0632
df = 1
p >.80
Φ^2 = .00316

bone to size of the desired artifact. These correlations, seen in Table 17, are based on 200 random pieces of bone and are clearly more significant.

DESCRIPTION OF ARTIFACTS

Of the sixty-four reconstructable artifacts recovered twenty-seven were designated as awls. These were long pointed artifacts, seventeen of which were round in cross section (Pl. XXV, *a-e*) while ten were rather flat and lenticular in cross section (Pl. XXV, *f-k*). There are no significant differences between these two types in metrical attributes. The unbroken specimens have a mean length of 7.76 cm (range: 4.13 to 9.29 cm) and a mean diameter or width of .61 cm (range: .37 to .92 cm). No bimodality was seen in the distribution of awl lengths which seemed to follow a normal curve. This may be a function of the rather small sample size, although the net-sinkers seemed to display such a functional dichotomy with an even smaller sample (cf. p. 142). Nineteen of these awls (over 70 per cent) exhibited numerous overlapping striations parallel to the long axis of the tool and three of these also showed helical or circumscribed striations around the distal portion of the tool, indicating that they were used functionally much as a modern awl or bodkin, to pierce skins or hides with a slight twisting motion. All of these awls display areas of polishing on both ends (where unbroken) but this may be as much the result of hand holding as of use. While similar implements have been reported from most sites in the Upper Great Lakes from all time periods, it is interesting to note that the deer ulna awls (with the proximal end of the ulna unaltered) reported from North Bay components (Mason,

TABLE 17

SIZE OF AVAILABLE BONE REFUSE AND WORKED BONE ARTIFACT SIZE (IN PERCENTS)

Artifact	Under 2 cm	2.1-5.0 cm	Over 5 cm
Mammal bone	20	30	50
Bird bone	70	15	15
Other bone	85	10	5
Worked bone artifacts	5	20	75

1966: 70-71; 1967: 324-25) or the antler splinter awls of some Point Peninsula components (Johnston, 1968: 113; Pl. 28, Fig. 2) do not find counterparts in the Middle Woodland components at Summer Island. Laurel sites in Ontario also lack these although this may be a factor of poor bone preservation (J. Wright, 1967: 97; Table 31).

Eight artifacts from the Middle Woodland component are also fully finished although all are broken. These resemble the flat worked bone awls with the addition of a single drilled hole (Pl. XXV, *l-s*). These artifacts are formally similar to what have been called "mat-sewing needles" (Mason, 1966: 72; Brose, 1968: 38; J. Wright, 1967: 40). Since there is no demonstrable reason for this appellation I would suggest that it is possible to regard these as some type of net-making shuttles. These are somewhat similar to modern wooden or plastic net shuttles used by the fishermen in this area. Six of these artifacts have a mean width of 6 mm (range: 3 to 8 mm) while two have a mean width of 8.5 mm. In both cases the shuttle or needle has a hole about 3.5 mm in diameter drilled through the tool at least 5 cm from one end. The single narrow shuttle or needle with an intact end is rather pointed while the single intact-ended wide shuttle is rather blunt. Most of these tools are very well polished but display few or no striations that cannot be attributed to their manufacture. The polish is probably indicative of having been held in the hand, and is consistent with either inferred function.

Four definite toggle head harpoons were recovered from the Middle Woodland levels at Summer Island (Pl. XXV, *t-w*) as well as five fragmentary points (Pl. XXV, *x-z*) that may have been part of such harpoons. These artifacts have been rather well described for the Upper Great Lakes since late Archaic times (Mason, 1965). The four examples from Summer Island all appear to have been made of deer antler tines. All have a fairly shallow socket at the proximal end, the maximum depth being at least 1.3 cm. In length these harpoons are at least 5.5 cm and all have a drilled line hole centered from 4.1 to 2.6 cm below the tip. This hole has a mean diameter of 3.8 mm (σ = .11 mm) and is countersunk with a mean diameter of 5.7 mm (σ = .37 mm). The two most complete specimens average 1.4 cm in diameter at their base. No polish or other signs of use were evident on any of these harpoon heads that could not be attributed to their manufacture. On the more complete examples the oblique spur at the base was clearly evident. The five broken antler tips previously mentioned did not display any evidence of socketing or drilled line holes, but as none exceeded 2.4 cm in length this need not exclude them from having formed part of a harpoon head. Two specimens seemed to display a slight groove at a distance of 1.8 to 2.0 cm below the tip, indicating that they may have functioned as a fish gorge. At best the interpretation of these artifacts is conjectural.

Similar antler tine toggle head harpoons have been reported from the Porte des Morts site (Mason, 1965; 1967: 323-24), at Spider Cave on Burnt Bluff (Cleland and Peske, 1968: 48-51), and from Laurel components in Minnesota (Wilford, 1955) and northern Ontario (Wright, 1967: 39). While socketed antler tine points are reported for Point Peninsula components (Johnston, 1968: Pl. 55; 3, 4) the most common harpoon seems to be the bilateral (or unilateral) barbed harpoon (Ritchie, 1964; Johnston, 1968) which becomes popular in the Upper Great Lakes only in the Late Woodland period (McPherron, 1967: 177).

Two rather questionable bone artifacts were recovered from the Middle Woodland component (Pl. XXV, *aa, bb*). These have at least formal resemblance to what have been called drifts or punches (Mason, 1966: 71; 1967: 324) or simply cut antler tines (Johnston, 1968: Pl. 28, 1). Formally the two artifacts from Summer Island do not seem to have much in common. Both display identical wear on one end, however, and seem to be functionally the same. The larger of the two is 11.3 cm long and 2.1 cm wide. It is made of a cut section of long bone from some large cervid, probably moose or elk. This tool is very dense and quite heavy. The smaller artifact is made from the antler of a deer and is 6.3 cm long and 9.5 mm in maximum diameter. Only the distal end of this latter implement shows signs of use while the heavier cut bone drift seems to have had two functionally equivalent utilized ends. Both artifacts display a rather distinctive wear on the working ends, consisting of small chips and short grooves in the edges and faces with short striations running from these indentations toward the end of the tool. These impressions overlap but all appear to have a consistent orientation with their long axis being perpendicular or slightly oblique from perpendicular to the long axis of the bone tool itself. These patterns of wear could have been produced by using these tools as hand-held retouchers or flakers. While the smaller implement may have been used as a punch or drift for controlled percussion flaking there is no evidence of battering on its proximal end. Both tools are assumed to have had the same function and their areal associations offer some confirmation for this hypothesis as both were recovered from areas with high frequencies of softhammer flat flakes and flakes of bifacial retouch.

Twenty-seven cut or ground beaver incisors (Pl. XXV, *cc-jj*) were recovered from this component. There were at least a dozen additional fragmentary and complete beaver incisors that bore no evidence of purposeful alteration. Twelve of the modified incisors were obliquely ground along a distal side (ten were right, two were left) to remove the labial and lingual portion of the incisor leaving a point. Five incisors had been transversely ground across the distal lingual portion to create a less acute-angled chisel-like edge. Twelve incisors had been vertically split and, on three of these, the distal portion had been ground somewhat obliquely on the broken surface to produce a thinner version of the first variety. These ground beaver incisors have been reported for Laurel components in Minnesota (Wilford, 1952: 10; 1955: 137), Michigan (Bettarel and Harrison, 1962: 39), Manitoba (MacNeish, 1958: 129), and Ontario (J. Wright, 1967: 38-39). They have also been reported from the Saugeen components at the Donaldson site (Wright and Anderson, 1963: 42) and the Inverhuron site (Kenyon, 1957: 16). Cut and ground rodent incisors are also reported from the Wickham site (Ritchie, 1946: 26) and other Point Peninsula components (Ritchie, 1965: 205-29) but in much lower frequencies than found in sites further west. Cut and/or ground rodent incisors are not commonly reported for either North Bay or Hopewell components.

The last bone artifact from the Middle Woodland component at Summer Island (Pl. XXV, *kk*) is a talon of a bald eagle (*Haliaetus leucocephalus*), broken where a hole had been drilled through from one side. The drill hole was approximately 4.1 mm in diameter. No functional interpretation is offered for this artifact and it is assumed to have been ceremonial in nature. Unperforated eagle talons have been reported from burial pit number 1 at the Serpent Mound site. Here they were associated with sherds of what seems to be transitional Middle to Late Woodland ceramics (Johnston, 1968: 48).

DISCUSSION

In general the worked bone industry from the Middle Woodland component at Summer Island seems quite similar to that from the Point Peninsula-Laurel components from New York to Manitoba. There is an apparent continuity in tool types and forms from the earlier Archaic complexes through the Late Woodland period (see McPherron, 1967: 176-79). Although many of the Archaic tools are copper this is probably due to the extremely poor bone preservation encountered in the earlier sites (Hruska, 1968; MacNeish, 1958: 129; Ritchie, 1965). The emphasis seems to have been on manufacturing implements from the available scrap bone following patterns whose wide distribution (with two exceptions) can be more closely correlated with geographical than with temporal changes. The two exceptions are the toggle head harpoon which seems to be quite restricted within the Upper Great Lakes and temporally rather limited even in this area, and the cut or ground rodent incisor which is reported only for the Middle Woodland period. Exceptions acknowledged, the emphasis must be still placed on the relative stability through time of the artifact assemblages within this large environmental zone of the Great Lakes-St. Lawrence drainage basin, and especially within the area of the Upper Great Lakes.

X

ECONOMIC ADAPTATION

FAUNA

FROM all excavation units and features stratigraphically assigned to the Middle Woodland component at the site 25,430 grams of identifiable bone, and 763 grams of unidentifiable bone were recovered. The breakdown by zoological classes was 13,667 grams of mammal bone, 9,356 grams of fish bone, 651 grams of bird bone, and 1,756 grams of other bone, primarily turtle. The majority of the 763 grams of unidentified bone is probably fish. Specific identification of all faunal remains has not been completed at this time but the fish and mammal bone have been identified by Mrs. Barbara Luxenberg (née Bird) of the Museum of Anthropology, The University of Michigan. While all minimal number of individuals (and thus the weight of available meat) have not been determined, it may be possible to obtain a more realistic picture of the focus of this economic adaptation by listing the frequency of identified bone for the various species recovered from this component.

Fish		
sturgeon	678	
walleye	18	
bass	5	
northern pike	2	
sucker	2	
gar	1	
drum	1	
		Total: 707
Mammal		
bear	8	
beaver	6	
deer	4	
moose	3	
muskrat	2	
otter	2	

Mammal (continued)			
porcupine	1		
rabbit	2		
human	1		
		Total:	29
Bird			
duck	8		
loon	1		
goose	1		
		Total:	10
Other			
turtle	17		
		Total:	17

Although bone preservation was quite good at Summer Island the faunal remains from the Middle Woodland component were extremely fragmentary. This was especially true of the bird and fish bone and has rendered these bones unidentifiable to a far greater degree than the mammal bone. The bias that this may introduce to the final analysis of the fauna will be increased by the greater amount of usable meat yielded by each individual which can be assigned to the identifiable mammalian fauna. This may result in a disproportionate decrease for the amount of non-mammal meat represented at the site.

The mammals recovered from the Middle Woodland component at Summer Island are essentially those found in or near Delta County today. The only exception is the moose which has been retreating north with the clearing of the forests that heralds the advance of civilization from the south (Burt and Grossenheider, 1956). The presence of the moose and porcupine indicates that at the time of occupation the forests around the site may have had a high percentage of conifers (Cleland, 1966: 145). The presence of deer and the absence of many Hudsonian mammals clearly indicates that these forests were of mixed composition, paralleling the modern situation (Dice, 1938). In general the seasonal inferences that can be made on the basis of the mammalian fauna indicate a spring or summer occupation. Cleland (1966: 163) has noted that the black bear hibernates from January until early spring and though it was probably hunted year-round, it could seldom be found during hibernation. Reliance on this mammal would thus argue for a site occupation between April and December. The presence of one portion of deer skull with the antler attached is evidence for occupation at some time during the late summer to spring period of the year, although a second fragment of deer skull has shed its antlers indicating a summer occupation. The large amount of identified beaver bone may also argue for a spring occupation (Cleland, 1966: 145).

The fish fauna of this component is distinctly lacustrine, and the majority prefer clean rocky bottoms with cool water and little rooted vegetation (Scott, 1954; Cleland, 1966). The sturgeon, walleye, and pike in particular are spring-spawning fish and can be netted or speared in the clear shoal waters where they run from April through June (Scott, 1954: 7, 75, 84). The total absence of any identified whitefish or lake trout (which spawn from October to December [Scott, 1954: 19, 34]) is negative evidence pointing to the spring-summer occupation of the site.

The avian fauna cannot greatly aid in fixing the season of occupation until the species of duck and goose are identified. It may be noted however that the loon can be found in the area year-round while, with the exception of teal, the ducks and geese are only transients in the late fall and spring. If Cleland's observation that, "at this latitude turtles are good indicators of summer occupation" (1966: p. 148) can be applied to Summer Island as well as to the Mero site, the faunal remains would suggest an occupation from the first spring thaw to the first frost.

FLORA

The floral remains from this component were identified by Daniel Caister and Volney Jones of the Museum of Anthropology Ethnobotanical Laboratory, The University of Michigan. These consisted of twelve fragments of hazelnut shell (*Corylus* sp.) and twenty-three chokecherry pits (*Prunus virginiana*). The hazelnuts are available August to September while the chokecherry ripens July to August (Yarnell, 1964: 59, 63). These would indicate that the occupation of the site extended throughout the summer. No cultigens were recovered from any deposits assignable to the Middle Woodland component.

Although considerable attention was given to the excavation of all features and to any area of the site that showed a denser texture than normal, no evidence was encountered for any sort of wild rice threshing pits (such as ethnographically reported for the Menominee [Hoffman, 1893]). The seeds of this plant are collected in September or later (Yarnell, 1964: 65). It may be that the inhabitants of the Middle Woodland component did not utilize this plant. A more reasonable assumption might be that the seasonal availability of wild rice probably marked the abandonment of the spring-summer fishing village.

ECONOMIC ADAPTATION

It is, perhaps, premature to attempt to characterize the subsistence pattern of the Middle Woodland component at Summer Island in terms of Cleland's (1966: 42-45) focal-diffuse continuum. The very definite predominance of sturgeon in the utilization of faunal resources clearly indicates that, whatever the amounts of available meat final analysis reveals, sturgeon fishing was a major subsistence activity at this component. Focal economies are characterized as those whose societies have directed their economic practices to the exploitation of one or a few similar kinds of an abundant resource (Cleland, 1966). Even if the bones from each of the mammal species could be assigned to a single individual, the amount of meat from one bear, one deer, and one moose could conceivably exceed the meat provided by several hundred fish. Nonetheless the economic emphasis during this occupation was clearly one based upon the availability of the spring-spawning sturgeon. This occupation must be considered primarily as a fishing site. Perhaps the larger mammals were hunted later in the summer when they had recovered from the winter and when the sturgeon had ended their spawning runs.

With this stipulation it is interesting to compare the rather focal nature of the economic pattern seen at Summer Island with the contemporary North Bay occupation of the Mero site (*ibid.:* 145-56). Quite clearly the Mero intermediate and lower middens (associated with the North Bay occupation) display a more diffuse economic pattern, with deer being the most important resource but with beaver and sturgeon also contributing. Cleland (1966) has described this as a summer occupation which for some reason did not make full use of the great amounts of fish which could be harvested during spring-spawning runs. If Mero and Summer Island are viewed as two types of functionally complementary sites, it is easy to see the Summer Island site representing the major spring-summer occupation for harvesting sturgeon while Mero may represent a short midsummer occupation by a small group who may have spent the earlier portion of the year at a site such as Summer Island.

There may also be early autumn sites for these people located at shallow inland lakes where the major subsistence resource would be wild rice, or located on shallow sandy or gravelly bays of the Great Lakes where fall-spawning whitefish, cisco, and lake trout could be taken (see Scott, 1954: 19, 21-22, 34). The latter type of site may be represented by the Heron Bay site and the Naomikong Point site on Lake Superior (Donald Janzen: personal communication; J. Wright, 1967: 41). The wild rice gathering sites would probably be similar to those reported for many of the Point Peninsula components in Ontario and upper New York State (Ritchie, 1946; 1949; 1965). Winter sites would probably be quite small and located along rivers or interior lakes. The major subsistence resources at these sites would most likely be mammals, probably the moose and beaver characteristic of the Canadian Biotic Province (Dice, 1938; Cleland, 1966). Numerous sites of this type have been reported from southern Ontario (J. Wright, 1967: 94).

The total economic pattern would thus place its reliance on numerous and varied subsistence resources at various times of seasonal availability. While any single site will produce archaeological evidence for what in Cleland's terms would be a focal economic pattern, the total adaptation of the culture would clearly be diffuse. Cleland noted this fact, and went on to state that this type of diffuse economic adaptation required the culture practicing it to have a large technological inventory and to be extremely mobile (1966: 44). This would go far to explain the wide distribution of sites showing similar archaeological styles in ceramics but quite definite differences in chipped stone and copper tools. Some of these can probably be interpreted as functional differences related to the different resources being exploited at different seasonal occupations. The mobility posited by Cleland is reflected in the thousand-mile range for similar archaeological materials in the Laurel to Point Peninsula continuum which occupies this ecologically homogeneous area of the Lake Forest Formation.

XI

FEATURES AND RADIOCARBON DATES

FEATURES

THE following features encountered in the excavation of the Middle Woodland component of the Summer Island site, were pedestaled and excavated as discrete provenience units. Both plan and profile drawings and photographs were obtained for each feature. Feature numbers were assigned serially to each feature as it was encountered regardless of horizontal or vertical location. These numbers serve merely to identify the feature and have no other significance.

To conserve space and avoid needless repetition all features will be discussed in tabular format as outlined below.

Feature number:	Identifying feature number, serially assigned
Definition:	Functional interpretation based on morphology, contents, and location of the feature
Excavation unit:	Coordinates of southwest corner of 5 by 5 foot unit or units in which the feature occurs
Location:	Association with other features and structures at the level
Size:	Maximum length x maximum width x maximum depth, measured from the highest level at which the feature was noted
Shape:	Relative shape in horizontal plane and vertical profile
Contents:	Material recovered from within feature boundaries, generally listed in the following sequence; 1) chipped stone tools, 2) retouched flakes, 3) bipolar cores, 4) weight of nonutilized chippage, 5) ground stone material, 6) bone tools, 7) mammal bone, 8) fish bone, 9) bird bone, 10) other bone, 11) copper material, 12) ceramics listed by number of sherds from named groups, 13) weight of fire-cracked rock fragments, 14) figure or plate designation, if any.

Within this table (18) most of the data is quite self-explanatory, although several features require somewhat greater explication than the format allows. The criteria employed in distinguishing the various pits were as follows: storage pits were generally poor in artifactual material. They had a dark soil layer at their bottoms indicative of some degree of organic decomposition. What material they did contain occurred in a single thin stratum superimposed over this darker lens. Above this these pits showed a rather large homogeneous stratum of sterile sand which practically filled the pit to the top. The refuse pits, on the other hand, were filled with a large number of strata alternating rather light colored sands with darker strata indicative of organic decomposition. Artifactual material occurred throughout these deposits. The refuse pits contained a considerable number of fragments of fire-cracked igneous rock and faunal remains indicating their use for some period of time as an area for rubbish disposal. As there was no significant association found between the shape and size of the pit and the function to which it was put, the assumption is that all of these pits were originally dug for storage purposes but most were subsequently used for the disposal of refuse. Hearths were distinguished from these pits by their larger more regular surface area, their lesser depth, and the fire-hardened, reddish sands that underlay their central basins. These hearths invariably had a layer of ash, large amounts of charcoal, and fire-cracked igneous rock associated with them.

RADIOCARBON DATES

The radiocarbon date of A.D. 250 ± 100 (M-1985) from the Middle Woodland component, referred to in the chapter on the ceramics, was obtained from a sample of cedar and aspen charcoal recovered from the southern hearth in Structure I (Feature 45). The radiocarbon date of A.D. 70 ± 280 (M-2073) was obtained from a sample of cedar twigs from the northern hearth in Structure I (Feature 12). The radiocarbon date of A.D. 160 ± 130 (M-2074) was obtained from a sample of unidentified charcoal from the hearth in Structure II (Feature 20). All dates show a clear overlap in the period A.D. 150 to A.D. 290. This is clearly an acceptable period for the occupation of this component and is in agreement with similar materials from Wisconsin (Mason, 1966) and Ontario (Wright, 1967; Johnston, 1968).

TABLE 18

MIDDLE WOODLAND FEATURES

F. No.	Definition	Excavation Unit	Location	Size	Shape	Contents
6	Storage pit (empty)	460E540	7 feet from entrance along W wall within Structure I	2 ft. by 1.5 ft. by 0.7 ft.	Oblong; steep-sided, asymmetrical	1 retouched flake; 17 grams chippage; 70 grams fish bone; 2 sherds Banked Punctate, plain tool (chevron); 2 sherds Linear Impressed, Dentate Stamp; 1 sherd Banked Stamp, Narrow tool (oblique)
15	Refuse pit	475E545	10 feet from entrance along E wall, within Structure I	1.5 ft. by 1.6 ft. by 0.6 ft.	Circular; steep-sided symmetrical flat-bottomed	1 utilized bladelet; 11 grams chippage; 3 sherds Banked Stamp, plain tool (oblique); 0.5 kg. fire-cracked rock, see Plate XXXVIII
46	Refuse pit	470E445-450	7 feet from entrance along E wall, Structure I	3.1 ft. by 2.8 ft. by 0.8 ft.	Circular; shallow, asymmetrical, round-bottomed	1 end scraper; 3 utilized flakes; 8 bipolar cores; 591 grams chippage; 20 grams mammal bone; 80 grams fish bone; 110 grams other bone; 1 sherd U.P. Plain; 1 sherd Linear Incised, simple (crisscross); 3 sherds Dragged Stamp, Dentate tool

TABLE 18 (Continued)

F. No.	Definition	Excavation Unit	Location	Size	Shape	Contents
5	Refuse pit	460E535	9 feet from entrance along SW wall, outside Structure I	2.9 ft. by 2.3 ft. by 2.2 ft.	Oval; steep-sided, symmetrical, round-bottomed	2 utilized flakes; 37 grams chippage; 9 grams mammal bone; 20 grams fish bone; 1 sherd Banked Stamp, dentate tool; 1 sherd Banked Stamp, Plain tool (oblique); 4 sherds Dragged Stamp, plain tool, see Plate XXVI, *a*
12	Hearth	480-485 E540	NW Focus of Structure I	3.9 ft. by 2.5 ft. by 1.5 ft.	Oval; steep-sided walls, symmetrical, round-bottomed	1 thumbnail scraper; 1 utilized flake; 35 grams chippage; 5 grams mammal bone; 6 sherds Linear Impressed, Braided Cord; 1 sherd Banked Stamp, narrow tool (oblique); 2 sherds Dragged Stamp, Plain tool (oblique); 1.5 kg. fire-cracked rock
45	Hearth	465-470E 540-545	SW Focus of Structure I	4.9 ft. by 3.9 ft. by 0.2 ft.	Oval; steep-sided, symmetrical round-bottomed	1 bifacial blank; 1 bipolar core; 121 grams chippage; 1 bone "mat" needle; 68 grams mammal bone; 135 grams fish bone; 1 copper awl; 13

45	(continued)					sherds Dragged Stamp, Dentate tool (oblique); 8 sherds Banked Stamp, narrow tool (vertical); 1 sherd Banked Stamp, Dentate tool; 24.1 kg. fire-cracked rock; 3 sherds Linear Impressed, Dentate Stamp
4	Internal platform	470E535	Between F. no. 45 and W wall 12 feet from entrance, within Structure I	3.7 ft. by 4.6 ft. by 0.2 ft.	Keyhole-shaped locus of postmolds about a burned area	190 grams mammal bone; 50 grams fish bone; 5.2 kg. fire-cracked rock; 2 sherds Linear Impressed, Braided cord; 1 sherd Linear Impressed, Dentate stamp, see Figure 16
38	Refuse pit	475-480 E550	2 feet SE of Ancillary Structure I *a*	1.9 ft. by 1.3 ft. by 1.2 ft.	Oblong; steep-sided, symmetrical round-bottomed	32 grams chippage; 20 grams fish bone; 2 sherds Linear Impressed Braided cord (vertical); 15 plain surface grit-tempered bodysherds; 2 sherds Linear Incised (crisscross); 4 sherds Linear Incised, Interrupted var.; 5 sherds Dragged Stamp, Plain tool

TABLE 18 (Continued)

F. No.	Definition	Excavation Unit	Location	Size	Shape	Contents
2	Drying rack	480E 525-530	Ancillary Structure I*b*	6.4 ft. by 2.4 ft. by 0.4 ft.	2 long parallel rows of postmolds	1 bifacial blank, 1 corner-notched projectile point; 4 utilized flakes; 1 utilized bladelet; 91 grams chippage; 450 grams mammal bone; 9 grams fish bone; 1 rolled copper bead; 4 sherds Banked Stamp Plain tool (chevron); 4 sherds Banked Stamp Dentate tool; 12 sherds Dragged Stamp Plain tool; 12 sherds Banked Stamp Plain tool (oblique); 6 sherds Banked Punctate Fingernail (oblique); 1.8 kg. fire-cracked rock
19	Refuse pit	505E535	Between F. no. 20 and N wall opposite entrance within Structure II	2.3 ft. by 1.8 ft. by 0.9 ft.	Circular; steep-sided asymmetrical round-bottomed	1 bifacial blank; 2 bifacial blades; 1 side-notched projectile point; 312 grams chippage; 5 grams mammal bone; 30 grams fish bone; 2 plain bodysherds; 8.5 kg. fire-cracked rock; chokecherry and hazelnut

42	SAME AS FEATURE NO. 19					
22	Refuse pit	500E520	16 feet from entrance dug under NW wall of Structure II from within	1.1 ft. by 0.9 ft. by 0.7 ft.	Circular; steep-sided asymmetrical round-bottomed	1 end scraper; 4 retouched flakes; 337 grams chippage; 1 bone awl; 180 grams fish bone; 17 plain surface grit-tempered bodysherds; 4 rimsherds U.P. Plain, unbossed (notched lip)
20	Hearth	500E 525-530	Center of Structure II	4.0 ft. by 3.3 ft. by 2.0 ft.	Oval; steep-sided, symmetrical round-bottomed	1 thumbnail scraper; 5 utilized blades; 37 grams chippage; 5 bipolar cores; 1 net sinker; 1 slate abrader; 2 bone awls; 40 grams mammal bone; 49 grams fish bone; 199 grams other bone; 3 sherds U.P. Plain (notched lip); 7 sherds Linear Impressed, Braided cord
29	Drying rack	490-500 E540	Ancillary Structure II*a*	4.9 ft. by 2.3 ft. by 0.4 ft.	2 parallel rows of post-molds	5 grams chippage; 10 grams mammal bone; 245 grams fish bone; 6 utilized bladelets; 3 bipolar cores; 1 ground-stone hammer; 1 ground-stone mortar and pestle; 2 sherds Banked Stamp, Dentate tool; 2 sherds Linear Incised, Interrupted var.

TABLE 18 (Continued)

F. No.	Definition	Excavation Unit	Location	Size	Shape	Contents
37	Drying rack	510E505	Ancillary Structure II*b*	4.7 ft. by 2.9 ft. by 0.4 ft.	2 parallel rows of postmolds	1 utilized bladelet; 54 grams chippage; 20 grams fish bone; 45 grams other bone; 4 sherds Banked Stamp, dentate tool; 2 misc. Punctate; 2 sherds Banked Stamp, Plain tool (chevron); 3 sherds Linear Incised (criss-cross); 2 sherds Linear Incised Interrupted; 3.5 kg. fire-cracked rock
23	Refuse pit	525E495	4 feet from entrance within Structure III, along SE wall	1.8 ft. by 1.5 ft. by 1.6 ft.	Oblong; very steep-sided, asymmetrical round-bottomed	1 bifacial blade; 2 bipolar cores; 88 grams chippage; 1 very abraded lump of specular hematite; 1 ground-stone mortar; 7 grams fish bone; 7 sherds Banked Stamp, Plain tool (oblique); 0.5 kg. fire-cracked rock
32	Refuse pit	530E495	4 feet from entrance within Structure III, along NE wall	2.7 ft. by 2.4 ft. by 0.6 ft.	Oblong; shallow, symmetrical, round-bottomed	18 grams chippage; 1 bone awl; 10 grams fish bone; 6 sherds Plain, unbossed (notched lip); 3 sherds

32	(continued)					Linear Impressed Dentate Stamp; 6 plain surface grit-tempered bodysherds; 5 kg. fire-cracked rock
43	Refuse pit	540E480	Along opposite wall 30 feet from entrance within Structure III	2.3 ft. by 2.2 ft. by 0.8 ft.	Circular; steep-sided symmetrical round-bottomed	2 utilized bladelets; 3 bipolar cores; 142 grams mammal bone; 145 grams fish bone; 8 plain surfaced grit-tempered bodysherds; 0.5 kg. fire-cracked rock
44	Storage pit	540E480	Along N wall 27 feet from entrance, within Structure III	1.4 ft. by 1.1 ft. by 0.6 ft.	Oval; steep-sided, asymmetrical, flat-bottomed	19 grams chippage; 10 grams fish bone; 11 plain-surfaced grit-tempered bodysherds; 1 kg. fire-cracked rock
31	Hearth	525-530 E490-495	SE Focus of Structure III	2.3 ft. by 1.7 ft. by 0.8 ft.	Oval; steep-sided, symmetrical, round-bottomed	11 grams chippage; 1 slate abrader; 1 abraded lump of specular hematite; 1 bone awl; 25 grams mammal bone; 1 rolled copper bead; 5 kg. fire-cracked rock; 2 sherds Banked Stamp, Plain tool (oblique); 7 sherds Dragged Stamp, Plain tool; 6 sherds U.P. Plain, unbossed, notched lip

TABLE 18 (Continued)

F. No.	Definition	Excavation Unit	Location	Size	Shape	Contents
40	Hearth	530E485	NW Focus of Structure III	3.9 ft. by 3.4 ft. by 0.9 ft.	Oval; steep-sided, symmetrical round-bottom	1 side scraper; 2 utilized bladelets; 278 grams chippage; 30 grams mammal bone; 115 grams fish bone; 4 sherds Dragged Stamp, Dentate tool; 1.9 kg. fire-cracked rock; 1 sherd Banked Stamp, plain tool (oblique); 3 sherds Banked Stamp, Dentate tool; 7 sherds Linear Incised, Interrupted var.
27	Area of packed and burred lime and clay	520E495	In entrance to Structure III	2.4 ft. by 1.6 ft. by 0.2 ft.	Oblong; very shallow, lenses out at edges	71 grams chippage; ground-stone hammer; block ground-stone anvil; 6 grams mammal bone; 5 grams fish bone; 5 sherds Banked Stamp, Plain tool (oblique); 3 sherds Banked Stamp, Plain tool (chevron); 35 kg. fire-cracked rock; 2 sherds Banked Stamp, Dentate tool; 2 sherds Linear Incised (criss-cross); 5 sherds U.P. Plain, unbossed

1	Drying rack	520E480	Ancillary Structure III	5.8 ft. by ? by 0.3 ft.	Two (?) parallel lines of postmolds	3 retouched flakes; 5 utilized bladelets; 6 bipolar cores; 728 grams chippage; 1 "net sinker;" 110 grams mammal bone; 48 grams fish bone; 1 copper fishhook; 125 sherds Dragged Stamp, Plain tool; 11 sherds Banked Stamp, Plain tool (chevron); 8 sherds Banked Stamp, Plain tool (oblique); 2.8 kg. fire-cracked rock; 2 sherds Narrow Banked Stamp
36	Refuse-filled depression	490E535	3 feet E of entrance to Structure II, between Structures I and II	3.3 ft. by 2.3 ft. by 0.2 ft.	Irregular; very shallow, asymmetrical, irregular bottom	1 end scraper; 4 retouched flakes; 40 grams chippage; 2 bone "mat needles;" 1 "net sinker;" 15 grams mammal bone; 35 grams fish bone; 20 grams other bone; 17 sherds Banked Stamp, Dentate tool; 1.5 kg. fire-cracked rock
35	Hearth	490-495 E540	8 feet SE of entrance to Structure II, between Structures I and II	1.8 ft. by 1.7 ft. by 0.2 ft.	Circular; very shallow, symmetrical, flat bottom	2 retouched flakes; 33 grams chippage; 1 bone drift; 5 grams mammal bone; 1 shell pottery-marker; 2 ceramic coils; 3 sherds Banked Punctate, Fingernail; 3 sherds

TABLE 18 (Continued)

F. No.	Definition	Excavation Unit	Location	Size	Shape	Contents
35	(continued)					U.P. Plain, unbossed; 5 sherds Dragged Stamp, Dentate tool; 6 sherds Dragged Stamp, Plain tool; 29 plain bodysherds; 6 kg. fire-cracked rock; see Plate III, *a*; also Plate XXVI, *b* and *c*
21	Area of packed and burred clay	495E540	Between entrance to Structure II and F. no. 49 and F. no. 35	3.3 ft. by 2.7 ft. by 0.3 ft.	Irregular; very shallow lenses out to edges	1 bifacial blank; 2 retouched flakes; 1 utilized bladelet; 14 bipolar cores; 370 grams chippage; 2 abraded ground-stone hammers; 1 block ground-stone anvil; 2 grooved abraders; 1 copper awl; 1 copper fish gorge; 3 rolled copper beads; 8 pieces copper scrap; 1 fragment amygdaloid epidote; see Plate XXIV
28	Area of packed clay	495E535	In entrance to Structure II	2.2 ft. by 1.5 ft. by 0.2 ft.	Oblong; very shallow lenses out to edges	13 grams chippage; 1 sherd Linear Incised, Interrupted (opposed); 3 sherds Banked Stamp, Plain tool (oblique); 1

28	(continued					sherd Dragged Stamp, Dentate tool; 1 sherd Linear Impressed, Braided cord
39	Storage pit	490-495 E535	3 feet S of entrance to Structure II between Structures I and II	1.2 ft. by 0.7 ft. by 1.0 ft.	Oblong; steep-sided, asymmetrical irregular bottom	2 Bifacial blanks; 1 bifacial side scraper; 11 retouched flakes; 8 bipolar cores; 822 grams chippage; 1 ground-stone hammer; 2 block ground-stone anvils; 1 antler punch; 20 grams fish bone; 1 sherd Banked Stamp, Narrow tool (horizontal); 5.2 kg. fire-cracked rock; 1 sherd Dragged Stamp, Dentate tool

XII

INTERPRETATIONS AND SPECULATIONS

ANALYSES of areal distributions of artifacts (Brose, n.d.*b*) have further clarified the nature of the Middle Woodland occupation of Summer Island. The community consisted of about thirty individuals, representing two extended families and two nuclear families, occupying four structures. Analysis of the areal distribution of various types of artifacts led to the inference that the preferred post-nuptial marriage pattern was patrilocality and that band exogamy and some form of cross-cousin marriage were practiced. Social organization does not seem to have reached any level beyond that of the patrilocal band. While one family apparently contained the leader of the band who provided for the less successful families there is no indication that this was due to ascribed status. It may merely have been due to his seniority.

On a more concrete level analyses have demonstrated that the basic economic unit in terms of subsistence activity was the household although the individual nuclear families appear to have been quite independent in the manufacture and processing of non-foodstuffs. While enterprises such as net fishing during the spawning runs may have involved the cooperation of the entire band, no archaeological evidence was recovered that would support this hypothesis.

The site was occupied from about the first spring thaw to the late summer. The major subsistence resource during the early part of this occupation, and indeed probably the principal reason for it, was sturgeon which were netted or speared as they spawned in the shallow water along the rocky shoals surrounding the island. Small mammals, possibly an occasional moose or deer, the results of miscellaneous hook-and-line and spear-fishing, and turtle added to the dried sturgeon probably supplied a great part of the diet through the midsummer. To this can probably be added many of the locally available plants (see Yarnell, 1964: 53-61). In the late summer and early autumn large mammals such as deer and bear, supplemented by the available plant foods (*ibid:* 61-73), were utilized. The site apparently was abandoned before the local spawning runs of lake trout and whitefish in October. This is assumed to indicate a reliance on some nonlocal resource then available. Wild rice is a good candidate. Analysis of the strata and structures quite definitely indicated that the site was not occupied for more than three or four seasons. No reason for its abandonment was apparent.

While faunal resources may have been difficult to obtain no such limitations seem to have been imposed upon the lithic materials. Vast amounts of chert débitage attest the easy availability of this stone. Although generally of low quality its great abundance made the search for more durable material uneconomical. The amounts of scrap copper recovered, often as sizeable pieces, may indicate that a feeling of affluence prevailed here as well. This is in marked contrast to those sites in Ontario where similar artifact styles occur at the same general time period. James Wright characterizes the Ontario Laurel components as small sites which

> rarely produce deposits that can be profitably excavated. . . . Subsurface features are rare and they generally consist of simple firestone concentrations interpreted as hearths. What little subsistence data are available suggests an economy centered on the hunting of moose and beaver, although regional and seasonal factors could play havoc with such a general observation, based as it is on very limited information. A characteristic that is difficult to qualify is the nature of the cultural debris itself. Large flakes, bone fragments artifacts and artifact fragments are in contrast to the preceding Archaic and following Late Woodland assemblages. Very small tools are abundant and the lithic and bone refuse have generally been reduced to minute fragments. In short, there appears to have been an extensive utilization of the raw materials with very little wastage. . . . This situation is quite contrary to that noted in the east with reference to the Point Peninsula and Saugeen foci [1967: 94].

While no data are given on the size of bone fragments or dēbitage, none of the finished artifacts are significantly smaller than their counterparts in the North Bay, Point Peninsula or Minnesota Laurel components. Nor are they noticeably smaller than their functional equivalents from Summer Island. With the exception of Heron Bay all of Wright's Ontario Laurel sites are poor indeed by comparison to Summer Island. While the Pelican Falls site may have as many as twenty vessels represented only two others have more than five (1967, passim). These sites are all quite small. Most excavated sites show a rather high frequency of projectile points and scrapers. Taken with Wright's characterization of the faunal remains, I would interpret these small sites as short-term fall and winter hunting camps occupied by a single family. The intensive utilization of raw materials at these sites may simply be a factor of temporarily limited access to the sources.

To some extent however, even the large sites such as Heron Bay and Pelican Falls (which probably represent multi-family summer and early fall fishing stations) seem to show a greater utilization of lithic material than the functionally equivalent Summer Island site. One explanation for this may be found in the relatively large numbers of scrapers that occur at the Ontario sites thus adding to the percentage of flaked stone showing evidence of deliberate work (Wright, 1967: 32, 64, 68). This is also the situation at the Naomikong Point site where over 1100 scrapers were recovered (Donald Janzen: personal communication). From these sites the frequency of bipolar cores is correspondingly low (Wright, 1967) while at Summer Island some evidence for the functional equivalence of bipolar cores and scrapers has been suggested (p. 227). Again, the bipolar core technique does not seem to have been of much importance in the North Bay components at the Mero or at the Porte des Morts sites (Mason, 1966; 1967).

Mason (1967: 333-34, 338-43) noted the regional diversity that characterized the lithic and copper industries of these Northern Tier Middle Woodland cultures, and added, "What is most distinctive of the Anderson-Nutimik-Laurel-[North Bay]-Saugeen-Point Peninsula continuum is of course the pottery." This situation has also been remarked upon by James Wright:

> Not only are many of the ceramic attributes unique to the [Laurel] tradition, but a substantial number exhibit a homogeneity which is quite surprising when one considers the extensive area involved (1967: 93).

Taken in conjunction with the variations noted in lithic and copper working (1967: 127-29) this leads Wright to see a movement of people into the area from the northwest. In the discussion of ceramics (p. 327) I rejected this interpretation in favor of viewing the ceramic continuum, albeit poorly understood, as a regional adoption of ceramic styles originated in the Illinois area. If the social structure deduced to have existed at Summer Island (Brose, n.d. *b*) can be imputed to similar sites throughout the Middle Woodland Lake Forest, a processual explanation is available to account for widespread homogeneity and regionally distinctive lithic traditions.

In his discussion of the composition of patrilocal bands Owen (1965: 678) indicates that the diversity between male and female "culture" could reach the point where, while all adult males were native speakers of one language some of the adult females were native speakers of different languages or dialects. Owen explains this, as a result of band exogamy and low population density which, "will inevitably lead to selection of mates from some distance, often fifty miles away or more" (1965: 683). The results of such a diffusion of females with their intendant cultural backgrounds would soon lead to the standardization of a ceramic design repetoire over large geographical areas while leaving a relatively stable male-related lithic industry to develop along more local lines. Such a movement of females would not lead to a total loss of ceramic attribute clusters (unless a totally random mating pattern were concomittant with patrilocal residence) any more than the lack of male movement would lead to unvarying and totally isolated lithic attribute clusters. It would, however, account for the widespread occurrence of quite similar ceramic modes such as are observed.

To carry these speculations further, some of these ceramic modes, while geographically widespread relative to much of the male-related artifact types, still show definite limits not all of which coincide. Granted the high degree of mobility that the economic pattern imposes upon these central-based wandering communities (Beardsley, *et al.*, 1955: 138-40) it would not be difficult to see ceramic styles diffuse quite rapidly (say within several generations) from one end of the Lake Forest to the other. If this had in fact occurred, and if ceramic styles ultimately derived from Illinois once entered such a system at either (or both) ends, the archaeological picture may well present the impression of a sweeping occupation of the central area by a cohesive culture which bears little relationship to the preceding Archaic occupation. This would be especially true if the economic patterns of that central area, in response to changing environmental conditions, were undergoing a readaptation towards a more diffuse economy with the intendant replacement of many of the older types of functional tools and the addition of several new ones (see Cleland, 1966: 42-45). The only movement of people this speculative model would require, is the seasonal movement of the exogamous patrilocal band to utilize the available resources of the Lake Forest Formation, and the postnuptial movement of women within that area.

PART III

THE UPPER MISSISSIPPIAN COMPONENT

XIII

THE NATURE OF THE COMPONENT

OCCURRENCE

SOME time after the Middle Woodland occupation previously described, the site was abandoned. Winds sweeping across the site from the harbor deposited a thin layer of beach sands in depressions and where vegetation existed to trap the developing dunes. In drier areas of the site, or with a decrease in atmospheric moisture, dune development slowed and aeolian erosion began to strip this recent sand level. This erosion was stopped by the development of a meadow soil in damper areas, perhaps indicative of a cooler moister climate. It was on this incipient soil which sporadically covered the backslope dunes that the second occupation of the site occurred. This occupation was characterized by a predominance of Upper Mississippian ceramics similar to those of the Oneota aspect (Griffin, 1943: 268-69, 286-302) especially those of the foci located in Wisconsin (Griffin, 1943; McKern, 1945). The strata associated with this Oneota, or Upper Mississippian component of the site were thin and quite discontinuous (depositional unit M) with their greatest density in northeastern and central Area "B." The deposits were characterized by thin irregular lenses of grayish brown sand. Although pits and postmolds intruded into and through the underlying pale brown sands and the earlier Laurel occupation, in most areas the grayish brown sands were simply a small, quite irregular, thin sheet lying directly upon the dense black Middle Woodland midden.

STRUCTURES, FEATURES, AND RADIOCARBON DATES

Postmolds originating in this unit were few and scattered. Although large areas were excavated where this component occurred most densely, no patterns could be determined. The majority of these postmolds seem to have been from 0.35 feet to 1.25 feet in diameter with a mean diameter of 0.62 feet. This is quite a large size for nonstructural posts (see p. 41) and it was expected, during the excavations of the site, that structural patterns would be found. Not only were no such patterns recovered, neither was there any recognizable correlation between the location of these posts and the features associated with this component. The features recovered are presented in Table 19 in basically the same format used to describe the Middle Woodland features (p. 151). The major difference is the elimination here of the "location" column, as no structural or areal relationship seems to exist for the Upper Mississippian features. Only a single feature requires any further comment. Feature 11 (Pl. XXXII) was the only recovery of a number of bivalves from any component of the site. All other bivalves recovered came from the four excavation units associated with this component immediately surrounding this feature. In all, at least forty-two individuals were represented. All were uncut although the large amount of charred organic material within Feature 11 indicates that they may have been steamed open. The associated chipped stone materials will be discussed in a later chapter.

Three radiocarbon dates were obtained from features associated with the Upper Mississippian component, all containing characteristic shell-tempered ceramics. A date of A.D. 1290±100 (M-2071) was obtained from a sample of charred mammal bone and charred twigs of spruce recovered from Feature no. 3. A date of 1290±200 (2Σ[M-2072]) was obtained from charcoal of an unidentified species recovered from Feature no. 14. A date of 370±140 B.C. (M-2070) was obtained from charred organic material (twigs, reeds, and grasses) recovered from Feature no. 11. This last date is clearly out of line with M-2071 and M-2072 which are quite reasonable in the light of similarly dated Oneota materials from Wisconsin (Hall, 1962; Mason, 1966). It is probably due to the inclusion in this feature of large amounts of mussel shell, presumably collected from the gravel bar to the northwest of the site. The waters of this area are rather basic with a high $CaCO_2$ content (Ayers, *et al.*, 1958) dissolved from the Middle Silurian Limestone series which comprises the local member of the Niagara Escarpment. The unreasonably ancient radiocarbon date probably represents leaching of $CaCO_2$ from the clamshells by ground water action and the contamination of the small charcoal fragments within the feature by this dead carbon.

TABLE 19

FEATURES OF THE UPPER MISSISSIPPIAN COMPONENT

F. No.	Definition	Excavation Unit	Size	Shape	Contents
3	Hearth	505E550	2.3 ft. by 2.5 ft. by 0.4 ft.	Very shallow gently rounded walls, irregular bottom	235 grams mammal bone; 45 grams fish bone; 237 sherds Koshkonong Bold representing a single vessel; 7.5 kg. fire-cracked rock; much ash and flecks of charcoal
9	Refuse pit	480E530	3.0 ft. by 1.0 ft. by 0.9 ft.	Asymmetrical pit with 1 steep irregular wall and 1 gradually sloping wall forming bottom	17 grams chippage; 2 bipolar cores; 1 fragment bone "mat-sewing" needle; 20 grams bird bone; 140 grams fish bone; 2 sherds Carcajou plain; 1 sherd Delta Collared; 2.5 kg. fire-cracked rock
10	Refuse pit	495E495	2.5 ft. by 1.9 ft. by 0.9 ft.	Asymmetrical pit with 2 steep walls flat bottom	26 grams chippage; 1 end scraper; 20 grams bird bone; 15 grams fish bone; 1.0 kg. fire-cracked rock
11	Refuse pit	485E535	0.7 ft. by 0.6 ft. by 1.2 ft.	Symmetrical steep-sided round bottom pit	175 grams chippage; 2 bipolar cores; 46 bivalve shells representing 16 individuals *Amblema costata plicata* (Say), and 7 individuals *Lampsilis siliquoidea*

TABLE 19 (Continued)

F. No.	Definition	Excavation Unit	Size	Shape	Contents
11	(continued)				(Barnes); 29 grams fish bone; 3 sherds Delta Collared; 1 sherd Carcajou Plain
14	Refuse pit	480E515	2.3 ft. by 2.4 ft. by 1.9 ft.	Symmetrical pit, bell-shaped, bottom rounded	10 grams chippage; 1 unnotched point; 12 grams bird bone; 20 grams fish bone; 7 shell-tempered bodysherds; 1.75 kg. fire-cracked rock; some charcoal
16	Storage pit	480E520	2.3 ft. by 1.4 ft. by 1.4 ft.	Asymmetrical pit 1 steep, 1 irregular wall, flat bottom	77 grams chippage; 1 bifacial blank; 2 pebble cores; 1 sherd Detour Trailed, 0.5 kg. fire-cracked rock
24	Refuse pit	520E495	0.9 ft. by 0.5 ft. by 0.5 ft.	Symmetrical with rounded walls and flattish bottom	24 grams turtle bone; 35 grams mammal bone; 6 shell-tempered bodysherds; 2.0 kg. fire-cracked rock
25	Hearth	500E495	1.0 ft. by 0.9 ft. by 0.2 ft.	Circular, shallow with flat bottom	3 grams chippage; 10 grams bird bone; 1 valve *Amblema costata* (Say); 1 shell-tempered bodysherd; 2.0 kg. fire-cracked rock

The pH of Feature no. 11 was 8.5 to 9.0, considerably higher than that of the surrounding soils.

SEASONALITY

In general the nature of the floral and faunal remains suggest that the site was occupied primarily in the late summer. At that season the bivalves would be the easiest to collect (Brose, n.d. *b*) although perhaps not at their most palatable. The only floral remains from this component, consisted of seven fragments of charred hazelnut shell (*Corylus* sp.). These nuts ripen in late August or early September (Yarnell, 1964: 63).

Apart from mollusks, the faunal remains have not, at this writing, been specifically identified. The weights of identifiable bone were available by order. From the Upper Mississippian component of the site 8256 grams of mammal bone, 3187 grams of fish bone, 269 grams of bird bone, and 697 grams of reptile and amphibian bone were recovered. An additional 312 grams were unidentifiable even as to order. Of all mammal remains deer, bear, and rabbit seemed to be the most abundant. Sturgeon, walleye, and bass were the most well-represented fish. Duck and turtle seem to have provided most of the remaining meat during this occupation. Until definite quantification for the weight of available meat represented by the minimal number of individuals of each species is completed, it is difficult to make precise statements as to the subsistence activity of the occupants. In general however, it appears that the site was not inhabited solely as a fishing station. It seems to have been a temporary camp occupied (as part of a seasonal cycle of utilizing various local resources) in the late summer or early autumn. A wide variety of faunal resources were apparently utilized during its occupation. The economic adaptation could be characterized as diffuse (Cleland, 1966: 42-45); however this may be a premature statement which will be altered when detailed analyses are completed.

XIV

DESCRIPTION AND ANALYSIS OF ARTIFACTS

CERAMICS

FROM the fifty-nine excavation units and features assigned to the Upper Mississippian component on the basis of stratigraphy, 16 minimal vessels, represented by 42 rimsherds, and 286 decorated bodysherds were recovered. An additional 110 undecorated bodysherds were recovered of which 61 were grit-tempered and cord-marked, and the remaining 49 were shell-tempered and smoothed. The distribution of these ceramics by types is shown in Table 20.

Four vessels, represented by six rimsherds and fifteen decorated bodysherds can be considered representative of Hall's (1962: 63-65, Pl. 25-28) type Carcajou Plain (Pl. XXVII, *a*-*e*). All vessels were shell-tempered and had a distinctly laminar paste texture. In hardness the sherds ranged from 2.0-2.5. Color was quite variable but exterior surfaces tended to be grayish brown to tan with fresh breaks showing an interior color somewhat lighter and more grayish. Surface finish on all vessels was smooth. All vessels were squat, globular, rounded-bottom pots with a rounded shoulder, constricted neck, and medium to high everted rim (Figure 15, *a*, *b*). Bodysherds below the neck ranged from 6.0 mm to 7.3 mm ($\overline{X}$ = 6.5 mm) in thickness. At the shoulder the sherds ranged from 5.9 mm to 6.2 mm ($\overline{X}$ = 6.0), and at the lip from 6.9 mm to 8.4 mm ($\overline{X}$ = 7.6 mm). No handles were observed on any of these vessels. The only decoration consisted of lip scalloping. On three vessels a dowel-like tool 5.9 mm to 6.2 mm wide has been impressed across the lip at intervals of from 7.3 mm to 9.5 mm to depths of about 3.1 mm. These impressions often have produced a small amount of extruded clay along the base of the exterior edge possibly indicating application from the interior. The fourth vessel of this type appears more definitely notched with a triangular tool. These notches are applied across the lip and often carry on along the exterior edge. They are 4.0 mm deep, 6.7 mm wide, and 5.9 mm to 7.1 mm deep.

TABLE 20

CERAMICS FROM UPPER MISSISSIPPIAN COMPONENT

Ceramic Variety	Rim-sherds	Decorated Bodysherds	Minimal No. of Vessels	Percentage of Minimal Vessels	No. of all Assignable Sherds	Percentage of all Assignable Sherds	Mean Vessel Occurrence Per Excavation Unit
Carcajou Plain	6	15	4	25.0	21	6.4	.119
Koshkonong Bold	15	163	3	18.7	178	54.3	.186
Delta Collared	19	78	6	37.5	97	29.6	.237
Pt. Detour Trailed	2	30	3	18.7	32	9.8	.119
TOTALS	42	286	16	99.9	328	100.1	$\overline{X}$ = .165

Unassignable cordmarked grit-tempered sherds = 61

Unassignable Plain shell-tempered sherds = 49

Total Sherds from Component = 438

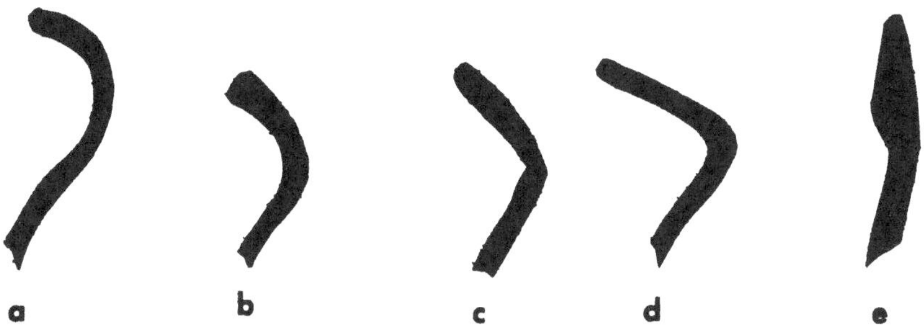

FIG. 15. Rim profiles of Upper Mississippian and Late Woodland Ceramics.

Similar ceramics have been reported from numerous sites in Wisconsin (Barrett and Skinner, 1932: Pl. 80, Fig. 2; Griffin, 1943: 293-97, Pl. 145, Figs. 31, 32; McKern, 1945: 149-50, Pl. 65, Figs. 6, 8; Hall, 1962: Pl. 25, *c*, *d*, 26, *b*, 27, 28, *a*; Mason, 1966: 168-70, Pl. 12, Fig. 2*c*, Pl. 13, Fig. 1, 2*a*, *c*). In northern Michigan similar ceramics have been reported from an ossuary at the Juntunen site (McPherron, 1967: 118-21, Pl. XXIII, *g*, *h*, *f*), the Backlund Mound Group, in Menominee County (Brose, 1968: 43, Fig. 7*b*, *c*), and from the upper level at the Ekdahl-Goudreau site (Prahl and Brose, n.d.).

Three squat globular vessels of Hall's (1962: 72-75, Pl. 36, *f*, *h*, 37, 72, 73) type Koshkonong Bold were represented by fifteen rimsherds, sixty-three decorated and one hundred undecorated bodysherds (Pl. XXVII, *f*-*i*). In terms of paste and tempering these sherds are identical to those previously described. Bodysherds ranged from 4.6 mm to 7.8 mm in thickness. At the shoulder these vessels were 5.2 mm to 6.0 mm thick while rims ranged from 7.0 mm to 8.3 mm just above the neck and from 4.7 mm to 5.9 mm at the lip. The everted lip on these sherds was rather flat (Fig. 15, *d*) and the lip edges were finger pinched (not scalloped) to produce alternately thin and thick areas. Where the lip had not been pinched an exterior fold of clay thickening the rim from 5.6 mm to 7.9 mm, about 16 mm high could clearly be seen. The vessel tended to split along this seam quite frequently. Decoration consisted of numerous vertical finger-trailed lines originating in the neck area somewhat below the finger pinched lip and extending downward to the upper shoulder area. These trailed lines are from 10.2 mm to 17.8 mm wide ($\bar{X}$ = 13.5) and are about 2.5 cm apart. These lines are all about

55.0 mm long and 3.5 mm deep. Numerous drilled holes occurred on the largest vessel of this type (rim diameter = 29.8 cm) both just below the rim where they are interpreted as suspension holes, and in a circular pattern of seven drilled holes all about 10.3 cm equidistant. These latter holes occurred below the shoulder and in the basal region on one side of the pot. These are tentatively interpreted as crack-lacing holes although the pattern taken by them lends little support to this view.

Similar ceramics have been recovered from east-central Wisconsin (McKern, 1945: Pl. 55, Fig. 10; Hall, 1962) and from west-central Wisconsin (Griffin, 1943: Pl. 141, Figs. 1-3). Griffin (1943: 284-86, Pl. 140, Figs. 4, 6) reported somewhat similar sherds from the Huber site, Cook County, Illinois, and Mason (1966: 168-71; Pl. XXII, Fig. 1, left center) described a few such sherds from the Door Peninsula of Wisconsin. McPherron reported finger-trailed Oneota ceramics from the Juntunen site (1967: 119) but these are not illustrated nor can many of these be located in the collections from the site in The University of Michigan Museum of Anthropology. Several sherds similar to Hall's type description were recovered in test pits at the Ekdahl-Goudreau site (Prahl and Brose, n.d.).

The last Oneota type at the Summer Island site has been designated Point Detour Trailed (Pl. XXVIII, *e-i*). The type consisted of three vessels represented by two rimsherds and thirty decorated bodysherds. In terms of paste and temper these vessels are similar to those previously described from this component. Vessels were all apparently squat globular pots with a constricted neck and sharply out-flaring (almost angular) rim and a slightly thickened, subrounded lip (Fig. 15, *c*). Bodysherds ranged in thickness from 2.5 mm at the neck to 7.0 mm at the base. Rimsherds ranged from 3.4 mm to 4.2 mm above the neck, to 5.1 mm at the lip. Decoration on these vessels was confined to the exterior surface between the plain lip and the shoulder. In general all lip to neck portions of sherds were also plain and decoration may have been confined to the neck-shoulder region of the vessel. No handles or lugs of any kind were apparent on this type. The decoration consisted of narrow trailed lines which varied in width from 1.5 mm to 5.8 mm ($\bar{X}$ = 4.2 mm), in depth from 0.1 to 0.7 mm, and in distance from each other from 2.5 mm to 1.0 cm. There was no noticeable cameo effect on the interior of these sherds. The trailed designs took the form of parallel oblique lines forming nested triangles or superimposed chevrons. No punctation was observed on any of these sherds.

Sherds similar to the Point Detour type from Summer Island have been reported as Orr focus pottery from the Midway site in west-central Wisconsin (Griffin, 1943: Pl. 141, Figs. 7, 10, 14, 15; Pl. 142, Figs. 25, 28-32) and as Grand River Trailed (Hall, 1962: 65-68, Pl. 21, *c-d*, 29*a*, 30-32) from central Wisconsin at the Carcajou Point site (ibid.) and at the Walker-Hooper site (Jeske, 1928: Pl. 32; Griffin, 1943: 293-97, Pl. 145, Fig. 2, 4, 6, 7; McKern, 1945: 149-50, Pl. 63, Figs. 3, 4). Point Detour Trailed is also quite similar to sherds from the Fisher site, LaSalle County, Illinois (Griffin, 1943: 274-77, Pl. 126, Fig. 3), to Hall's Category A unclassified Mississippian ceramics (1962: 58-59, Pl. 20, Figs. *d*, *e*). Resemblances also exist to the more angular designs on some of the Diamond Bluff Trailed ceramics (Maxwell, 1950: 427-33; Hall, 1962: 129, 171-73, Pl. 56, 61, Fig. *a*) although the Point Detour Trailed ceramics show a higher, possibly more everted rim.

The final ceramic type recovered from this component consisted of six grit-tempered, cordwrapped-paddle malleated vessels represented by nineteen rimsherds and seventy-eight bodysherds (Pl. XXVIII, *a-d*). The paste was a somewhat sandy clay with a slightly laminar, but generally quite compact, texture. Hardness on the Moh's scale ranged from 2.5 to 3.5. Colors on exterior and interior surfaces were gray to brown with interior cores light to dark gray. Temper represented about 40 per cent aplastic by volume and consisted of particles of crushed granitic grit ranging from 2.1 mm to 3.9 mm in diameter ($\bar{X}$ = 2.4 mm). Vessels seemed to be globular to slightly elongated with a rounded base, slightly constricted neck, and slightly everted collared rim (Fig. 15, *e*). Bodysherds ranged in thickness from 4.8 mm to 7.9 mm ($\bar{X}$ = 6.0 mm). At the shoulder thickness ranged from 5.5 mm to 7.0 mm ($\bar{X}$ = 6.3 mm). At the lower edge of the thickened collar thickness ranged from 7.6 mm to 8.8 mm ($\bar{X}$ = 8.0 mm) thinning to the lip ranging from 5.4 mm to 7.9 mm ($\bar{X}$ = 6.0 mm). Exterior surface finish consisted in offset and obliterating cord-wrapped paddle impressions. This cord, 2.1 mm in diameter, was composed of a ${}^{Z}_{Z}S$ twist, and was wrapped around the paddle about four times per centimeter. The lips were flattened and crossed by oblique ${}^{S}_{S}Z$ twisted cord-wrapped stick impressions about 1 mm wide and 3.8 mm apart. No castellations of any sort were observed on these vessels. The collar appears to have been constructed by folding the rim. It thickened gradually from the lip to its maximum thickness of 9.2 mm at about 23.3 mm below the rim. Below this it abruptly thinned to the bodysherd thickness below. No other decoration occurred anywhere on these vessels. This type is designated as Delta Collared.

Similar ceramics described as the plain (and uncastellated) variety of Aztalan Collared have been reported from the Carcajou Point site (Hall, 1962: 83). It is somewhat like what has been described as Point Sable Collared from Aztalan and from the Point Sauble site (Baerreis and Freeman, 1958: 52-58), and from the Heins Creek and Mero sites (Mason, 1966: 20-21, 133-37, Pl. XX) although these ceramics all seem to have exterior twisted-cord decoration on the collars, and many have interior decorations as well. Perhaps the closest affinities for the Delta Collared vessels are found to the south and east in Michigan. From the Juntunen site, where McPherron recovered sherds of Point Sable Collared (1967: 110-11), his type Bois Blanc Braced Rim, Corded Collar variety (1967: 105-6) is formally identical to the type Delta Collared. Despite Fitting's disclaimers of equivalence between his Spring Creek Collared and Aztalan Collared (1968: 24), the two types are rather similar. Spring Creek Collared diverges from the Aztalan collared in having a thinner profile, no castellations, and no elaborate decorations (Fitting, 1968). The Spring Creek Collared is thus formally similar to the Delta Collared type (ibid.: Pl. IV, center row).

CHIPPED STONE

The distribution of the 13,403 pieces of chipped stone weighing 20,304 grams are represented in Table 21 according to those categories described for the Middle Woodland chipped stone (p. 181). Of the 108 bipolar cores recovered, 27 were subjected to microscopic examination. No definite traces of use were discovered on the seven (out of twenty-eight) opposed point, two (out of eight) point-ridge, or two (out of eight) point-area cores. On six of the fifteen (out of sixty) opposed ridge cores examined there were transverse striae along one edge with numerous small chips removed from a concave surface at these points. These were all very small examples of the opposed ridge bipolar core, all looking longitudinally broken (Pl. XXIX, *a*, *b*). These implements may have functioned as curved chisels of some sort. The single ridge-area core examined showed no evidence of use.

The single bifacial scraper from this component (Pl. XXIX, *c*) was 4.9 cm long, 3.1 cm wide, and 1.4 cm thick. It was formally identical to the bifacial blanks from this component but bore signs of heavy transverse striations along both edges as

TABLE 21

CHIPPED STONE DISTRIBUTION FROM UPPER MISSISSIPPIAN COMPONENT

Category	Number	Percentage of Total Number	Weight (Grams)	Percentage of Total Weight	Percentage of Non-type 1 Chert
Flakes:					
Decortication	794	5.92	4229	21.12	15.0
Block	3102	23.14	5237	25.69	10.1
Flat	8254	61.65	3700	18.27	9.4
Cores:					
Pebble	440	3.29	2925	14.48	4.5
Block	579	4.33	1808	8.94	1.0
Bipolar	108	0.81	1305	6.48	6.9
Bifaces:					
Scraper	1	0.01	14	0.07	0
Blade	2	0.01	37	0.18	0
Blank	3	0.02	79	0.39	33.3
Projectile Point	13	0.09	174	0.85	8.9
Unifaces:					
End scraper	10	0.07	97	0.48	10.0
Side scraper	4	0.03	53	0.26	0
Notched scraper	1	0.01	14	0.07	0
Bladelet	30	0.23	136	0.65	27.8
Utilized flake	62	0.46	645	3.13	10.4
TOTAL	13403	100.07	20453	101.06	

well as along its base indicating that it may have had its point set into a handle. The bifacial blades from the component were both about 5.5 cm long, 2.5 cm wide and 0.6 cm thick (Pl. XXIX, *d, e*). Both were ovate points and both were slightly asymmetrical with one edge rather straight and quite sharp while the other edge was considerably more excurvate and showed clear longitudinal striations along the narrower two-thirds. No polish or gloss occurred on the straight edge although the curved edge showed slight gloss on high ridges extending to the longitudinal midline. The wear patterns confirm the use of these implements as blades, and while the butt was not markedly thinned they were apparently not hand held.

Three bifacial blanks (Pl. XXIX, *f, g*) were recovered from the Upper Mississippian component. In length these ranged from 4.2 cm to 5.7 cm, in width from 2.4 cm to 2.8 cm, and in thickness from 0.6 cm to 1.3 cm. All were rather ovate in shape while two had convex bases and one had a broken base. These all appear to have been unused either as knives or as scrapers.

On two of these preforms the hinging out at inclusions clearly showed why further work was abandoned. The third blank seems to have been made of a rather high quality flint and was probably lost before it could be further worked into a projectile point or used as a knife or scraper.

Thirteen projectile points were recovered from this component of the site. A metrical analysis for these points is presented in Table 22 and several of them are illustrated in Plate XXIX, *h-m*. Most of these points are easily classifiable as Madison points (Ritchie, 1961). On one of these points two distinct side notches have been made about 4.2 mm up from the base. This point thus resembles the notched triangular points from the Cahokia site and from the related Rock River focus site at Aztalan (Titterington, 1938; Maher and Baerreis, 1958). The projectile points varied considerably in quality of workmanship. Some were quite crude while others displayed considerable symmetry and quite fine retouching. In general the cruder points were more laterally convex while the finer ones tended to be slightly concave.

The ten end scrapers recovered from this component (Pl. XXX, *a-g*) were rather variable in size and amount of retouch. While only two (Pl. XXX, *c*, *e*) displayed major areas of cortex

TABLE 22

ONEOTA COMPONENT PROJECTILE POINTS

Catalog Number in situ	Length	Width	Thickness
74902	3.58	1.53	0.40
74459	. . .	. . .	0.45
74404	4.28	2.55	0.82
74394	8.54	3.80	1.10
74589	6.80	3.58	1.06
74350	5.75	3.46	1.03
75261	7.70	3.28	0.80
75188	. . .	2.75	1.06
75177	6.69	. . .	0.45
75290	2.92	1.67	0.80
75131	1.91	1.29	0.39
74984	2.47	1.70	0.36
75131	1.76	1.04	0.39
MEAN	4.76	2.42	0.70
σ	1.30	0.46	0.14

the others ranged from rather crudely retouched bipolar cores (Pl. XXX, *a*) to thin, finely flaked elongated end scrapers (Pl. XXX, *b*). Three of the four side scrapers from this component are illustrated in Plate XXX, *h-j*. All seem to have been made on randomly chosen large flakes. They differ from the utilized flakes only in the amount of deliberate retouch and in their larger size. The single notched scraper from the component (Pl. XXX, *k*) displayed large areas of gloss on the surfaces indicating that it was probably hand held. The metrical data for all of the scrapers recovered from this component are presented in Table 23. The relative frequency of end scrapers and projectile points may, in fact, reflect the sexual composition on the function of the site. They most certainly cannot be abstracted from these cultural matrices and used to create chronological seriations (cf., Hall, 1962: 121-23; Mason, 1966: 180-81).

From the Upper Mississippian component of the site thirty bladelets (Pl. XXX, *l-y*) were recovered. Six of these were on exotic materials while the remainder were of local cherts. Microscopic analysis of ten of these bladelets failed to indicate any signs of use. Although one of them (Pl. XXX, *u*) looked as though one end had been modified into a small drill, no wear patterns were discovered to support the initial observation. Many of these bladelets were clearly flakes derived from the bipolar core preparation (e.g., Pl. XXX, *l*, *n*, *w*). The mean length for the Upper Mississippian component bladelets was 2.38 cm (σ = 0.5043 cm) and the mean width was 0.92 cm (σ = 0.2631 cm).

Sixty-two utilized flakes were recovered from this occupation. The mean weight for these flakes was 10.40 grams. Since forty of them were flat flakes they clearly represent a deliberate selection of the largest flakes from that category. A typical utilized flat flake is illustrated in Plate XXX, *z*.

PECKED AND ROUGH STONE

Only six items of pecked and/or ground stone were recovered from this component. Two notched pebble net-sinkers were found in excavating units in the 500E580 block. These were not associated with each other, or indeed with anything else save fire-cracked rock and Carcajou Plain potsherds. In overall length these net-sinkers were 7.93 cm and 7.09 cm. In weight they were 103 and 98 grams. In length between notches they were 7.45 and 6.69 cm, in notch width 1.42 cm and 0.97 cm, and in notch depth 1.03 and 1.03 cm respectively. Comparison

TABLE 23

UPPER MISSISSIPPIAN SCRAPERS
(Measurements In Centimeters)

UMMA Cat. Number	Max. Length	Max. Width	Thickness at Scraping Edge	Length of Scraping Edge	Degree of Arc on Working Edge	Cortex Present	Flint Type
74657	3.64	2.32	0.60	2.32	40	No	B
74905	2.02	2.45	0.59	2.45	85	No	B
75300	2.10	1.72	0.65	1.67	50	No	B
75299	2.32	2.45	0.46	2.45	75	No	B
74988	2.83	1.88	0.53	1.88	40	No	B
74988	3.17	2.50	0.77	1.59	30	Yes	B
74567	2.49	2.81	0.50	2.49	60	No	B
74155	5.46	3.19	0.93	3.76	180	Yes	B
74155	3.29	2.72	0.50	2.59	55	No	B
74170	. . .	2.32	0.55	1.55	70	No	B
74170	. . .	2.30	0.47	2.30	45	No	B
75147	2.87	1.43	0.30	1.47	-25	No	B
75287	2.17	2.10	0.63	2.10	65	No	B
75290	. . .	1.76	0.58	1.76	60	No	B
75255	2.58	2.68	0.53	2.39	60	No	B
MEAN	2.92	2.31	0.57	2.18	65		
σ	.55	.29	.06	.21	33		

of these figures with Table 13 and Figures 15 and 16 indicates that these closely compare to the Middle Woodland net-sinkers. This may indicate an optimum size for net sinkers to be employed in the offshore fishery in the Summer Island area, or it may more reasonably be considered evidence that these artifacts properly belong to the earlier component.

Two fragments of slate were recovered from the Upper Mississippian component both of which bore clear evidence of their use as abraders (Pl. XXXI, *c*, *n*). The larger of these had one rounded edge which was well worn and highly polished. This may have been used for burnishing pottery (although no polished ceramics were recovered) or perhaps for softening hides or thongs. The smaller fragment has one end crossed by numerous small ($\overline{X}$ = 1.3 mm) grooves and notches all of which showed faint transverse striations. I interpret this artifact as a sharpener for circular bone awls. The other two pecked stone artifacts were large abraders, both of which showed sharply defined well-grooved facets on several surfaces (Pl. XXXI, *a*, *b*). These would ordinarily be defined as "manos" but the implication of agriculture this term carries inveighed against its use in this case where no evidence for agriculture exists. They may well have served a similar function in processing locally available vegetal foods however.

Twelve whole and fragmentary worked bone tools were recovered from levels assigned to the Upper Mississippian component at the site. Of these, five (Pl. XXXI, *d*, *e*, *g-j*) were split-bone awls, bearing the wear patterns indicative of their use. In length the awls which were unbroken ranged from 4.33 cm to 8.45 cm ($\overline{X}$ = 6.95 cm). The three flat awls averaged 0.66 cm in width and 0.37 cm in thickness. The two round awls averaged 0.41 cm in maximum diameter. Four of the worked bone tools were split-bone netting needles and had a shape quite similar to the flat bone awls (Pl. XXXI, *j-m*). The reconstructed specimen had a length of 7.58 cm. These needles had a mean width of 0.58 cm and a mean thickness of 0.32 cm. The holes were all drilled from one side and none appeared "countersunk." Mean diameter of these holes was 3.1 mm.

Three broken points made of the antler tine of a deer were recovered from this component (Pl. XXXI, *i*, *g*, *r*). As all were fragmentary, metrical analysis would add little to their interpretation. None, however, were socketed nor was there any indication of lateral line-holes which would have indicated their use as toggle-head harpoons.

COPPER

Three pieces of scrap copper (weight = 12.2 grams) were recovered from the deposits assigned to the Upper Mississippian component. The only finished copper artifact was a rolled copper bead, in all respects identical to the narrow rolled copper beads from the earlier component from which it is assumed to have been derived. With this possible exception copper-working appears to have suffered a great decline in the post-Middle component at Summer Island.

XV

CERAMIC RELATIONSHIPS, INTERPRETATIONS AND CONCLUSIONS

ONE of Fitting's conclusions resulting from his distinguishing Aztalan Collared from Spring Creek Collared was that the former is a later local type dated at A.D. 1100-1300, while the Spring Creek ceramics were seen as generalized early Late Woodland types dating A.D. 960±75 (M-512) related to the earlier Mackinac wares at Juntunen (Fitting, 1968: 24, 65-67). The Delta Collared type might then have been expected to have occurred after the Spring Creek date and the early Bois Blanc phase date of A.D. 1070±75 (M-1140 [Crane and Griffin, 1961]). This is somewhat late when compared to the A.D. 720±150 date for the early Late Woodland ceramics at the Heins Creek site (I-678 [Mason, 1966: 27-28]), but not unreasonably so. The lack of any stratification distinguishing the Late Woodland and Mississippian components of the Mero site may indicate that these were not separate occupations. At Summer Island there is no question that the Upper Mississippian and the Delta Collared ceramics are coeval, and that they post-date A.D. 1200. This mixture of early Late Woodland with Upper Mississippian ceramics is not uncommon in northern Wisconsin (Barrett and Skinner, 1932; Wittry, 1959*c*; McKern, 1928; Hall, 1962). It has also been reported in northern Michigan (McPherron, 1967; Brose, 1968) although at a somewhat later date. The Oneota ceramics from Summer Island clearly relate to the Koshkonong focus (Hall, 1962: 100-9) which, at Carcajou Point has been dated to A.D. 998±250 (M-786) and A.D. 1028±250 (M-785). The Point Detour Trailed ceramics may relate to the early Oneota Diamond Bluff Trailed, or to some examples of the later Oneota Fisher Trailed ceramics. While presumably early Late Woodland types such as the Madison Plain, Hahn Cord Impressed and Heins Creek Cord Impressed were recovered from the sites on the Door Peninsula (Mason, 1966: 151-53) they occurred only in the 1963 surface collections at Summer Island. Sherds formally identical to Heins Creek Cord Impressed from Wisconsin have been identified at the upper levels of the Ekdahl-Goudreau site where they were associated with plain-surfaced notched-lip Oneota ceramics and collared Late Woodland ceramics similar to those from Summer Island. Ceramics that appear to represent the local equivalent of the Bois Blanc wares from the Juntunen site were also present at Ekdahl-Goudreau (Prahl and Brose, n.d.).

In south-central Wisconsin ceramic styles related to the Effigy Mound ceramics have been identified as Madison wares (Mason, 1966: 151; Wittry, 1959*c*). Madison Cord Impressed is one of the earliest types of this ware (Griffin, 1964: 247). Mason would also include Madison Plain, Hahn Cord Impressed, Point Sable Collared and Aztalan Collared within this ceramic ware (Mason, 1966: 15). This "tradition" may have developed in late Middle Woodland times, but its most widespread occurrence, especially as far as the northern Lake Michigan basin, seems to be a Late Woodland phenomenon (Griffin, 1964: 247-48; Mason, 1966: 152-53; Wittry, 1959*c:* 218). This contention is reinforced by the Kolterman Mound date of A.D. 766±250 (M-398) for a feature containing Madison Cord Impressed (Wittry, 1956: 133). Hall (1962: 82-83) has postulated a Late Woodland seriation of Madison Cord Impressed-Aztalan Collared-Hahn Cord Impressed-Point Sable Collared. Mason (1966: 158) accepts this developmental sequence but would interpose his Heins Creek wares between the earliest Madison wares and the later Lake Michigan wares.

The exact nature of Mississippian expansion into this area is unclear. Griffin has seen a spread of Old Village to Aztalan from Cahokia (1964: 250-51). The spread of Mississippian cultures is presumed to have extended to the agricultural limits, and the subsequent climatic deterioration (post-1200) created a somewhat degenerate Oneota in marginal areas (Griffin, 1960: 27). Bennett had taken this same position (1952: 119) based on Trappist-Late Developed Oneota contemporaneity. This however, was based on the Crable site which seems rather late (Smith, 1951: 39) for a discussion of Oneota development. (If the early date obtained on shell is rejected, the Crable radiocarbon dates cluster at A.D. 1330±220 [M-553], A.D. 1420±220 [M-554], and A.D. 1328±200 [M-550] [Crane and Griffin, 1958].) Hall has posited a development of Koshkonong-Grand River Oneota directly out of Old Village (1962: 103-9), although he sees a possible stage similar to Silvernale or Apple River (1962: 120). Bennett states that no affiliations of Apple River to Grand River can be perceived (1952: 125).

While most traditional interpretations have brought Oneota out of Cahokia by Aztalan, Hall has recently proposed that the C^{14} dates for Carcajou Point make both Cahokia and Aztalan too late (1966: 7). Hall has posited the Cahokia Old Village, as defined by Powell and/or Ramey Incised, is a phenomenon of the twelfth to thirteenth century A.D. (1966: 3). The early dates for Cahokia Old Village (A.D. 825±75 [M-1294], A.D. 895±75 [M-129] [Crane and Griffin, 1963: 237]) are assigned by Hall to the series of dates from the Merrill tract (15A) obtained on features lacking Ramey Incised (Hall, 1966: 8). These have been assigned to a pre-Old Village "Pulcher Phase" between A.D. 900-1050. Hall derives this complex from some nebulous Lower Mississippi culture area and thus considers the Rock River and Monks Mound Aspects as contemporary with each other (1966: 6-7). This would make sense of the cluster of C^{14} dates A.D. 1100-1300 for Aztalan (WIS-63, 68, 73, 74, M-1214) which have been associated with Old Village manifestations. To agree with Hall's interpretation and to accept the earliest dates for Carcajou Point (1962: 86) and the latest dates for Old Village (1966: 7) one must not only derive Koshkonong-Grand River from a movement around the American Bottoms or through the Pulcher phase Cahokia, one must also account for the sudden development of an Old Village complex at Aztalan whose close neighbors were sharing a cultural complex apparently only reached farther south some two hundred years later. It is also curious that no material related to lower Mississippi cultures is reported for any early component of Wisconsin Upper Mississippian. Sherds of definite Middle Mississippian ceramics have been found throughout the northern Lake Michigan area indicating that such influence was at least present in areas of Upper Mississippian development. Sherds of Ramey Incised have been reported from Big Lake Butte des Morts (Wittry, 1963: Fig. 17, *d*), and the Juntunen site on Bois Blanc Island (McPherron, 1967: 119-21) perhaps soon after A.D. 835±150 (although control is poor and Griffin feels these date to A.D. 1100 [1964: 250]). Several of these grit- or shell-tempered Oneota ceramics illustrated by McPherron can be related to presumably early types found in eastern Wisconsin, particularly those of the Koshkonong focus. McPherron's ceramic type (Pl. XXIII, *g*) would seem to be a grit-tempered variety of Carcajou Plain (Hall, 1962: 63, Pl. 28). The sherd illustrated as UMMA Catalog No. 65118 seems to be closely related to Hall's (1962: 68, Pl. 34, 29) Category F; a form of Grand River Plain. Plate XXIII, *j* seems to fall into Hall's category U (Pl. 40, E). I have examined several sherds which McPherron does not illustrate and would relate UMMA Catalog No. 41532 to a definite type that Hall calls Category R (1962: Pl. 38, *c*, p. 80), and UMMA Catalog No. 40724 seems to be a good example of the shell-tempered Diamond Bluff Trailed (Hall,

1966: Pl. 56, Fig. B). Both of these sherds were from the surface collections at the Juntunen site. Hall himself has identified sherds of Ramey Incised and Aztalan-like Ramey Incised from features associated with the Koshkonong phase he has dated to about A.D. 1000 (Hall, 1962: 59; Crane and Griffin, 1959: 179). The early dates from both Aztalan and Carcajou Point are quite close (A.D. 750±150 [M-1037] and A.D. 890±80 [WIS-77]), although both are rather early in terms of Cahokia. This has led Hall to claim that the Koshkonong focus represents the earliest Wisconsin Oneota manifestation (1962: 125-26). Having related Koshkonong to Grand River and having described the Koshkonong focus as earlier (1962: Pl. 83) Hall has set up the Oneota plain as a horizon-marker for emergent Upper Mississippian (1962: 125-28). That Koshkonong and Grand River are closely related foci is obvious from the definition of the former (Hall, 1962: 100). There are two significant ceramic differences between these foci (and apparently no nonceramic differences): the Koshkonong Plain wares have no lip notching (which Mason suggests may be a case of free variation, 1966: 184) and the Koshkonong focus shares the ceramic type Koshkonong Bold with the Lake Winnebago focus. This type is absent from the Grand River focus. Indeed, it was nearly absent from these former foci as well: in the Lake Winnebago focus six vessels have been identified from all collections, while this type comprised only 2.5 per cent of Koshkonong focus vessels (if one pot of uncertain provenience is included in this focus [Hall, 1962: Table 15, p. 73]). With these exceptions the Koshkonong focus does not differ at all from Grand River.

The Koshkonong-Grand River foci differ from other Wisconsin Oneota foci by the far greater frequency of Oneota Plain wares in the former. Hall would maintain that this plain, loop-handled, unnotched Oneota is representative of an early horizon and not a regional variety. This concept of Oneota development is clearly invalid outside of Wisconsin. The Leary site in Nebraska has shell-tempered Oneota ceramics with less than half having lip notching, and over 60 per cent plain. This would be a middle Oneota by Hall's standards yet Hill and Wedel (1936: 59) considered it to have been protohistoric and it has been dated to A.D. 1205±70 and A.D. 1360±70 in its earliest and middle phases (WIS-151, 155, unpublished). At the Fanning site in Kansas, a single component site where plain rims and bodies account for 594 out of 632 provisional vessels (Wedel, 1959: 145), there is no question about temporal placement as "objects of European origin [were] found at a number of points in our excavations" (Wedel, 1959: 166). The Blue Earth-Correctionville-Orr foci are a typical Oneota manifestation. The Blue Earth and Correctionville ceramics are characterized as highly decorated with incisions and having wide-strap handles. The later phases of Blue Earth, such as the Bartron site, are less flamboyantly decorated and loop handles predominate (Wilford, 1955: 140-41). The later Orr focus ceramic complex, the vessels of which are less highly decorated, dates A.D. 1420±70 (WIS-61) at the Midway Village site. The Silvernale and Cambria foci are believed to ante-date Blue Earth-Orr in Minnesota (Wilford, 1955: 131, 138; Table 6). While loop handles predominate on Cambria ceramics, strap handles are presumably also present (Wilford, 1955: 138-39). Most Cambria type A nad B vessels have a variety of decoration and type C is characterized as always having broad-tailed or incised lines (Wilford, 1955: 139). The Cambria ceramics are compared to Middle Mississippi in decorative motifs. The Silvernale focus, which even Hall had considered early (1962: 101), is characterized by Wilford as commonly having much decoration clearly related to Aztalan or Monks Mound (1955: 140). At the Diamond Bluff Mound Group Maxwell has recovered decorated early Orr focus ceramics associated with Ramey Incised, Powell Plain and Madison wares (Maxwell, 1950: 430-31).

To the northeast of Carcajou Point the Lake Winnebago focus ceramics at sites such as Lasley's Point are boldly decorated and strap-handled. These ceramics may have developed as early as A.D. 990±70 (WIS-50) or be late as A.D. 1440 (G. Richard Peske: personal communication). The developing "emergent Oneota" at Carcajou Point has yielded five C^{14} dates on basically plain, loop-handled Oneota ceramics: A.D. 890±80 (WIS-77), A.D. 998±250 (M-786), A.D. 1028±250 (M-785), A.D. 1528±250 (M-747), and Modern (W-76). These Koshkonong focus dates do not seem to seriously predate other Oneota sequences. I would suggest that while Carcajou Point may represent an early component, the Oneota Plain ceramics may be considered geographical variations as much as a horizon marker. As a hypothesis for discussion of the Upper Mississippian developments in this marginal area I would propose the following: Middle Mississippian complexes such as Old Village, were present from Cahokia through Eveland to Aztalan by A.D. 1100. At this time Upper Mississippian complexes were developing in overlapping areas to the north (Carcajou Point, Lasley's Point), the west (Mohler site), and the northeast (based on C^{14} dates of A.D. 1160±110 [M-1593]; and A.D. 1170±110 [M-1592] for Fisher Noded at the Lawrence site). I would assume that Cambria,

Silvernale, Apple River, and Spoon River foci had early Upper Mississippian components by this time also. Even if this hypothesis is correct it does not account for the expansion of Mississippian culture which must have occurred A.D. 900-1000. It should, nonetheless, be clear that Oneota does not seem to represent a later (agri-) culturally deprived development by a refugee group from Aztalan. Oneota is seen to have been initiated prior to the climatic deterioration of 1200 A.D. (Griffin, 1960) and the Orr and Koshkonong foci are still in areas of 160 or more frost-free days (USDA Yearbook, 1941). To reduce this to 140 days, which are required for reliable mazie agriculture (Yarnell, 1964), would require climatic deterioration on a scale never inferred (Griffin, 1961). Cleland (1966: 84-90) has suggested that by A.D. 1200 each of the Wisconsin Oneota foci had adapted to a local specialization of a mixed hunting-agricultural economy. The Oneota peoples occupying the Door Peninsula were considered to have had an economy oriented towards aquatic resources (1966: 87), although faunal analyses of the Mero and Heins Creek sites do not strongly support this position (1966: 145-51).

The Mero complex Oneota is defined as a Koshkonong-like complex but having at least 40 per cent of the vessels grit-tempered. Of these only 1.7 per cent had any decoration below the lip. Less than half that amount are cordmarked (Mason, 1966: 160-63). Mason (1966: 175-87) has stated that in general decorative mode and frequency the Mero complex is closely related to Koshkonong-Grand River foci Oneota. His reservation of similarity to Lake Winnebago on the basis of the degree of rim eversion does not seem necessary: Hall has indicated a rather wide range of rim flare for his Grand River and Carcajou Plain types (1962: 64, 69). With the exception of the rather high frequency of grit temper, the Mero Complex duplicates the Summer Island component, and could be easily placed in the Grand River or Koshkonong foci. Mason has noted the replacement of grit temper by shell temper through time in the Mero Complex Oneota (1966: 160-61). This is not duplicated at any of the Koshkonong or Grand River focus sites where variations in temper have no temporal significance and where grit tempering never attains more than 2 per cent for any type (Hall, 1962: 53). The only Upper Mississippi ceramic sequence of which I am aware that duplicates this shift from grit to shell temper over time is the Baum focus of the Fort Ancient Aspect (Griffin, 1943: 36-69). In this focus there seems to be some evidence for a development from Baum Cordmarked or Incised with 85 per cent grit temper through Anderson Cordmarked and Incised where grit and shell seem to be in free variation, to Madisonville Cord-Marked which is always shell tempered. This progression was considered to represent the fusion of an early diffused Middle Mississippi culture with local Woodland groups and a development along Mississippian lines to the protohistoric Madisonville focus (Griffin, 1943: 307-8). The Fisher Focus, to which Fort Ancient is most closely compared (Griffin, 1943: 283), shows a reversal of this development with the shell-tempered Fisher Trailed (which was dated in two features at the Lawrence site to A.D. 1170±110, A.D. 1160±110, and A.D. 1260±110 [M-1592-95, Crane and Griffin, 1966: 267]) replaced by a somewhat less elaborately decorated, but clearly descendant, grit-tempered Langford Trailed which is in turn replaced by a plain, smooth, Oneota-form, grit-tempered, Langford Plain (J. W. Griffin, n.d.: 18, 21-22). The last occupation at the Fisher Site is represented by grit-tempered, cordmarked, corded-rim ceramics with a distinctly Woodland vessel form. I would tend to consider the Fisher site as representing a culture which received strong influences from a well-developed Middle Mississippian complex, but continued to develop along Lake Woodland lines. If these speculations on the Baum and Fisher foci are correct, the Mero Complex Oneota ceramics may represent a Woodland population strongly influenced by Koshkonong-Grand River Oneota developing a distinctive complex along the lines of greater Mississippianization. The shell-tempered Lake Winnebago focus ceramics were considered by Mason to represent a possible intrusive occupation (1966: 161) but they may represent a final occupation by the same group shifting to the nearby "classic Oneota" as a step in this ceramic development. Lack of good stratigraphic association at Mero has left this problem unanswered, although the two types do appear to occur in this way at Summer Island.

The Point Sable site, at the bottom of Green Bay, seems to represent a relatively permanent campsite whose Oneota component ceramics are completely shell-tempered although in terms of form and decoration it seems to duplicate the Mero Complex (Mason, 1966: 179). Joan Freeman (cited in Mason, 1966: 180) has assigned this Point Sable Oneota to an early Lake Winnebago focus and seems to see it as a development out of Grand River. I have already reviewed my reasons for considering the Wisconsin Oneota foci to be relatively contemporaneous. I would consider the Point Sable component to be as much representative of its geographical position between Mero and Lake Winnebago as representative of some point on a theoretical developmental diagram (cf., Hall, 1962: Pl. 83).

The relationship of Upper Mississippian to Late Woodland is seen to be one of replacement in northeastern Wisconsin at Point Sable and Mero. At Juntunen, McPherron (1967) has interpreted the Oneota component as a brief occupation of people (from Mero?) rather than a blending of traditions. He noted that no Late Woodland relationships connect Juntunen to the west. The Oneota vessel in the dated Late Woodland Juntunen phase ossuary thus remains enigmatic.

At Summer Island the Upper Mississippian component seems to be quite similar to the Point Sable component, and both are much more alike than either is to the geographically intervening Mero complex. This is principally due to the presence of Madison Cord Impressed ceramics and the high frequency of grit-tempered Oneota vessels at Mero. If the latter is interpreted as local variation in ceramics, all three components are clearly related. The Upper Mississippian ceramics at these sites have been postulated to have been in the area from about A.D. 1000 through A.D. 1500 or later. The Woodland materials from these sites do not display major differences in time although a sequence can be created with the Mero site ceramics apparently relating to the early Late Woodland types developing in eastern Wisconsin some time after A.D. 700, the Point Sable ceramics having affinities with types that presumably developed into the later Aztalan types some time before A.D. 950, and the Summer Island type, Delta Collared, being youngest, relating to Spring Creek Collared post-A.D. 960 and Bois Blanc Corded Collar after A.D. 1070. There is, nonetheless, enough continuity and contemporaniety in all the ceramics to consider these three sites as closely related in time as in space. All three seem to show a rather diffuse economic pattern utilizing all the available resources of the Green Bay-Lake Michigan area (Cleland, 1966; Mason, 1966: 179-82). No evidence of agriculture exists, archaeologically or through analytical faunal inference, and some degree of seasonal mobility is expectable. Under these conditions the Upper Mississippian component of Summer Island can be interpreted as a number of short-term occupations in the late summer by a small group whose cultural heritage continued the use of local lithic industries and included a ceramic complex that displayed both locally developing Woodland ceramics and ceramics derived from the Upper Mississippian cultures which had originated to the south but had moved into the Green Bay region several hundred years earlier. The economic pattern displayed by this group certainly owes as much to the local Woodland hunters and fishers as it does to whatever forefathers may once have hoed corn along the Mississippi River.

XVI

THE PROTOHISTORIC COMPONENT

INTRODUCTION

THE final aboriginal occupation of Summer Island occurred during the deposition of geological unit N. The occupation appears to have been centered in Area "B" (Fig. 3) on the surface of a partially vegetation-stabilized sand dune about twenty feet above the level of Summer Harbor. Much of the component had been severely disturbed by subsequent plowing. To a great extent, the aboriginal artifacts described in this section were recovered from unit N or from features originating at that level. Mixed within this dark brown stratum were several distinctive types of aboriginal ceramics as well as a large amount of European-manufactured trade material. This situation occurred in several areas of the site in pits intruding into earlier deposits. Only in Area "B," however, was the area of continuous midden large enough so that postmolds originating in that level could be followed to infer structural patterns, or could features be correlated with structures. After troweling through this level, floors were shovel-shaved and features such as pits and postmolds could clearly be seen as fine-textured dark brown circles on the medium grayish brown sands below.

STRUCTURES

The pattern taken by postmolds originating at the protohistoric level can be seen in Figure 16. There is evidence for a structure about eighteen feet north-south by about twelve feet east-west. There is some suggestion of an entrance in the center of the eastern wall. The north wall of the structure has undergone a fair amount of post-for-post replacement, and there probably has been one complete rebuilding of the south wall about 2.5 feet further south than it originally was. Small interior posts seem to form a semicircle around the northern half (Feature No. 30) and may have been a wind screen of some sort. A majority of the other interior posts seem to cluster around the refuse pit

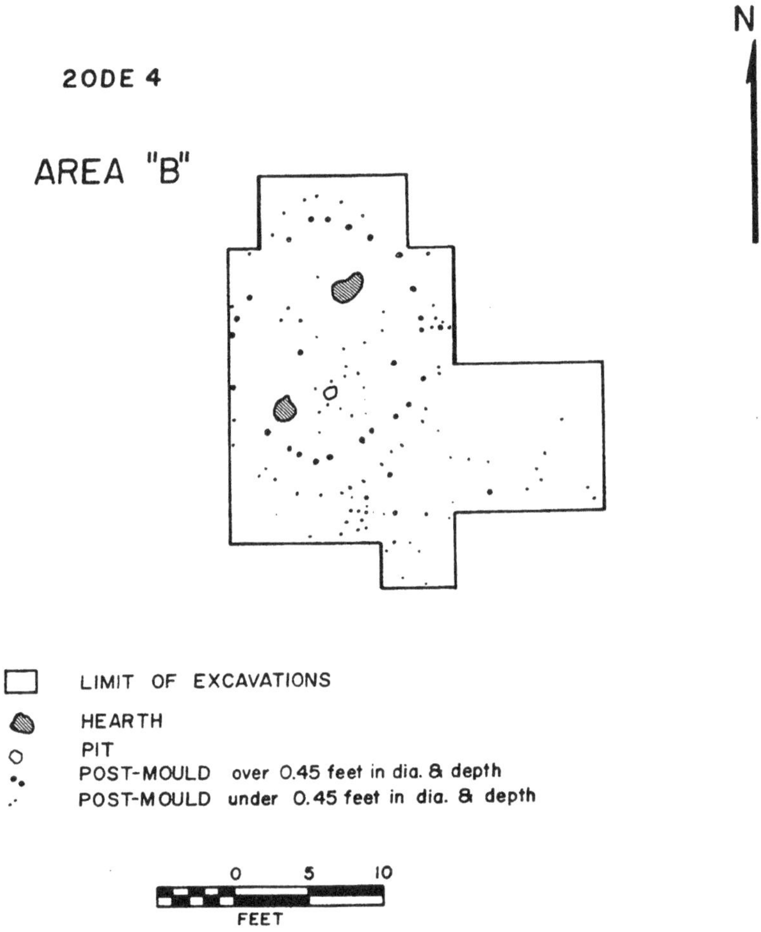

FIG. 16. Protohistoric structure in Area "B."

(Feature No. 34) just northeast of the smaller hearth (Feature No. 33). No functional reason for such a pattern suggests itself. Alternately, the posts can be viewed as a line running northwest-southeast separating the structure into two more or less equal areas, each with a centrally located hearth. On this view, the structure may have housed an extended family or possibly two related nuclear families.

FEATURES

Nine features were assigned to this component. All originated in dark brown sands below the plow zone. No evidence of intrusion into this thin stratum from the overlying unit was noted. The date for these features is presented in Table 24. While most data is self-explanatory, several require further discussion. The squash seeds from Feature No. 34 were identified by Mr. Volney Jones of The University of Michigan Museum of Anthropology. The charred mammal bone from Feature No. 47 was identified by Dr. William Burt of The University of Michigan Museum of Zoology. A sample of this charred bone was submitted to The University of Michigan Radiocarbon Laboratory. The date on this sample was 230±100 B.P., or A.D. 1620±100 (M-2014). Ceramic sherds could be fitted together from Features 17 and 47; from Features 13, 17, and 41; from Features 13 and 47; and from Features 34 and 41, indicating that this was probably a contemporaneous occupation of the site.

ABORIGINAL ARTIFACTS

Ceramics. From the protohistoric component at Summer Island, 66 sherds representing 13 vessels were recovered. These ceramics have been described in detail by Brose (n.d. *c*). Thirteen rim sherds and 31 body sherds represented four vessels of the type Bay de Noc Notched Lip (Pl. XXXIII, *a-e*; Fig. 17, *b*). This type consists of small globular grit-tempered cordmarked vessels

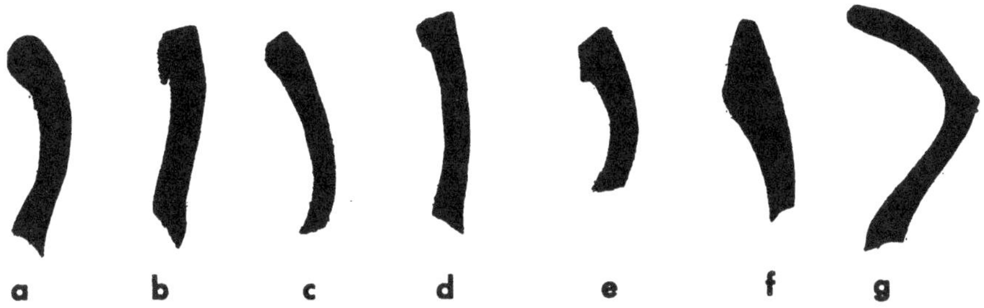

FIG. 17. Rim profiles of protohistoric ceramics.

TABLE 24

FEATURES OF THE PROTOHISTORIC COMPONENT

F. No.	Definition	Excavation Unit	Location	Size	Shape	Contents
13	Refuse pit	480E 510-515	No association with known structures	4.3 ft. by 2.7 ft. by 1.7 ft.	asymmetrical pit with 2 steep walls, uneven flat bottom	12 flat flakes; 2 decortication flakes; 1 pebble core; 1 notched triangular point; 47 grams mammal bone; 1 human incisor; 4 sherds Summer Island Cordmarked; 1 sherd Garden Incised; 1 Iroquoian sherd; 2 glass beads; 1 iron fishhook; 1 copper bead; 2 Oneota sherds; 1 Middle Woodland sherd
17	Refuse pit	460E545	No association with known structures	3.6 ft. by 1.9 ft. by 1.1 ft.	asymmetrical pit with 2 steep walls, uneven flat bottom	7 decortication flakes; 8 flat flakes; 2 bipolar cores; 1 end scraper, 1 bifacial blade; 6 bladelets; 29 grams fish bone; 40 grams mammal bone; 1 iron needle; 1 brass thimble; 4 glass beads; 4 sherds Summer Island Cordmarked; 1 sherd Grand River Plain; 3 Middle Woodland sherds

18	Storage pit	460E550	No association with known structures	2.8 ft. by 2.2 ft. by 0.8 ft.	asymmetrical pit with 1 steep, 1 gently curved wall, flat bottom	12 flat flakes; 49 grams fish bone; 0.75 kg. fire-cracked rock
30	Hearth	685E430	North hearth in structure, 8.0 ft. from entrance	3.4 ft. by 2.7 ft. by 0.9 ft.	symmetrical gently rounded walls, flat bottom	26 decortication flakes; 37 block flakes; 89 flat flakes; 1 bifacial blade; 4 bladelets; 1 triangular point; 1 copper bead; 2 brass kettle fragments; 1 clasp-knife blade; 20 grams fish bone; 30 grams mammal bone; 4.25 kg. fire-cracked rock
33	Hearth	685E435	South hearth in structure, 12.3 ft. from entrance	2.9 ft. by 2.3 ft. by 0.9 ft.	symmetrical gently rounded walls, flat bottom	13 decortication flakes; 67 flat flakes; 3 bipolar cores; 1 bifacial blank; 2 lead balls; 1 gunflint; 40 grams mammal bone; 5.0 kg. fire-cracked rock
34	Refuse pit	690E435	In south-center of structure, between F. no. 33 and entrance	1.2 ft. by 1.1 ft. by 0.7 ft.	asymmetrical pit with 2 steep curved walls	17 decortication flakes; 35 flat flakes; 17 block flakes; 1 bifacial blank; 2 triangular points; 2 block cores; 1 bipolar core; 3 sherds Bay de Noc Notched Lip; 1

TABLE 24 (Continued)

F. No.	Definition	Excavation Unit	Location	Size	Shape	Contents
34	(continued)					sherd Summer Island Cordmarked; 1 sherd Garden Incised; 1 copper bead; 1 lead ball; 28 charred squash seeds [*Curcurbita pepo*], small variety
41	Storage pit	545E495	No association with known structures	2.7 ft. by 2.2 ft. by 1.4 ft.	Bell-shaped pit with gently rounded walls and floor	4 decortication flakes; 10 flat flakes; 1 block flake; 1 end scraper; 27 grams mammal bone; 10 grams bird bone; 3 sherds Garden Incised; 3 sherds Bay de Noc Notched Lip; 1 sherd Lake Winnebago Trailed; 2 glass beads; 1 iron awl
47	Hearth	510E550	On far SE edge of component; no association with known structures	2.2 ft. by 2.1 ft. by 0.7 ft.	Symmetrical gently rounded walls, flat bottomed pit	3 flat flakes; 1 decortication flake; 1 bipolar core; 1 end scraper; 1 slate abrader; 278 grams charred mammal bone; (Bear [*Ursus americanus*] and Elk [*Cervus canadensis*]); small flecks of charcoal; 1 sherd Summer Island Cordmarked; 5

47	(continued)					sherds Bay de Noc Notched Lip; 3 sherds Lake Winnebago Trailed; 7.05 kg. fire-cracked rock

with finger crimped or alternate two edged notched lips. In general, this type shows close resemblances to the Type II pottery recovered from the Bell site just south of Big Lake Butte des Morts, Wisconsin (Wittry, 1963: 25-26; Fig. 13*b*, 16) and to some of the pottery from the Dumaw Creek site, Michigan (Quimby, 1966*b*: 64-72; Fig. 31). It is also similar to ceramics from surface collections at the Juntunen site (McPherron, 1967: Pl. XXIII, *h*, *j*).

Sixteen body sherds and ten rim sherds represented three vessels of Garden Incised (Pl. XXXIII, *f-h*; Fig. 17, *a*, *c*). These vessels were similar to sherds of Bay de Noc Notched Lip but had an upper smoothed rim with single or double incised or trailed chevron motif lines. These ceramics are reminiscent of some of the Bell site Type I ceramics in technique (Wittry, 1963: 22-25; Fig. 13, *c*), although the motif resembles late Upper Mississippian motifs from the area such as Lake Winnebago Trailed, and Perrot Punctate (Hall, 1962, I: 171-74, 175-77; II: Pl. 74-76, 41, 61-62). The lip treatment of these vessels is identical to those described for many of the Dumaw Creek rim sherds by Quimby (1966*b*: 67, 70, 71-72). There are also similarities to the Langford Trailed ceramics from Starved Rock, Illinois (Brown, 1961: 31-35).

The last group of three vessels made on the previously described paste were represented by 17 body sherds and 5 rim sherds classified as Summer Island Cordmarked. These were characterized by strong predominantly vertical cordwrapped paneled impressions extending from the base to the out-flaring thickened lip (Pl. XXXIII, *i*, *j*, *k*; Fig. 17, *d*) These ceramics are identical to sherds in the collection of The University of Michigan Museum of Anthropology from both Dumaw Creek and the Moccasin Bluff site overlooking the St. Joseph River in Berrien County, Michigan. These ceramics also correspond to descriptions of Dumaw Creek material published by Quimby (1966*b*: 67-72), and are somewhat similar to sherds of the terminal Late Woodland Swanson Cordmarked from Starved Rock (Brown, 1961: 39-41). Two vessels assigned to the protohistoric component were also grit tempered although the paste was much more compact. Both vessels, represented by one rim sherd each, had smoothed over surfaces so it can not be determined whether the panel had been wrapped at all, and if so with what. The first vessel seems quite similar to illustrations of Huron Incised (MacNeish, 1952: 34; Pl. X, Fig. 4) as well as some variance of Lawson Incised (MacNeish, 1952: 14; Pl. I, Fig. 6-9). This vessel is illustrated on Plate XXXIII, *l* and rim profile on

Figure 17,*f*. The second vessel is similar to the named type Sidey Notched, as illustrated by Wintemberg (1946: 162-80). The vessel (Pl. XXXIII, *m;* Fig. 17, *e*) from the Protohistoric component at Summer Island displayed somewhat squared high castellations. Similar ceramics have been reported from numerous late sites between Toronto and Lake Simcoe in Ontario (MacNeish, 1952; Wintemberg, 1939, 1946), as well as from Isle Royale, Michigan (Bastian, 1963: Pl. 15). Both of these vessels are presumed to represent early historic Huron or Neutral ceramics.

At least one vessel of Lake Winnebago Trailed (Pl. XXXIII, *n,o*) is represented by eleven body sherds and four rim sherds from the Protohistoric component. This shell-tempered vessel is squat and globular with a constricted neck and a sharply inverted rim (Fig. 17, *g*) the lip of which is decorated with shallow finger impressions creating a scalloped look. In all respects, this vessel can be considered to conform to the type Lake Winnebago Trailed as defined by Hall (1962, I: 171-74). Similar ceramics have been reported from numerous sites along the western shore of Lake Michigan.

In general, this ceramic assemblage is unified by its temporal position. The Bay de Noc and Summer Island ceramics can be associated with the Bell site Type II ceramic dated A.D. 1680-1730 (Wittry, 1963: 56) and with the Dumaw Creek ceramics dated A.D. 1680±75 (M-1070) which Quimby feels are probably pre-1620 (1966*b:* 80). The Iroquian ceramics are similar to those occurring in postcontact or immediately precontact Huron village sites in Ontario (Wintemberg, 1946; MacNeish, 1952). The Upper Mississippian vessel is a type which "must have reached its peak of popularity late in the Protohistoric period" (Hall, 1962: 155). These ceramics agree with radiocarbon dates and European trade goods from Summer Island.

Lithic Artifacts. The lithic material from the Protohistoric component probably represents some degree of admixture with earlier materials. Caution must be exercised in the interpretation. The descriptive categories used (Table 25) are those previously defined for the Middle Woodland component of the site. In general, the chippage indicates a good deal of primary and secondary knapping with a rather large block core utilization. Beyond these qualifications, the chippage shows quite similar trends, toward utilization of locally available raw material and a rather generalized tool assemblage, much like the earlier components at the site.

Of the 131 bipolar cores recovered, 46 were of the opposed ridge variety. Twenty-three of these were examined for signs of

TABLE 25

CHIPPED STONE DISTRIBUTION FROM PROTOHISTORIC COMPONENT

Category	Number	Percentage of Total Number	Weight (In Grams)	Percentage of Total Weight	Percentage of non-Type 1 Chert
Flakes:					
Decortication	1042	6.45	7184	29.37	12.4
Block	3981	24.28	6182	25.08	9.1
Flat	9877	60.45	4215	17.08	7.3
Cores:					
Pebble	295	1.80	1881	7.65	9.8
Block	874	5.30	2837	11.48	9.0
Bipolar	131	0.81	1141	4.63	8.3
Bifaces:					
Scraper	9	0.05	138	0.56	0
Blade	4	0.02	53	0.21	25.0
Blank	6	0.04	236	0.96	16.5
Projectile point	17	0.10	201	0.81	6.0
Unifaces:					
End scraper	16	0.09	157	0.64	6.3
Side scraper	5	0.03	69	0.28	0
Notched scraper	4	0.02	29	0.12	0
Bladelet	35	0.24	68	0.27	20.0
Utilized flake	82	0.50	284	1.15	7.4
TOTAL	16378	100.18	24675	100.29	

use. Fourteen showed no evidence of any use that could be demonstrated not to be a result of the manufacturing processes. All nine remaining cores showed evidence of limited use as wedges or heavy scrapers. Four of these were made on opposed ridge bipolar cores (Pl. XXIV, *k*) while the remaining five were rather amorphous (Pl. XXIV, *o*). The bifacial blades (Pl. XXIV, *f*) all showed some signs of use as knives. Of the six bifacial blanks, two each were convex, concave, and straight-based (Pl. XXIV, *g-i*).

The seventeen projectile points recovered from this component (Table 26) can be classified as rather carelessly made (Pl. XXIV, *a-e*). Seven of these points show primary flaking only on one surface, the other face having only slight marginal retouch. The points are similar to those illustrated from Dumaw Creek (Quimby, 1966*b*: 20-27) and with a length to width ratio of .61, seem similar to the major type from the Bell site (Wittry, 1963: 28-29). These points all fall within the range of Ritchie's Madison type (1961: 33-34). The metric data for unifacial scrapers recovered from this component are presented in Table 27 and a number of these illustrated in Pl. XXXIV, *j, l-n*. The

TABLE 26

LATE WOODLAND PROJECTILE POINTS

Catalog Number	Length	Width	Thickness
74170	2.90	0.61	0.40
74140	1.96	1.43	0.39
74325	. . .	. . .	0.34
74325	. . .	. . .	0.36
74325	2.33	1.12	0.43
74325	1.64	1.05	0.33
74175	4.90	2.97	0.49
74294	3.60	2.89	1.59
74294	3.43	3.46	1.03
75138	5.62	3.33	0.73
75138	. . .	1.38	0.30
75130	. . .	1.37	0.37
75136	4.46	2.23	1.18
74428	5.56	2.89	1.44
75190	3.67	2.75	1.06
75190	. . .	2.00	0.99
75178	1.62	1.08	0.34
MEAN	3.47	2.10	0.69
σ	0.78	0.46	0.22

TABLE 27

LATE WOODLAND SCRAPERS
(Measurements In Centimeters)

UMMA Cat. Number	Max. Length	Max. Width	Thickness at Scraping Edge	Length of Scraping Edge	Degree of Arc on Working Edge	Cortex Present	Flint Type
74878	2.36	1.81	0.70	1.81	50	No	B
74656	3.70	3.05	0.72	3.05	0	No	B
74903	1.84	2.12	0.50	1.85	-40	No	B
74857	2.69	2.49	0.60	2.49	75	No	B
74858	2.85	2.97	0.80	2.77	60	Yes	B
74503	2.80	1.81	0.54	1.22	-20	No	B
74571	2.79	2.80	0.51	2.54	-10	No	B
74478	3.88	2.14	0.73	1.87	30	No	B
74437	3.04	1.92	0.81	1.92	40	No	B
74607	2.22	1.85	0.26	2.22	-35	No	B
74004	1.42	2.07	0.32	1.91	70	No	A
74428	3.18	1.75	0.76	2.29	60	No	B
74428	3.15	2.41	0.57	2.98	90	No	B
74428	2.38	2.46	0.60	2.63	90	No	B
74444	2.10	1.48	0.38	1.91	140	No	B
74325	1.83	1.96	0.33	1.53	50	No	B
74209	4.13	2.49	0.96	2.99	70	Yes	B
74230	2.56	2.23	0.69	2.10	0	No	B
74252	2.77	3.32	0.42	1.54	30	No	B
75129	2.76	2.59	0.66	2.59	0	No	B
75258		2.35	0.48	2.25	0	No	B
75189	3.44	2.90	0.65	2.90	105	No	B
75190	1.85	1.80	0.59	1.77	60	No	B
75148	3.51	2.79	0.71	1.43	20	Yes	B
75187	3.33	2.41	0.40	2.41	0	No	B
75187	4.78	3.63	0.75	2.42	0	No	B
MEAN	2.86	2.36	0.60	2.24	67	. . .	. . .
σ	.56	.29	.10	.30	24	. . .	. . .

bladelets from this component (Pl. XXIV, *q-z*) show the same association between shape and material as did those of earlier components.

Only five pieces of ground stone could be assigned to this component. Aside from a questionable fragment of drilled slate (Pl. XXXV, *a*), the major artifact types consisted of a small fragment of abrading stone (Pl. XXXV, *b*), and two ground-stone celts (Pl. XXXV, *c, d*). The larger of these celts is similar to the smaller celt reported for Dumaw Creek (Quimby, 1966*b:* 34, Fig. 10, left). Two fragments of specular hematite were also recovered from this component.

Copper. Ten aboriginal artifacts of native copper were recovered from features pertaining to this component. Three of these were rolled copper beads similar to those from the Middle Woodland component of the site (Pl. XXV, *e*). Similar beads have been recovered from the Late Woodland Juntunen site (McPherron, 1967: 171; Pl. XXXIII). They are also similar to beads recovered from burials at Dumaw Creek (Quimby, 1966*b*: 39-40; Fig. 13, 15).

Three copper awls (Pl. XXXV, *f*) were recovered from this component as well. All had been constructed with the fold-and-hammer technique noted for the Middle Woodland component. Four rolled copper points (Pl. XXXV, *g*) from this component were at first thought to be recut and rolled brass kettle fragments. Specific gravity analysis indicated that these were copper. Two of these points were wrapped around a single oxidized fragment of iron. All four points appear similar in size and shape. Quimby (1966*b*: 42) has reported similar artifacts from Dumaw Creek as tinkling cones. The last aboriginal artifact from the protohistoric component (Pl. XXV, *h*) is interpreted as an effigy snake. This artifact was composed of a copper sheet folded and hammered into a squared bar pointed on one end. The artifact was bent at five alternating 60 degree angles located 7, 16, 27, 43, and 54 mm. from the rounded point. In its final form, this implement resembles snake effigies reported from Dumaw Creek (Quimby, 1966*b:* 42; Fig. 16), from the terminal Woodland-Upper Mississippian Anker site in Chicago (Bluhm and Liss, 1961: 126; Fig. 66, *a*), and from a late component of the Madisonville site northeast of Cincinnati, Ohio (Griffin, 1943: 128). Similar artifacts are represented in northeastern Iowa (M. M. Wedel, 1959: 72) and in Wisconsin at Upper Mississippian sites of late aspect (McKern, 1945).

EUROPEAN ARTIFACTS

Trade Beads. From features and units of the protohistoric component, forty-nine glass beads and eight shell beads were recovered. A detailed description of these is to be found in Brose (n.d. *c*). Four of the beads were opaque red glass tubes, two were dark blue opaque, and one was an opaque white glass bead tube similar to the red beads described above. Two were round tubular polychrome beads with longitudinal red stripes on a dark blue background. A single polychrome spheroidal bead with white and blue opaque spiral stripes was also recovered. Two were small "melon" beads of a solid dark blue color and nine were barrel-shaped opaque to translucent blue glass beads. There was a single oblate spheroidal transparent amber bead and a large translucent amber-colored spun glass bead as well as three opaque white glass elliptical beads, two faceted beads, one white and one blue, and sixteen small "seed" beads of dark opaque blue and ten small seed beads of opaque white. Beads of these types have been recovered from numerous sites in northern Michigan, Canada, upstate New York, Wisconsin, and Illinois (Brose, n.d.*c*). All of these beads seem to date from the period A.D. 1625 to 1745. Several of these are much more restricted in their temporal distribution, and clearly indicate occupation during the A.D. 1650 to 1690.

Ten drilled shell wampum beads were also recovered from this component. Wampum of this type was manufactured at least as early as A.D. 1650 and as late as A.D. 1850.

Other Artifacts. Nine iron artifacts of European manufacture were recovered from the Protohistoric component of Summer Island. These consisted of two rectangular and rounded awls, one barbed iron fishhook, two knife blades, what seems to be the bale to a kettle, an iron needle, and an iron hinged fragment. Fourteen brass artifacts of European origin were excavated from this component as well. A brass hawk-bell, four tinkling cones (probably cut from kettles), a brass thimble, and several fragments of brass kettles with rolled rims, as well as two fragments of small brass rings presumed to have been Jesuit in origin were recovered. A single gunflint was recovered from Area "B" in deposits assigned to the Protohistoric component. The last three artifacts of European origin from the component, were three lead balls made in a pliers-type mold. At least two different calibers are represented.

In terms of the trade goods recovered, the last aboriginal occupation of Summer Island seems to have occurred sometime during the last half of the seventeenth century A.D. Although the diagnostic European artifacts from this component have been reported from sites in the Great Lakes as early as A.D. 1625 or as late as A.D. 1730, this in no way detracts from the more limited dates of occupation proposed here. Of the sixty-nine such artifacts, nearly 80 per cent can be classified as articles of personal adornment. The remaining articles are those that eventually replaced native manufactures completely. At this point in time and space, chipped flint still occurs in a higher frequency than gun parts. Aboriginal ceramics are still more evident than brass kettles, and iron knives have not yet replaced native stone tools. The greatest change in the native tool kit is probably the replacement of bone awls and needles by their iron counterparts. If any conclusions may be drawn from these observations, it may be that those tools more directly concerned with subsistence are those most governed by tradition and least amenable to change. Whether this can be taken to indicate that women are more conscious of new fashions or more desirous of them, is not clear. It is clear however, that the Protohistoric component at Summer Island represents a group whose material culture had not been altered too greatly by European contact.

ECONOMY

From the Protohistoric component of the site 13,273.0 grams of mammal bone, 196.0 grams of bird bone, 832.9 grams of fish bone, and 289.0 grams of other bone were recovered. The preliminary analysis clearly shows the major food resource to have been whitetail deer, elk, black bear, rabbit, and beaver. Fish, bird, and turtle provided only secondary roles in the subsistence of the group.

Most of the fish present in this area were not extensively exploited. The fishing industry seen in faunal remains seems to have been confined to weedy shallow waters which even today support large populations of bass and pike.

The mammal fauna is noteworthy because of the presence of elk and the absence of moose. Given the aboriginal environment of Summer Island moose would have been the major large herbivore present (Dice, 1938: 504), and elk would not have been expected much nearer than the southern edge of the Canadian Biotic Province in northeastern Wisconsin. The presence of charred elk bone in association with the Lake Winnebago Trailed and Summer Island Cordmarked ceramics (Feature 47) indicates that the protohistoric group possibly spent part of their seasonal round in that part of Wisconsin.

The faunal remains from this component confirm the hypothesis that the occupation was primarily a summer one. The botanical remains recovered from features consist of eight charred fragments of hazelnut shell, two chokecherry seeds, and twenty-eight charred seeds identified by Mr. Volney Jones as squash (*Cucurbita pepo*). The hazelnut and chokecherry both ripen in late August or early September (Yarnell, 1964: 59, 63). The agricultural products played a minor role, if in fact they were not imported onto the site by members of this group from agricultural sites of earlier seasons, or imported by outsiders in trade for furs or meat. The view of a minor role for agriculture is reinforced by the diffuse nature of the economy (Cleland, 1966: 44-75) as seen in the large numbers of quite different animal species utilized as food.

In general, the best interpretation of this component would seem to be an occupation of a small number of patrilocal and probably patrilineal families most of whom may have been patrilineally related but who were beginning to be identified more by territory than by family (Hickerson, 1960). The occupation took place during the late spring to early fall period of the year. While on the Island, the major subsistence activity was the hunting of deer and fur-bearing mammals on the nearby islands and mainland. These hunting parties were probably composed of a few patrilineally related males. Some fishing and possibly limited agriculture was practiced by members of the group remaining on the island. The major resource of the island, fish, was under-exploited, and one might assume that the economy had to some extent been readapted to meet the demands of the growing fur trade, stimulated by European goods from the east. In this respect, Summer Island with its central location and well-protected harbor would be an ideal point from which trade could move into Bay de Noc, Green Bay, and western Lake Michigan. With the onset of winter, the group probably abandoned the island, probably for the more open ground to the immediate southwest of Green Bay where they might engage in hunting elk or bison, or where a larger "parent" agricultural village (such as the Bell site) might be located.

XVII

CONCLUSIONS

SUMMARY

IN the preceding chapters three stratified aboriginal occupations of the Summer Island site were analyzed in terms of material culture, economic adaptation, and social organization.

The earliest occupation occurred during the latter part of the Middle Woodland period and has been dated at A.D. 250±100 (M-1985), A.D. 70±280 (M-2073), and A.D. 160±130 (M-2074). This component of the site appears to have been occupied for three or four years from April through September. There appear to have been between twenty-five and forty inhabitants representing six families of a small exogamous, patrilocal band. The site at this time seems to have been primarily a fishing station where the spring-spawning sturgeon were taken by netting and spearing. During the later part of the summer bear and beaver were hunted or trapped and some line fishing was practiced. The seasonal abandonment of the site coincides with the availability of wild rice, and it has been suggested that this was the reason for the departure of the inhabitants.

During this Middle Woodland occupation the prevalent styles of ceramic decoration demonstrate the participation of these people in what has been called the Northern Tier Middle Woodland tradition (Mason, 1967: 338) which extended across the ecologically similar Lake Forest Biotic Province from Lake Winnipeg to the St. Lawrence estuary. The regional cultures of this wide area, described as Nutimik-Anderson, Laurel, North Bay, and Point Peninsula, all share rather distinctive techniques of ceramic decoration characterized by banked and dragged stamping, linear stamping, and various dentate impressions on conoidal smooth-surfaced vessels.

The chipped stone industry seen in this component is characterized by the use of a bipolar core technique in addition to block and pebble core utilization. These varied manufacturing processes are interpreted to be primarily a result of the extensive utilization of the locally available chert which occurs as glacially eroded and redeposited nodules of varying sizes and shapes. The projectile points ranged in shape from stemmed through side-notched, and little standardization of shape was evident. Scrapers were predominantly the small unifacial "thumbnail" variety (55 per cent) although other types occurred. The production of chipped stone tools appears to have been an individual male activity and all phases of the processing were carried out on the site.

Copper-working was of some importance during this occupation and all postextractive phases of production appear to have been performed as group activity by several related males. Ceremonial, ornamental, and utilitarian artifacts were made of copper and the effects of annealing on the ductility of the metal were appreciated.

Some use was made of available scrap bone for the production of needles, awls, and net-shuttles, while antler was modified for use as harpoon-heads and drifts. Ground-stone artifacts were rare although beach pebbles were slightly modified for use as net-sinkers, hammers, anvils, and mortars.

The second occupation of the site occurred during the Late Woodland period and dates to A.D. 1290±100 (M-2071, 2072). This component of the site apparently represents a number of short-term midsummer occupations by small family groups. No population estimates are available for these groups, and their social organization is unknown. The site at this time appears to have been utilized as a temporary base camp sustained by collecting mollusks from the gravel shoal to the north and fish from the weedy shallows of the harbor to the east of the site, while deer and small mammals could be hunted either on the island or on the nearby Garden Peninsula.

The ceramics from this component clearly indicate that the inhabitants were related to other Oneota peoples of the Green Bay region whose culture was incorporating the ceramics of the resident early Late Woodland tradition and the intrusive Mississippian tradition. The Point Sable site might be typical of the more permanent villages of such people.

In terms of technology the chipped stone industry of this component is quite similar to the earlier Middle Woodland occupation. Bipolar, block, and pebble cores were all worked from the local chert nodules. Projectile points were all triangular in shape and most were quite poorly finished. While one projectile point could be characterized as a side-notched Cahokia point, the others were all classified as Late Woodland Madison points. The predominant scraper type (77 per cent) was the unifacial "thumbnail" scraper although most of the other types noted in the earlier component were present. All phases of lithic production occurred at the site, apparently all performed by individual males. Different areas of the site appear to have been utilized for different phases of this production. Bone tools, while not as frequent as earlier, were well represented. Copper-working seems to have suffered a great decline and no copper artifacts can be securely assigned to this component.

The third and last aboriginal occupation of the site occurred in the protohistoric period and has been dated at A.D. 1620±100 (M-2014), but may have occurred several decades later. The site at this time period was occupied from the summer through the fall probably by several extended patrilocal families with a total population of from twenty to thirty individuals. The site seems to have functioned primarily as either a base camp from which small groups of males hunted deer and fur-bearing mammals on the mainland and nearby islands, or as a rendevous point for those aborigines engaged in a European-stimulated fur trade, or (probably) both.

In this component the aboriginal ceramics show cultural relationships with several other mutually unrelated, late prehistoric groups in the areas around the Lake Michigan basin. Other ceramics, types common in southern Ontario, may indicate the directions taken by trade or the actual presence of refugee potters on the island as a result of postcontact population displacements.

The chipped stone industry of this component is similar in production techniques to the earlier occupations. As in these the emphasis was on the utilization of locally available raw materials. Projectile points are all small, triangular, and poorly made. Scrapers are still predominantly (60 per cent) the small "thumbnail" variety, although all types present in the earlier components are represented here also. Copper-working seems to be practiced again although the disturbed nature of the deposits makes judgment difficult as to whether all postextractive production stages were actually performed at the site. Copper artifacts of ceremonial, ornamental, and utilitarian nature are present. Worked bone, in contrast to the earlier occupations is almost nonexistent. For the first time ground-stone celts, inferred to be woodworking tools, are present.

The most distinctive aspect in the material culture of this component is, of course, the European-manufactured material present. Glass beads were the most frequent, but tinkling cones, bells, and a brass ring were among the ornamental artifacts while iron awls, needles, knives, brass kettles and a brass thimble indicated the presence of more functional trade goods. Gunflints, lead shot, and gun parts clearly demonstrated the use of firearms by these people.

While European material acculturation does not seem to have been strong enough at this time to totally destroy the aboriginal ethnic styles of the inhabitants, the lack of precise historical documentation and the population displacements caused by the fur trade have prohibited the application of the "direct historic approach" with any accuracy and the ethnolinguistic affiliation of the inhabitants is unknown.

COMPARISON

In a comparative discussion of the ecological adaptation and settlement patterning of the three aboriginal occupations at Summer Island several factors must be considered. First, of course, is the tentative nature of conclusions based upon the uncompleted faunal analyses. Second, the acculturated nature of the protohistoric component render questionable many of the analytical methods that would otherwise be employed. Third, and perhaps most important, is the fact that the ethnography to which references are made and from which models may be derived, cannot be known to reflect the aboriginal pattern, although it has been suggested to be closer than it might at first seem (Brose, n.d.*b*).

While recognizing that the weights of bone only vaguely reflect the amount of available meat, they are the only data currently available for the faunal remains of all zoological classes recovered from the site. Since soil conditions were relatively conducive to bone preservation at all components this information should at least be capable of showing relative differences in the utilization of the faunal resources in the different components. As Table 28 indicates these differences are highly significant. They clearly are not the result of sampling error, although they are not particularly strong. These differences are clearly due to a decrease in the weight of fish and a corresponding increase in the weight of mammal bone from the site through time. When the utilization of shellfish is also considered as a characteristic of the Upper Mississippian occupation that component seems to be displaying a clearly diffuse economic pattern at the site, while the Middle Woodland occupation seems to be a focal fishing economy and the Protohistoric component seems to have a focal hunting economic adaptation (Cleland, 1966: 42-46). These

TABLE 28

COMPARISON OF FAUNAL REMAINS FROM ABORIGINAL COMPONENTS AT THE SITE

Component	Mammal	Fish	Bird	Other	Total
Middle Woodland					
wt. in grams	13667	9356	651	1756	25430
percentage of wt. O/E	53.6/70.4	36.7/22.6	2.5/2.0	6.8/4.9	100/100
Upper Mississippian					
wt. in grams	8256	3187	269	697	12409
percentage of wt. O/E	66.6/70.4	25.3/22.6	2.2/2.0	5.9/4.9	100/100
Late Woodland (Protohistoric)					
wt. in grams	13273	832	196	289	14589
percentage of wt. O/E	91.0/70.4	5.7/22.6	1.3/2.0	2.0/4.9	100/100
Total					
wt. in grams	35196	13375	1116	2732	52428
percentage of wt. O/E	211.2	67.7	6.0	14.7	300

$\chi^2 = 36.773$

$df = 6$

$p = <.001$

$\Phi^2 = .1226$

differences in site utilization are reinforced by the index computed for each component, as the total number of identified fish bones divided by the total number of identified mammal bones. These indices are 24.4 for the Middle Woodland component, 3.18 for the Upper Mississippian component, and 2.99 for the Protohistoric component. Since the Protohistoric component is thought to represent a base camp for male hunting parties, it is possible that only the pelts and choicest cuts were returned to the island. If this is correct the actual index for this component should probably be somewhat lower. If these economic pattern indices are correct they indicate the increasingly important role hunting attained through time at this site.

It is interesting to compare these results with the index Fitting (n.d.) has derived by dividing the number of unifacial tools by the number of bifacial tools. The index should reflect the ratio of hunting activities to other types of economic activity, particularly fishing. The ratios at Summer Island are 4.95 for the Middle Woodland component, 2.47 for the Upper Mississippian component, and 3.09 for the Protohistoric component. Since at this last component iron knives have replaced bifacial flint knives and firearms have replaced some number of bifacial projectile points, this figure should actually be considerably lower than 3.09. Since the exact correction factor is unknown this uniface/biface ratio cannot be applied to this component without obtaining elevated figures. These ratios indicate that the Middle Woodland component would clearly represent a fishing site while the Upper Mississippian component is neither a fishing nor a hunting site.

INTERPRETATIONS

While it thus seems safe to characterize these components at Summer Island as representing, respectively, a focal fishing, diffuse, and focal hunting adaptations, it has been noted that these do not characterize the economic adaptation of the entire culture (see also Cleland, 1966; McPherron, 1967: 299; Fitting, n.d.). The location and function of seasonally complementary sites have been mentioned in the preceding chapters for each of the three components. The available data has led to the conclusion that at all three components cultures with a diffuse economic adaptation are represented. What is being viewed, in this interpretation, are changes in the settlement patterns through time. The occupation of the three components at Summer Island are seasonally each successively later than the occupation of the previous component. During the period represented by the Upper Mississippian component the spring sturgeon spawning run was not being utilized fully. This must mean that some other resource capable of supporting a somewhat large group was being utilized. Two possibilities suggest themselves. If the inhabitants had spent the late fall and winter hunting on the prairies to the southwest, enough meat may have been preserved to sustain a group at a larger village through the spring. Alternately, if agricultural villages existed to the south or the mainland in Wisconsin, the group would not have left for summer hunting until the crops had been planted after the last frost. This would easily account for their arrival on the island after the spring spawning.

The Protohistoric component's seasonal occupation of the site may have been delayed for much these same reasons. The fur trade has been suggested as the most logical explanation for the extended occupation on the island as a rendezvous in the late fall. A location whence, initially the canoe brigades left for the French colonies, and where later the French themselves arrived to trade.

It has been seen that while ceramic styles changed so completely that the assemblages of sequent components are completely different, the same replacement does not characterize lithic industries at the site. To test the possibility that the similarity of the lithic industries in these components is due to the mixing of earlier materials in the later occupations (as has been suggested) a comparison of the percentages of the categories of débitage recovered from each component was attempted. The results of this comparison (Table 30) are inconclusive. The null hypothesis, that no significant difference exists in the distribution of the categories of chippage from these three components, can be accepted. Whether this indicates that the last two components contain a substantial amount of material derived from the earliest occupation, or whether the lithic traditions in the northern Lake Michigan area were rather conservative cannot be determined from Summer Island alone. Comparison with other sites in this region indicates that a conservative lithic tradition is the most economical answer (Binford and Quimby, 1963; McPherron, 1967; Fitting, n.d.). In this respect it is interesting to note (Table 31) that types of unifacial scrapers do not seem to display significant variations in relative frequency through time at Summer Island, and therefore in this region are not a sensitive indicator of chronological position (cf. Mason, 1966: 180-81; Hall, 1962: 121-22; J. Wright, 1967: 102-3).

TABLE 30

DISTRIBUTION OF CHIPPED STONE BY PERCENTAGE OF WEIGHT FROM ABORIGINAL COMPONENTS OF SUMMER ISLAND

Component	Decortication Flakes	Block Flakes	Flat Flakes	Pebble Cores	Block Cores	Bipolar Cores	All Bifaces	All Unifaces	Total
Protohistoric O/E	29.4/ 25.8	25.1/ 24.2	17.1/ 19.8	7.7/ 10.6	11.5/ 9.4	4.65/ 5.7	2.46/ 1.4	2.46/ 3.15	... 100
Upper Mississippian O/E	21.1/ 25.8	25.7/ 24.2	18.3/ 19.8	14.5/ 10.6	8.9/ 9.4	6.5/ 5.7	1.51/ 1.4	4.59/ 3.15	... 100
Middle Woodland O/E	27/ 25.8	22/ 24.2	24/ 19.8	9.5/ 10.6	7.7/ 9.4	4.05/ 5.7	0.28/ 1.4	2.41/ 3.15	... 100
TOTAL	77.5	72.8	59.4	31.7	28.1	15.2	4.32	9.46	300

χ^2 = 10.5237

df = 14

p = <.70

ϕ^2 = .0350

TABLE 31

TYPES OF SCRAPERS BY CULTURAL COMPONENT

Component	Middle Woodland O/E	Upper Mississippian O/E	Late Woodland O/E	Total
End scrapers	16/17.74	10/7.95	15/15.30	41
Side scrapers	4/2.59	0/1.60	2/2.24	6
Notched scrapers	2/2.59	1/1.60	3/2.24	6
Multiple scrapers	7/6.05	2/2.72	5/5.22	14
TOTAL	29	13	25	67

$x^2 = 5.038$

df = 6

p = .50

The increase in ground stone in the last occupation is taken to indicate the slightly different functional uses to which the site was being put. This may also be the explanation for the decrease in copper-working seen in the Oneota component although the Mississippian intrusion into the northern Lake Michigan area may have temporarily disrupted previous exchange networks.

The conservatism of lithic industry in comparison to the changing ceramic styles is seen to be a result of the prevailing type of social organization which seems relatively consistent through time. This social structure, which was predominantly one of patrilocal exogamous bands, has been noted to favor relatively conservative regional male-related traditions while creating optimum conditions for diffusion and change in the results of female-related activity (Owen, 1965).

That this form of social organization is inferred to have been prevalent in the northern Lake Michigan area for so long (Brose, n.d.*b*) may be attributed to the facility it displays in adapting to the demographic character required of societies with a diffuse economic adaptation. While this should not be taken as the total acceptance of a theory of economic determination (cf. Service, 1962: 72-76) it does indicate an appreciation for the fact that this form of economic adaptation in this area requires great mobility and changing residential groups. Though this need not necessitate a social organization formed along the lines of a patrilocal band, it may well prevent the development of more complex levels of socio-cultural integration. While some evidence for a shift away from this pattern can be seen in the Upper Mississippian component of the site where the economic pattern was inferred to include larger winter villages to the south, the introduction of the European fur trade permitted its readoption as the most efficient way in which to utilize the newly emphasized resources of this area.

REFERENCES

Ayers, John C.
1965 The Climatology of Lake Michigan. Great Lakes Research Division, Publication No. 12. The University of Michigan. Ann Arbor.

Ayers, J. C., D. C. Chandler, G. H. Lauff, C. F. Powers, and E. B. Henson
1958 Currents and Water Masses of Lake Michigan. Great Lakes Research Institute, Publication No. 3. The University of Michigan. Ann Arbor.

Baerreis, David and Joan Freeman
1958 Late Woodland Pottery in Wisconsin as seen from Aztalan. The Wisconsin Archeologist, Vol. 39, No. 1, pp. 35-61. Lake Mills.

Barrett, A. and A. Skinner
1932 Certain Mounds and Villages of Shawanoe and Oconto Co. Bulletin of the Public Museum of Milwaukee. Vol. 10, No. 3. Milwaukee.

Bastian, Tyler
1963 The Archaeology of Isle Royale. National Park Service Report (ms). Ann Arbor.

Beardsley, Richard K., Preston Holder, Alex D. Krieger, Betty J. Meggers, and John B. Rinaldo
1955 Functional and Evolutionary Implications of Community Patterning. *In*: Seminars in Archaeology, edited by Robert Wauchope. Society for American Archaeology, Memoir 11, pp. 129-57. Salt Lake City.

Bennett, John
1952 The Upper Mississippi Valley. *In*: Archaeology of The Eastern United States, edited by J. B. Griffin. University of Chicago Press. Chicago.

Bettarel, Robert and Sidney Harrison
1962 An Early Ossuary in Michigan. Michigan Archaeologist, Vol. 8, No. 2, pp. 37-42. Ann Arbor.

Binford, Lewis R. and George I. Quimby
1963 Indian Sites and Chipped Stone Materials in the Northern Lake Michigan Area. Fieldiana, Anthropology, Vol. 36, No. 12, pp. 277-307. Chicago.

Black, Robert F.
1966 Valders Glaciation in Wisconsin and Upper Michigan—A Progress Report. Great Lakes Research Division, Publication No. 15, pp. 169-75. The University of Michigan. Ann Arbor.

Blalock, Hubert M., Jr.
1960 Social Statistics. McGraw-Hill Inc. New York.

Bluhm, Elaine A. and Allen Liss
1961 The Anker Site, Chicago Area Archaeology. Bulletin Illinois Archaeology Survey, No. 3. Urbana.

Brandon, Jay
1968 Excavations at the Lamb Site. The Wisconsin Archeologist, Vol. 49, No. 1, pp. 1-31. Lake Mills.

Brose, David S.
1965 Infra-red Photography: An Aid to Stratigraphic Interpretation. Michigan Archaeologist, Vol. 10, No. 4. Ann Arbor.
1966*a* The Valley Sweets Site, Saginaw Co., Michigan. The Michigan Archaeologist, Vol. 12, No. 1, pp. 1-24. Ann Arbor.
1966*b* Excavations in Fort Mackinac: 1965. The Michigan Archaeologist, Vol. 12, No. 2, pp. 88-102. Ann Arbor.
1968 The Backlund Mound Group. The Wisconsin Archeologist, Vol. 49, No. 1, pp. 34-52. Lake Mills.
1970 A Cumulative Percentile Analysis of Beach and Dune Sands in Northern Lake Michigan. The Ohio Journal of Science. In press. Columbus.
n.d.*a* The Ceramics from the Goodwin Gresham Site, Iosco Co., Michigan. *In*: The Goodwin-Gresham Site. The Wisconsin Archeologist. In press. Lake Mills.
n.d.*b* Middle Woodland Cultural Ecology and Social Organization in the Upper Great Lakes. Case Western Reserve University Papers in Anthropology, No. 1. In press. Cleveland.
n.d.*c* Summer Island III: An Early Contact Period Site in the Upper Great Lakes. Journal of the Society for Historic Archaeology, Vol, IV. In press. Lansing.
n.d.*d* The Molluscan Fauna From the Schultz Site, 20SA2, Saginaw County, Michigan. Unpublished Manuscript on file in The University of Michigan Museum of Anthropology. Ann Arbor.

Brown, James A.
1961 The Zimmerman Site. Illinois State Museum, Reports of Investigations No. 9. Springfield.
1962 Notes and News. American Antiquity, Vol. 28, No. 1, p. 120. Salt Lake City.

Bunting, Brian T.
1965 The Geography of Soils. Aldine. Chicago.

Bunzel, Ruth (editor)
1929 The Pueblo Potter. Columbia University, Contributions To Anthropology, No. 8. New York.

Burlington, Richard S.
1956 Handbook of Mathematical Tables and Formulas. Handbook Publishers Inc. Sandusky.

Burt, William H.
1954 The Mammals of Michigan. University of Michigan Press. Ann Arbor.

Burt, William H. and Richard P. Grossenheider
1956 A Field Guide to the Mammals. The Riverside Press. Cambridge.

Callender, Charles
1962 Social Organization of the Central Algonkian. Papers of the Public Museum of Milwaukee. Milwaukee.

Changnon, Stanley A., Jr.
1966 Effect of Lake Michigan on Severe Weather. Great Lakes Research Division, Publication No. 15, pp. 220-37. University of Michigan. Ann Arbor.

Cleland, Charles E.
1966 The Prehistoric Animal Ecology and Ethnozoology of the Upper Great Lakes Region. Anthropological Papers, Museum of Anthropology, University of Michigan, No. 29. Ann Arbor.

Cleland, Charles E. and G. Richard Peske
1968 The Spider Cave Site. *In*: The Prehistory of the Burnt Bluff Area, assembled by James E. Fitting. Anthropological Papers, Museum of Anthropology, University of Michigan, No. 34, pp. 20-60. Ann Arbor.

Channen, E. R. and N. D. Clarke
1965 The Copeland Site: A Precontact Huron Site in Simcoe County, Ontario. Anthropological Papers, National Museum of Canada, No. 8. The Queens Printer. Ottawa.

Coe, Joffre L.
1964 Formative Cultures of the Carolina Piedmont. Transactions of the American Philosophical Society, n.s., Vol. 54, Pt. 5. Philadelphia.

Cook, S. F. and Robert F. Heizer
1965 The Quantative Approach to the Relation Between Population and Settlement Size. Report of the University of California Archaeological Survey, No. 64. Berkeley.

Crane, H. R. and J. B. Griffin
1958 University of Michigan Radiocarbon Dates III. Science, Vol. 128, pp. 1117-23. Washington, D.C.
1959 University of Michigan Radiocarbon Dates IV. American Journal of Science, Radiocarbon Supplement 1, pp. 173-98. New Haven.
1960 University of Michigan Radiocarbon Dates V. American Journal of Science, Radiocarbon Supplement 2, pp. 31-48. New Haven.
1961 University of Michigan Radiocarbon Dates VI. Radiocarbon, Vol. 3, pp. 105-25. New Haven.
1963 University of Michigan Radiocarbon Dates VIII. Radiocarbon, Vol. 5, pp. 228-53. New Haven.
1964 University of Michigan Radiocarbon Dates IX. Radiocarbon, Vol. 6, pp. 1-24. New Haven.
1966 University of Michigan Radiocarbon Dates XI. Radiocarbon, Vol. 8, pp. 256-85. New Haven.

Cushing, Edward J.
1965 Problems in the Quarternary Phytogeography of the Great Lakes Region. *In*: The Quarternary of the United States, edited by H. E. Wright, Jr. and David G. Frey. Princeton.

Dailey, R. C. and J. V. Wright
1955 The Malcolm Site. Transactions of the Royal Canadian Institute. Vol. 31, Pt. I, pp. 24-68. Toronto.

Damann, Kenneth E.
1966 Plankton Studies of Lake Michigan. Great Lakes Research Division, Publication No. 15, pp. 9-17. The University of Michigan. Ann Arbor.

Dice, Lee R.
1938 The Canadian Biotic Province with special Reference to the Mammals. Ecology, Vol. 19, No. 4, pp. 503-14. Urbana.

Driver, Harold E. and William C. Massey
1957 Comparative Studies of North American Indians. Transactions of the American Philosophical Society, N.S. Vol. 47, Pt. 2. Philadelphia.

Eggan, Fred
1966 The American Indian. Aldine. Chicago.

Emerson, J. N.
1955 The Kant Site: A Point Penninsula Manifestation in Renfrew County, Ontario. Transactions of the Royal Canadian Institute, Vol. 31, Pt. 1, pp. 3-23. Toronto.

Farrand, William R.
1962 Post-Glacial Uplift in North America. American Journal of Science, 260, pp. 181-89. New Haven.

Fenner, Gloria J.
1963 The Plum Island Site, La Salle County, Illinois. Reports on Illinois Prehistory: I. Illinois Archaeology Survey, Bulletin No. 4. Urbana.

Fitting, James E.
1965*a* Middle Woodland Manifestations in Eastern Michigan. Paper presented at 30th Annual Meeting: S.A.A. Urbana.
1965*b* Late Woodland Cultures of Southeastern Michigan. Anthropological Papers, Museum of Anthropology, University of Michigan, No. 24. Ann Arbor.
1968*a* The Spring Creek Site. *In:* Contributions to Michigan Archaeology. Anthropological Papers, Museum of Anthropology, University of Michigan, No. 32, pp. 1-78. Ann Arbor.
1968*b* Northern Lake Michigan Lithic Industries. *In:* The Prehistory of the Burnt Bluff Area, assembled by James E. Fitting. Anthropological Papers, Museum of Anthropology, University of Michigan, No. 34, pp. 116-33. Ann Arbor.
n.d. The Lithic Industries of the Schultz Site, 20SA2, Saginaw County, Michigan. Manuscript on file, University of Michigan Museum of Anthropology. Ann Arbor.

Fitting, James E., Jerry DeVisscher, and Edward J. Wahla
1966 The Paleo-Indian Occupation of the Holcombe Beach. Anthropological Papers, Museum of Anthropology, University of Michigan, No. 27. Ann Arbor.

Flanders, Richard
n.d. A Comparison of Some Hopewell Materials from Michigan and Illinois. Unpublished Ph.D. Thesis; University of Michigan, Department of Anthropology. Ann Arbor.

Flint, Richard F.
1957 Glacial and Pleistocene Geology. John Wiley and Son. New York.

Fogel, Ira L.
1963 The Dispersal of Copper Artifacts in the Late Archaic Period of Prehistoric North America. The Wisconsin Archeologist, Vol. 44, No. 3, pp. 129-79. Lake Mills.

Friedman, G. M.
1961 Distinction between Dune, Beach, and River Sands from Their Textural Characteristics, Journal of Sedimentary Petrology, 31, pp. 514-29. Menasha.

Frye, John C., H. B. Willman, and Robert F. Black
1965 Outline of Glacial Geology of Illinois and Wisconsin. *In*: The Quarternary of the United States, edited by H. E. Wright, Jr., and David C. Frey. Princeton University Press. Princeton.

Griffin, James B.
1943 The Fort Ancient Aspect. University of Michigan Press. Ann Arbor.
1952 Some Early and Middle Woodland Pottery Types in Illinois. *In*: Hopewellian Communities in Illinois, edited by Thorne Duell. Science Papers, Illinois State Museum, Vol. 5, pp. 93-129. Springfield.
1960 Climatic Change: A Contributory Cause of the Growth and Decline of Northern Hopewell Culture. The Wisconsin Archeologist, Vol. 41, No. 1, pp. 21-23. Lake Mills.
1961 Some Correlations of Climate and Cultural Change in Eastern North American Prehistory. Annals of the New York Academy of Science, Vol. 95, Article 1, pp. 710-17. Albany.
1962 A Discussion of Prehistoric Similarities and Connections Between the Arctic and Temperate Zones of North America. Technical Paper No. 11, Arctic Institute of North America, pp. 154-81. Montreal.
1964 The Northeast Woodlands. *In*: Prehistoric Man in the New World, edited by Jesse D. Jennings and Edward Norbeck, pp. 223-58. University of Chicago Press. Chicago.
1965*a* Prehistory in the Northeast Woodlands. *In*: The Quarternary of the United States, edited by H. E. Wright, Jr. and David G. Frey. Princeton.
1965*b* Ceramic Complexity and Cultural Development: The Eastern United States as a Case Study. *In*: Ceramics and Man, edited by Frederick R. Matson. Viking Fund Publications in Anthropology No. 41, pp. 104-13. New York.
1967 Eastern American Archaeology: A Summary. Science, Vol. 156, No. 3772, pp. 175-91. Washington, D.C.

Griffin, John W.
n.d. The Fisher Site. Unpublished 1946 Masters Thesis on file at the University of Chicago. Chicago.

Grigor'ev, G. P.
1967 A New Reconstruction of Above Ground Dwelling of Kostenki I. Current Anthropology, Vol. 8, No. 4, pp. 344-49. Utrecht.

Hall, Robert L.
1962 The Archaeology of Carcajou Point, 2 vols. University of Wisconsin Press. Madison.
1966 Cahokia Chronology. Mimeographed copy of paper presented at 1966 meeting of Central States Anthropological Society. St. Louis.
1967 Those Late Corn Dates: Isotopic Fractionation as a Source of Error in Carbon-14 Dates. The Michigan Archaeologist, Vol. 13, No. 4, pp. 171-80. Ann Arbor.

Hand, Bryce M.
1967 Differentiation of Beach and Dune Sands Using Settlings Velocities of Light and Heavy Minerals. Journal of Sedimentary Petrology, Vol. 37, No. 2, pp. 514-20. Menasha.

Harding, Thomas
1967 Voyagers of the Vitiaz Strait/A Study of a New Guinea Trade System. University of Washington Press. Seattle.

Harrison, Sidney
n.d. Petrological Identification of Archaeological Materials. Unpublished 1963 manuscript in files of University of Michigan Museum of Anthropology. Ann Arbor.
1966 The Schmidt Site (20SA192), Saginaw County, Michigan. The Michigan Archaeologist, Vol. 12, No. 2, pp. 49-70. Ann Arbor.

Hawkins, Arthur S.
1964 The Mississippi Flyway. Waterfowl Tomorrow, pp. 185-207. United States Department of the Interior. Washington, D.C.

Hickerson, Harold
1960 The Feast of the Dead Among the 17th Century Algonkians of the Upper Great Lakes. American Anthropologist, Vol. 62, No. 1, pp. 81-107. Menasha.
1962 The Southwestern Chippewa. Memoirs of the American Anthropological Association, No. 92. Salt Lake City.
1967 Some Implications of the Theory of Particularity, or "Atomist" of Northern Algonkians. Current Anthropology, Vol. 8, No. 4, pp. 313-44. Utrecht.

Hill, Asa T. and Waldo Wedel
1936 Excavations at the Leary Indian Village and Burial Site, Richardson County, Nebraska. Nebraska History Magazine, Vol. XVLI, No. 1. Lincoln.

Hinsdale, W. B.
1931 Archaeological Atlas of Michigan. University of Michigan Press. Ann Arbor.

Hockett, Charles
1964 Proto-Central Algonkian Kinship. *In*: Explorations in Cultural Anthropology, edited by Ward Goodenough. pp. 762-89. Columbia University Press. New York.

Hoffman, W. J.
1893 The Menomini. Bureau of American Ethnology, Fourteenth Annual Report. Washington, D.C.

Hough, Jack L.
1958 The Geology of the Great Lakes. University of Illinois Press. Urbana.
1963 Prehistoric Great Lakes of North America. American Scientist, Vol. 51, No. 1, pp. 84-109. Easton.

Hruska, Robert
1967 The Riverside Site: A Late Archaic Manifestation in Michigan. The Wisconsin Archeologist, Vol. 48, No. 3, pp. 145-260. Lake Mills.

Hubbs, Carl L. and Karl F. Lagler
1961 Fish of the Great Lakes Region, 2nd edition. University of Michigan Press. Ann Arbor.

Janzen, Donald
1968 Excavations and Survey at Burnt Bluff in 1965. *In*: The Prehistory of the Burnt Bluff Area, assembled by James E. Fitting. Anthropological Papers, Museum of Anthropology, University of Michigan, No. 34, pp. 61-94. Ann Arbor.

Jeske, John
1928 The Grand River Mound Group. Bulletin Publication of the Museum of Milwaukee, Vol. 3, No. 2. Milwaukee.

Johnson, L., Jr.
1961 The Yarbrough and Miller Sites of Northeast Texas, with a Preliminary Definition of the Lattarpe Aspect. Bulletin of the Texas Archaeological Society, Vol. 32, pp. 141-284. Austin.

Johnston, Richard B.
1968 The Archaeology of the Serpent Mounds Site. Royal Ontario Museum, Occasional Papers No. 10. University of Toronto Press. Toronto.

Jones, Volney
1968 Four Textile Products from the Burnt Bluff Site (B-95), Michigan. *In*: The Prehistory of the Burnt Bluff Area, assembled by James E. Fitting. Anthropological Papers, Museum of Anthropology, University of Michigan, No. 34, pp. 95-97. Ann Arbor.

Jury, Wilfrid
1941 Clearville Prehistoric Village Site in Oxford Township, Kent County, Ontario. University of Western Ontario, Bulletin of the Museum, No. 2. London, Ontario.

Jury, Wilfrid and Elsie Jury
1952 The Burley Site. University of Western Ontario, Museum of Archaeological and Pioneer Life, Bulletin 9. London, Ontario.

Kent, B. and D. Griffin
n.d. Field Notes for Delta County Islands, 1961. U. P. Survey. Manuscript on file in The University of Michigan Museum of Anthropology. Ann Arbor.

Kenyon, Walter
1957 The Inverhuron Site. Royal Ontario Museum of Anthropology and Archaeology, Occasional Paper 1. Toronto.
1961 The Swan Lake Site. Royal Ontario Museum of Anthropology and Archaeology, Occasional Paper 3. Toronto.

Kidd, Kenneth E.
1949 The Excavation of Ste. Marie I. University of Toronto Press. Toronto.

Krumbein, W. C. and F. J. Pettijohn
1938 Manual of Sedimentary Petrography. Appleton-Century-Crofts, Inc. New York.

Lee, Thomas E.
1965 A Point Peninsula Site, Manitoulin Island, Lake Huron. Bulletin of the Massachusetts Archaeological Society, Vol. 26, No. 2, pp. 19-29. Attleboro.

Lee, G. B., W. E. Janke, and A. J. Beaver
1962 Particle-size Analysis of Valders Drift in Eastern Wisconsin. Science, Vol. 138, pp. 154-55. Washington, D.C.

Leechman, Douglas and Fredrica de Laguna
1949 The Parker Site. Annual Report of the National Museum of Canada, 1947-48. Bulletin 113 of the National Museum of Canada. Ottawa.

Libby, Arnold
1952 Radiocarbon Dating. Third Edition. University of Chicago Press. Chicago.

Lippincott, Kerry A. and Elaine Bluhm Herold
1965 Archaeological Investigations along the Henderson Creek Drainage. Middle Woodland Sites in Illinois, Illinois Archaeological Survey, Bulletin No. 5, pp. 68-95. Davenport.

MacLean, N. W.
1963 Modern Pseudo-Warping around Lake Erie. Great Lakes Research Division, University of Michigan. Proceedings of Smith Conference, Great Lakes Research Publication 10, pp. 156-68. Ann Arbor.

MacNeish, Richard S.
1952 Iroquois Pottery Types. National Museum of Canada, Bulletin No. 124. Ottawa.
1958 An Introduction to the Archaeology of Southeast Manitoba. National Museum of Canada, Bulletin 157. Ottawa.
1964 Investigations in Southwest Yukon: Archaeological Excavations, Comparisons, and Speculations. Papers of the Robert S. Peabody Foundation, Vol. 6, No. 2. Andover.

McGregor, John C.
1958 The Pool and Irving Villages/A Study of Hopewell Occupation in the Illinois River Valley. University of Chicago Press. Chicago.

McKern, W. C.
1928 The Neale and McClaughry Mound Groups. Bulletin, Public Museum of Milwaukee, Vol. 3, No. 3. Milwaukee.
1945 Preliminary Report on the Upper Mississippi Phase in Wisconsin. Bulletin, Public Museum of Milwaukee, Vol. 16, No. 3. Milwaukee.

McPherron, Alan L.
1967 The Juntunen Site and the Lake Woodland Prehistory of the Upper Great Lakes Area. Anthropological Papers, Museum of Anthropology, University of Michigan No. 30. Ann Arbor.

Maher, Robert F. and David A. Baerreis
1958 The Aztalan Lithic Complex. The Wisconsin Archeologist, Vol. 39, No. 1, pp. 5-26. Milwaukee.

Martin, Helen
1936 Centennial Geological Map of the Northern Peninsula of Michigan. Department of Conservation, Geological Survey 33, Pub. 39. Lansing.

Mason, Ronald J.
1965 Wisconsin Middle Woodland Toggle Head Harpoons. The Michigan Archaeologist, Vol. 11, No. 34, pp. 156-64. Ann Arbor.
1966 Two Stratified Sites on the Door Peninsula, Wisconsin. Anthropological Papers, Museum of Anthropology, University of Michigan No. 26. Ann Arbor.
1967 The North Bay Component at Porte Des Morts Site. The Wisconsin Archeologist, Vol. 48, No. 4, pp. 267-344. Lake Mills.

Matson, Fredrick
1937 An Analysis of the Younge Site Ceramics. *In*: The Younge Site, by E. F. Greenman. Occasional Contributions, Museum of Anthropology, University of Michigan No. 6. Ann Arbor.

Maxwell, Moreau S.
1950 A Change in the Interpretation of Wisconsin's Prehistory. Wisconsin Magazine of History, Vol. 33, No. 4, pp. 427-33. Madison.

Mitchell, Barry M.
1966 Preliminary Report on a Woodland Site near Deep River, Ontario. National Museum of Canada, Anthropological Papers, No. 11. Ottawa.

Morgan, Lewis H.
1881 Houses and House-Life of the American Aborigenes. U. S. Geographical and Geological Survey of the Rocky Mountain Region. Contributions to North American Ethnology, Vol. IV. Government Printing Office. Washington, D.C.

Morse, Dan F.
1963 The Steuben Village and Mounds/A Multi-Component Late Hopewell Site in Illinois. Anthropological Papers, Museum of Anthropology, University of Michigan, No. 21. Ann Arbor.

Munsell
1954 Munsell Soil Color Charts. 1954 Edition. Munsell Color Co., Inc. Baltimore.

Murdock, George P.
1949 Social Structure. The Free Press, Collier-MacMillan. New York.

Murie, Olas J.
1958 Field Guide to Animal Tracks. The Riverside Press. Cambridge.

Odum, Eugene P.
1959 Fundamentals of Ecology. 2nd Edition. W. B. Saunders Co. New York.

Owen, Robert C.
1965 The Patrilocal Band: A Linguistically and Culturally Hybrid Social Unit. American Anthropologist, Vol. 67, No. 5, pp. 675-90. Menasha.

Papworth, Mark L.
n.d. Late Archaic Sites in the Saginaw Valley, Michigan. Unpublished Ph.D. dissertation, 1967. Department of Anthropology, University of Michigan. Ann Arbor.

Peske, G. R. and D. Higgins
n.d. Field Report of the 1961 U. P. Survey. Manuscript on file at the University of Michigan, Museum of Anthropology. Ann Arbor.

Pilling, Arnold R.
1966 Life at Porter Site 8, Midland County, Michigan. The Michigan Archaeologist, Vol. 12, No. 4, pp. 235-48. Ann Arbor.

Prahl, Earl J. and David S. Brose
n.d. The Ekdahl-Goudrean Site. Unpublished manuscript at The University of Toledo. Toledo.

Prahl, Earl J. and W. R. Farrand
1968 The Geology of Burnt Bluff. *In:* The Prehistory of the Burnt Bluff Area, assembled by James E. Fitting. Anthropological Papers, Museum of Anthropology, University of Michigan No. 34. Ann Arbor.

Pratt, Peter P.
1961 Oneida Iroquois Glass Trade Bead Sequence/1585-1745. Fort Stanwix Museum, Color Guide Series No. 1. Onondaga Printing Co. Syracuse.

Quimby, George I.
1957 An Old Copper Site at Port Washington. The Wisconsin Archeologist, Vol. 38, No. 1, pp. 1-5. Lake Mills.
1960 Indian Life in the Upper Great Lakes. University of Chicago Press. Chicago.
1963 Late Period Copper Artifacts in the Upper Great Lakes Region. The Wisconsin Archeologist, Vol. 44, No. 4, pp. 193-98. Lake Mills.

1966*a* Indian Culture and European Trade Goods. University of Wisconsin Press. Madison.
1966*b* The Dumaw Creek Site. Fieldiana: Anthropology, Vol. 56, No. 1. Chicago.
n.d. The Woodland Pattern in Michigan. Unpublished masters thesis, 1935, University of Michigan, Department of Anthropology. Ann Arbor.

Ridley, Frank
1954 The Frank Bay Site, Lake Nipissing, Ontario. American Antiquity, Vol. 20, No. 1, pp. 40-50. Salt Lake City.

Ritchie, William A.
1946 A Stratified Prehistoric Site at Brewerton, New York. Rochester Museum of Arts and Sciences, Research Records No. 8. Rochester.
1949 An Archaeological Survey of the Trent Waterway in Ontario, Canada and its Significance for New York State Prehistory. Rochester Museum of Arts and Sciences, Research Records No. 9. Rochester.
1954 Dutch Hollow, An Early Historic Period Seneca Site in Livingston County, New York. Researches and Transactions of the New York State Archaeological Association, Vol. 13, No. 1. Albany.
1961 A Typology and Nomenclature for New York Projectile Points. New York State Museum and Science Service, Bulletin 384. Albany.
1965 The Archaeology of New York State. Natural History Press. New York City.

Ritchie, William A. and R. S. MacNeish
1949 The Pre-Iroquoian Pottery of New York State. American Antiquity, Vol. 15, No. 2, pp. 97-124. Menasha.

Roosa, William B.
1966 The Warner School Site. The Michigan Archaeologist, Vol. 12, No. 1, pp. 25-34. Ann Arbor.

Rostlund, Erhard
1952 Freshwater Fish and Fishing in Native North America. University of California Geographical Publication No. 9. University of California Press. Berkeley.

Rouse, Irving
1939 Prehistory in Haiti: A Study in Method. Yale University Publications in Anthropology, No. 21. New Haven.

Schoolcraft, Henry R.
1851 Personal Memoirs of a Residence of Thirty Years with the Indian Tribes on the American Frontiers. Lippincott, Grambo and Co. Philadelphia.
1953 Narative Journey of Travels, edited by Mentor L. Williams. Michigan State College Press. East Lansing.

Scott, W. B.
1954 Freshwater Fishes of Eastern Canada. University of Toronto Press. Toronto.

Semenov, S. A.
1964 Prehistoric Technology, translated by M. W. Thompson. Barnes and Noble. New York City.

Service, Elman R.
1962 Primitive Social Organization. Random House. New York.

Sinclair, William C.
1960 Reconnaissance of the Ground-Water Resources of Delta County, Michigan. Michigan Geological Survey Program, Report No. 24. Lansing.

Smith, Hale G.
1951 The Crable Site, Fulton County, Illinois. Anthropological Papers, Museum of Anthropology, University of Michigan, No. 7. Ann Arbor.

Spaulding, Albert C.
1953 Statistical Techniques for the Discovery of Artifact Types. American Antiquity, Vol. 18, No. 4, pp. 305-13. Salt Lake City.

Speth, John
n.d. Suggestions for the Geologic Sampling of Michigan Sites. Unpublished manuscript on file at the University of Michigan, Museum of Anthropology. Ann Arbor.

Steinbring, Jack
1967 A Copper "Gaff Hook" from Ontario. The Wisconsin Archeologist, Vol. 48, No. 4, pp. 345-58. Lake Mills.

Stoltman, James B.
1962 A Proposed Method for Systematizing the Modal Analysis of Pottery and its Application to the Laurel Focus. Unpublished masters thesis, University of Minnesota. Minneapolis.

Stuiver, Minze and Hans Suess
1966 On the Relationship Between Radiocarbon Dates and True Sample Ages. Radiocarbon, Vol. 8, pp. 534-40. New Haven.

Taggart, David W.
1967 Seasonal Patterns in Settlement, Subsistence and Industries in the Saginaw Late Archaic. The Michigan Archaeologist, Vol. 13, No. 4, pp. 153-70. Ann Arbor.

Thwaites, Ruben G., editor
1959 The Jesuit Relations and Allied Documents, 1610-1791, 73 Vols. Burroughs Bros. New York City.

Titiev, Mischa
1943 The Influence of Common Residence on the Unilateral Classification of Kindred. American Anthropologist, Vol. 45, Oct.-Dec., pp. 511-30. Menasha.

Titterington, Paul F.
1938 The Cahokia Mound Group and Its Village Site Materials. Published by the author. St. Louis.

United States Department of Agriculture

1941 Climates of the United States. Yearbook of Agriculture, 1941, pp. 701-47. Government Printing Office. Washington, D.C.

1962 Soil Survey Manual. U. S. Department of Agriculture, Handbook No. 18, 3rd edition. Agricultural Research Administration, U.S.D.A. Washington, D.C.

Waterman, T. T.

1925 North American Indian Dwellings. Annual Report of the Smithsonian Institute, 1924, pp. 461-85. Washington, D.C.

Wayne, William J. and James H. Zumberge

1965 Pleistocene Geology of Indiana and Michigan. *In*: The Quarternary of the United States. Edited by H. E. Wright, Jr., and David G. Frey. Princeton.

Wedel, Mildred Mott

1959 Oneota Sites on the Upper Iowa River. The Missouri Archaeologist, Vol. 12, No. 2-4, pp. 1-181. Columbia.

Wedel, Waldo

1959 An Introduction to Kansas Archaeology. Bureau of American Ethnology. Bulletin 176. Washington, D.C.

White, Anta M., Lewis R. Binford, and Mark L. Papworth

1963 Miscellaneous Studies in Typology and Classification. Anthropological Papers, Museum of Anthropology, University of Michigan, No. 19. Ann Arbor.

White, Marian E.

1967 An Early Historic Niagara Frontier Iroquois Cemetery in Erie County, New York. New York State Archaeological Association, Research and Transactions, Vol. XVI, No. 1. Rochester.

Wilford, Lloyd A.

1951 The Prehistoric Indians of Minnesota: The Mille Lacs Aspect. The Minnesota Archaeologist, Vol. XVII, No. 3, pp. 9-16. Minneapolis.

1952 The Prehistoric Indiana of Minnesota. The Minnesota Archaeologist, Vol. 18, No. 2, pp. 4-15. Minneapolis.

1955 A Revised Classification of the Prehistoric Cultures of Minnesota. American Antiquity, Vol. 21, No. 2, pp. 130-42. Salt Lake City.

Wintemberg, W. J.

1939 The Lawson Prehistoric Village Site, Middlesex County, Ontario. National Museum of Canada, Bulletin 94. The Queens Printer. Ottawa.

1946 The Sidey-Mackay Village Site. American Antiquity, Vol. 11, No. 3, pp. 154-82. Menasha.

Wittry, Warren

1956 The Kolterman Mound C^{14} Date. The Wisconsin Archeologist, Vol. 37, No. 4, pp. 131-34. Lake Mills.

1957 A Preliminary Study of the Old Copper Complex. The Wisconsin Archeologist, Vol. 38, No. 4, pp. 204-21. Lake Mills.

1959*a* The Raddatz Rock Shelter, Sk5, Wisconsin. The Wisconsin Archeologist, Vol. 40, No. 2, pp. 33-69. Lake Mills.

1959*b* Archaeological Studies of Four Wisconsin Rock Shelters. The Wisconsin Archeologist, Vol. 40, No. 4, pp. 137-268. Lake Mills.

1959*c* The Wakanda Park Mound Group. The Wisconsin Archeologist, Vol. 40, No. 3, pp. 95-116. Lake Mills.

1963 The Bell Site. The Wisconsin Archeologist, Vol. 44, No. 1, pp. 1-57. Lake Mills.

Wobst, H. Martin

1968 The Butterfield Site. *In*: Contributions to Michigan Archaeology. Anthropological Papers, Museum of Anthropology, University of Michigan, No. 32, pp. 173-275. Ann Arbor.

Wright, Gary A.

1967 Some Aspects of Early and Mid-17th Century Exchange Networks in the Western Great Lakes. The Michigan Archaeologist, Vol. 13, No. 4, pp. 181-97. Ann Arbor.

Wright, James V.

1964 The Ontario Iroquois Tradition. National Museum of Canada, Bulletin 210. Ottawa.

1967 The Laurel Tradition and The Middle Woodland Period. National Museum of Canada, Bulletin 217. Ottawa.

Wright, James V. and James Anderson

1963 The Donaldson Site. National Museum of Canada, Bulletin 184. Ottawa.

Yarnell, Richard A.

1964 Aboriginal Relationships between Culture and Plant Life in the Upper Great Lakes Region. Anthropological Papers, Museum of Anthropology, University of Michigan, No. 23. Ann Arbor.

PLATE I

A

B

Views of the Summer Island site. U.M.M.A. Neg. Nos. 16522-23.

PLATE II

a

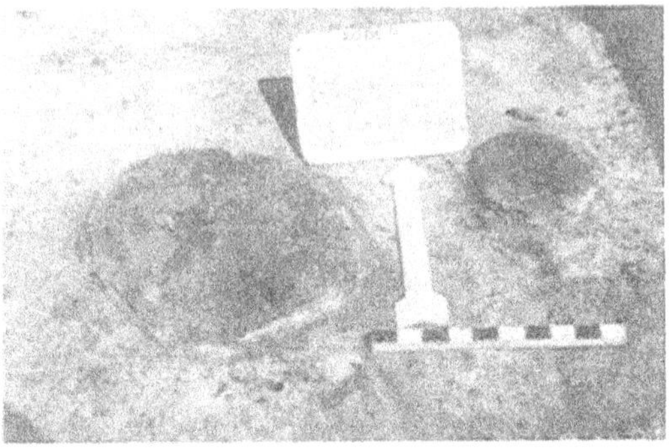

b

c

Middle Woodland midden and post molds. U.M.M.A. Neg. No. 16524.

PLATE III

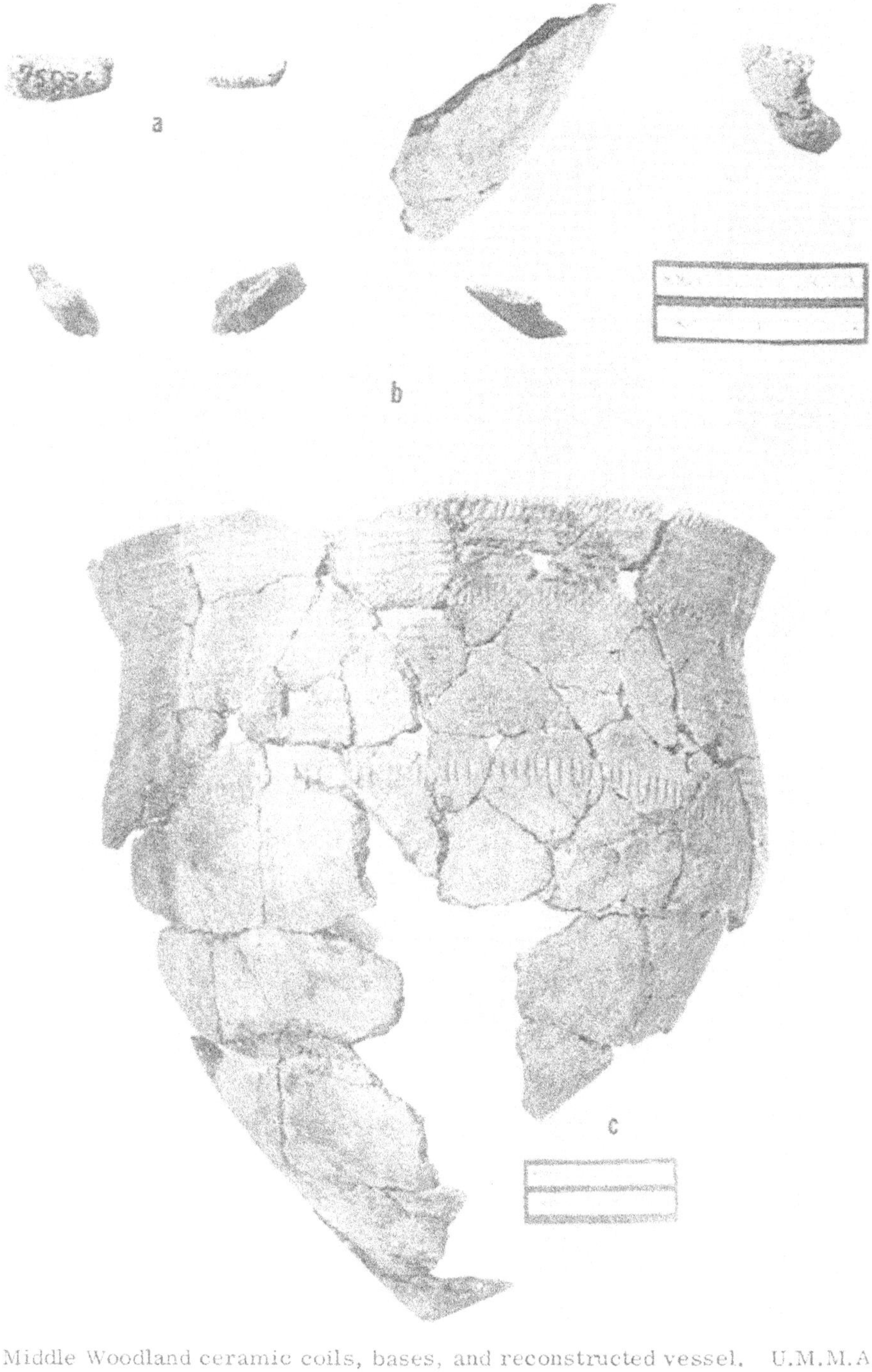

Middle Woodland ceramic coils, bases, and reconstructed vessel. U.M.M.A. Neg. No. 16525.

PLATE IV

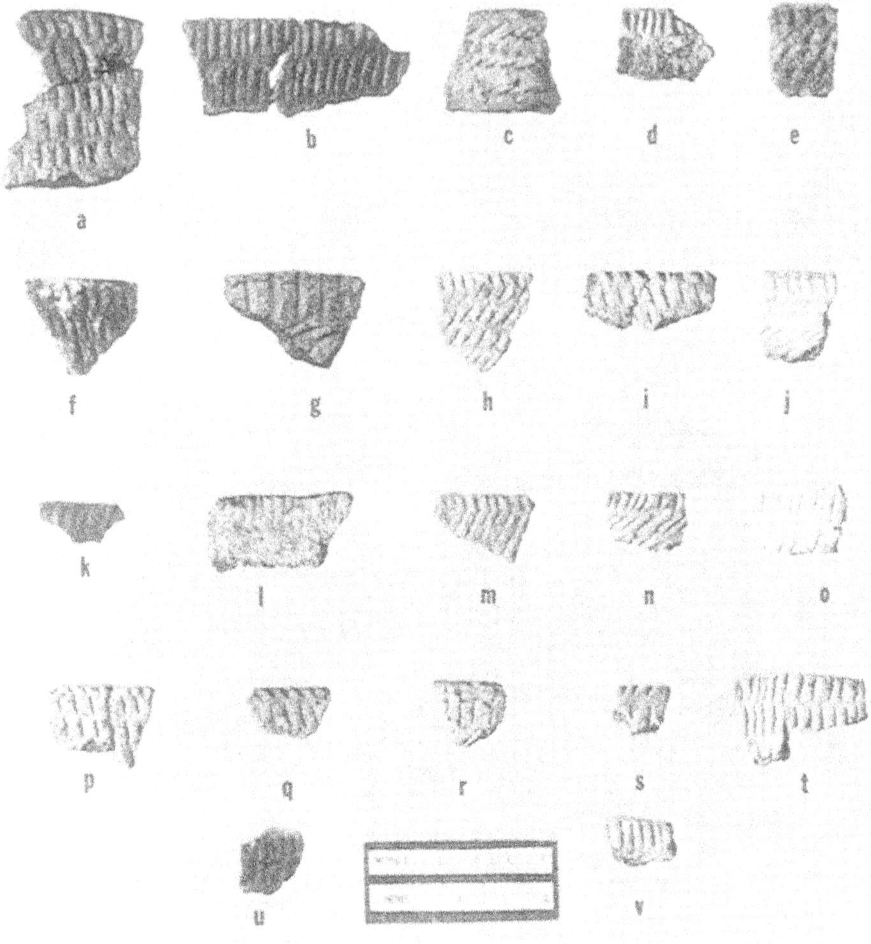

Banked stamp, plain tool (oblique) ceramics. U.M.M.A. Neg. No. 16526.

PLATE V

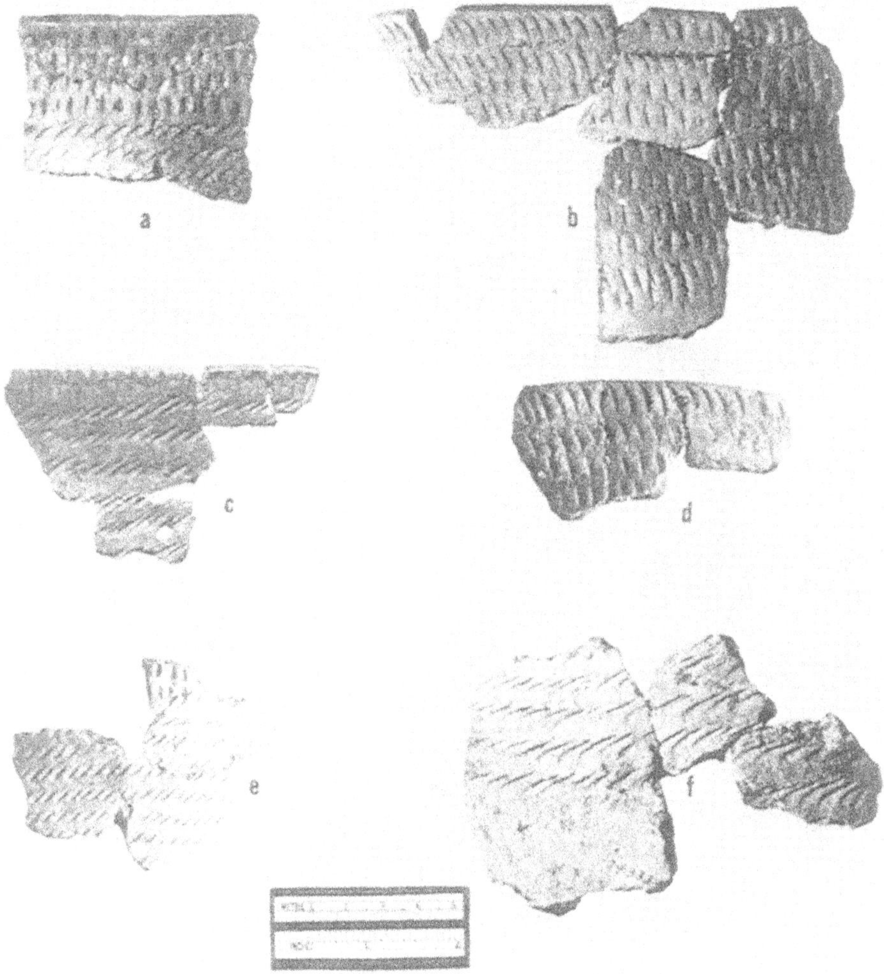

Banked stamp, plain tool (oblique) ceramics. U.M.M.A. Neg. No. 16527.

PLATE VI

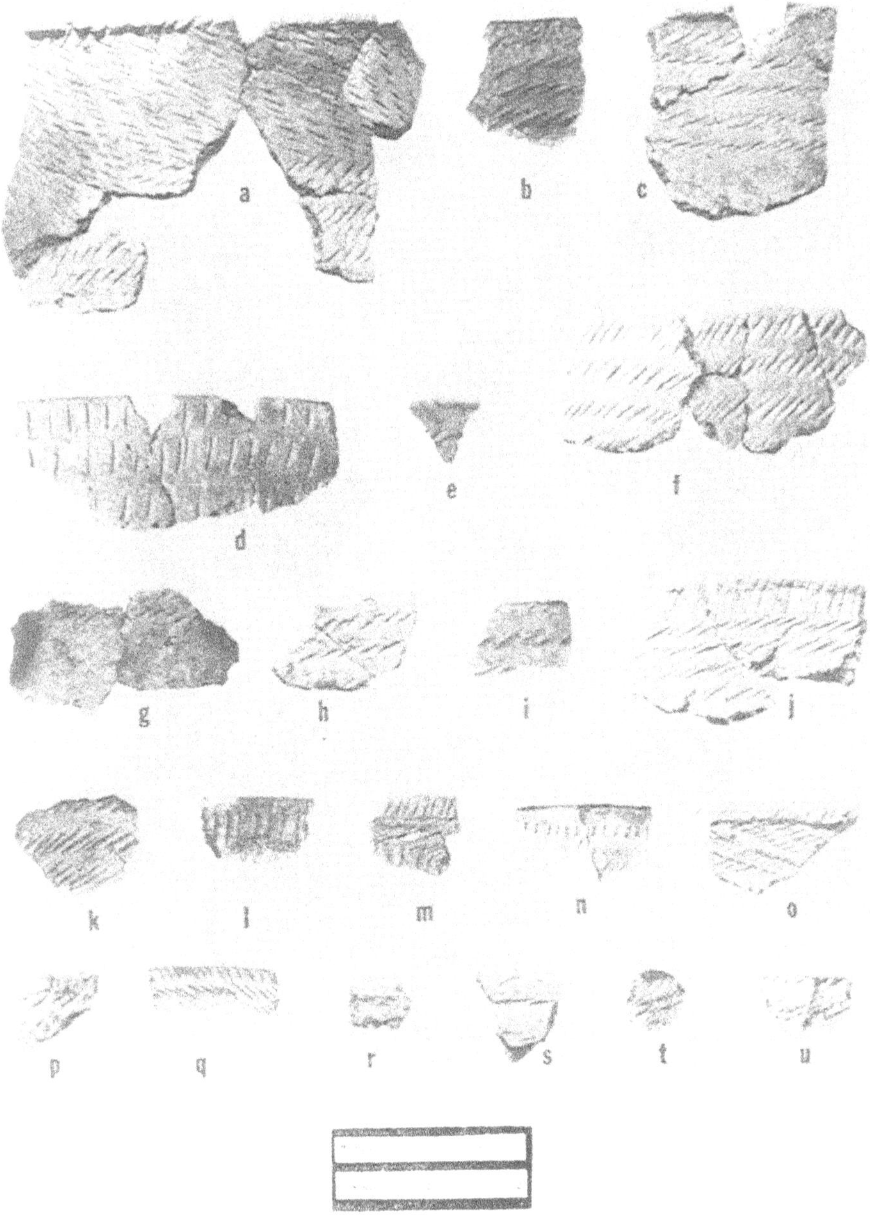

Banked stamp, narrow tool (vertical) ceramics. U.M.M.A. Neg. No. 16528.

PLATE VII

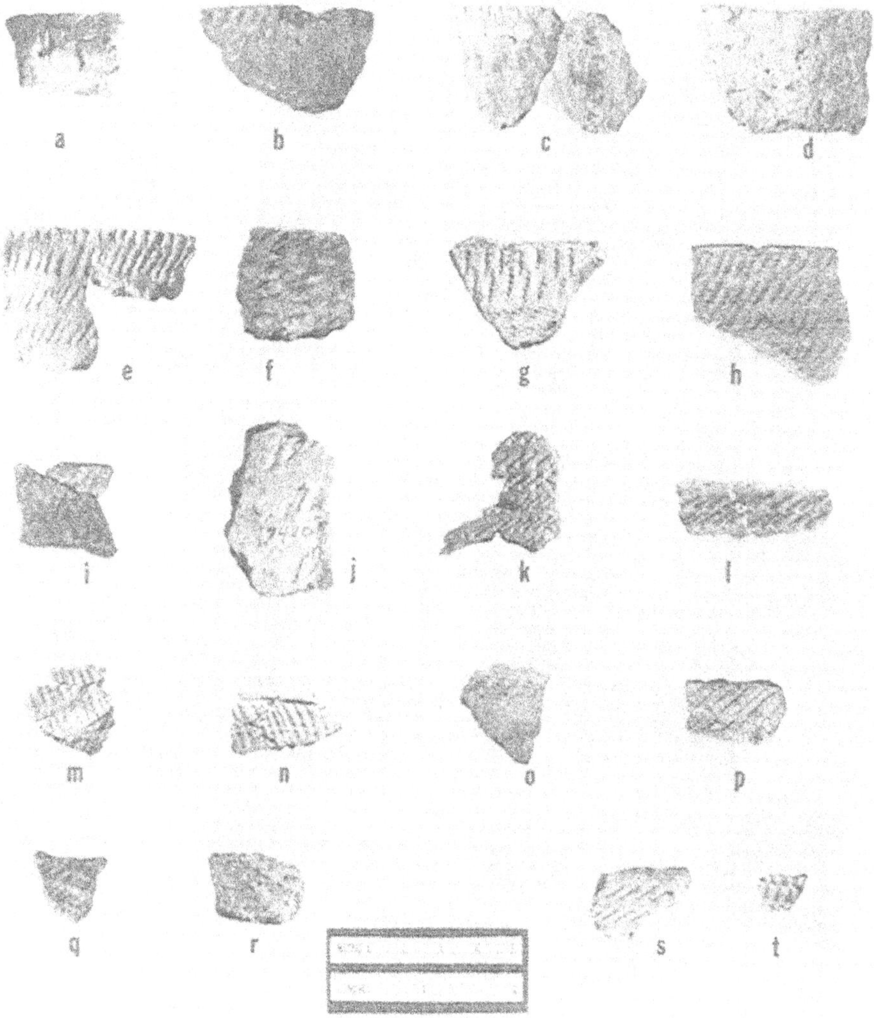

Plain and banked stamp, dentate tool ceramics. U.M.M.A. Neg. No. 16529.

PLATE VIII

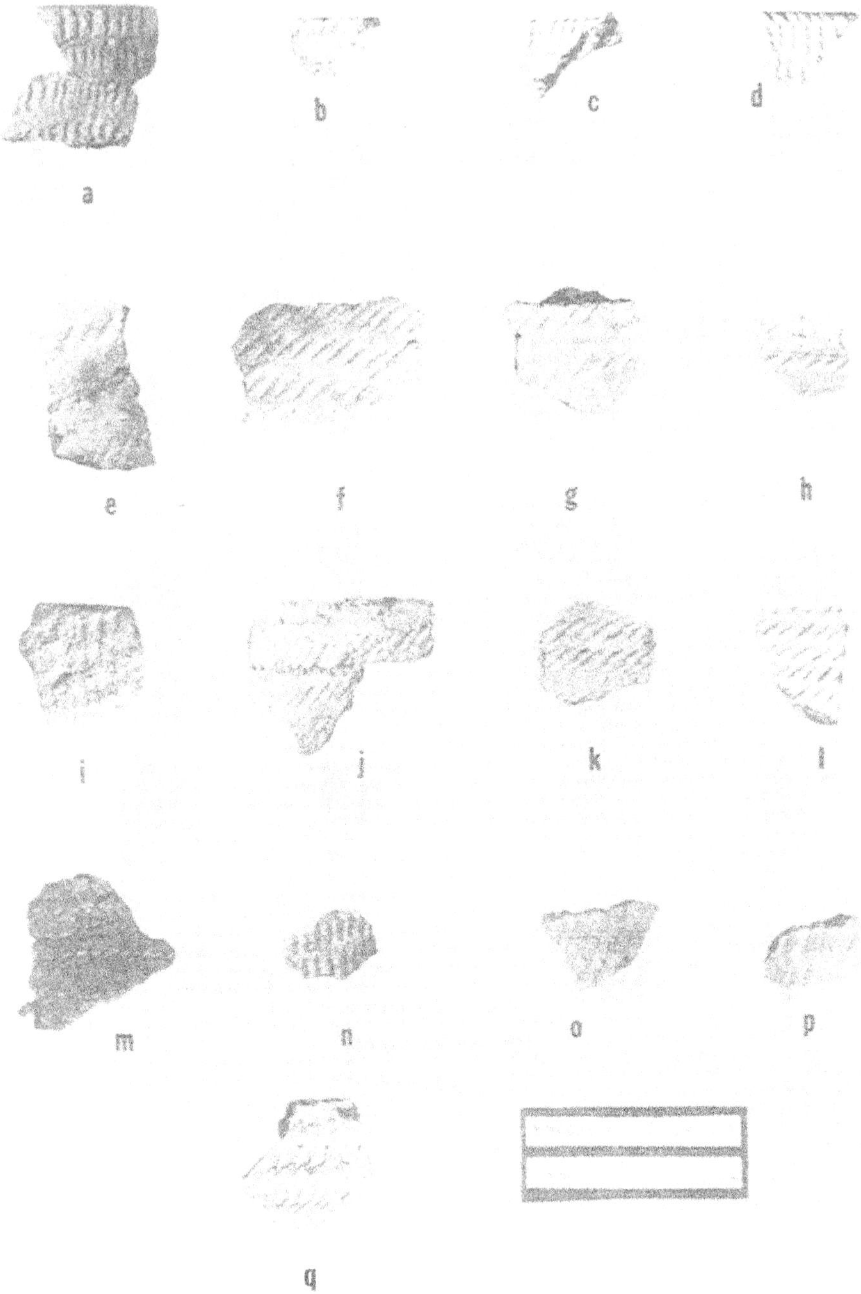

Dragged stamp, dentate tool ceramics. U.M.M.A. Neg. No. 16530.

PLATE IX

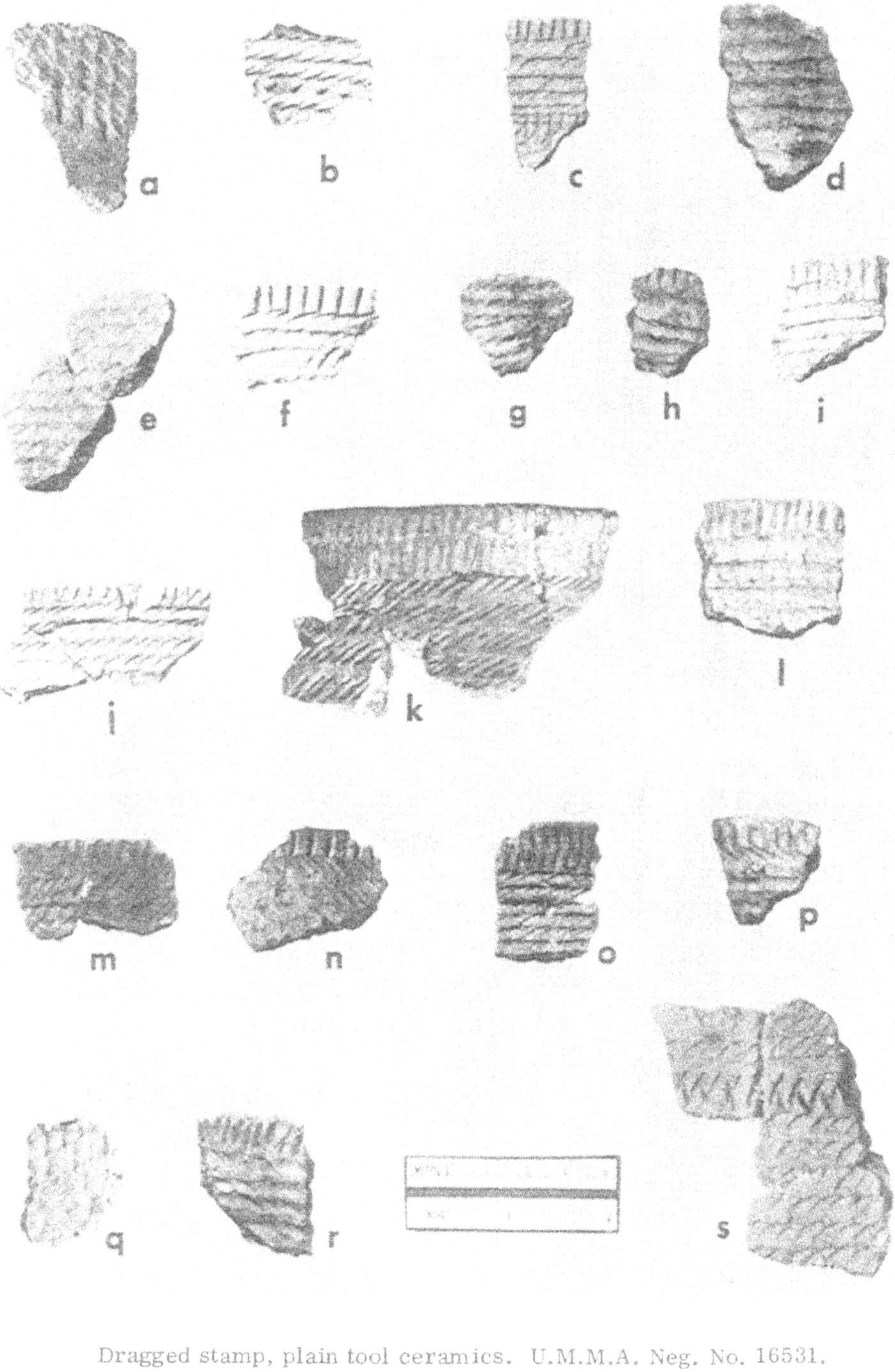

Dragged stamp, plain tool ceramics. U.M.M.A. Neg. No. 16531.

PLATE X

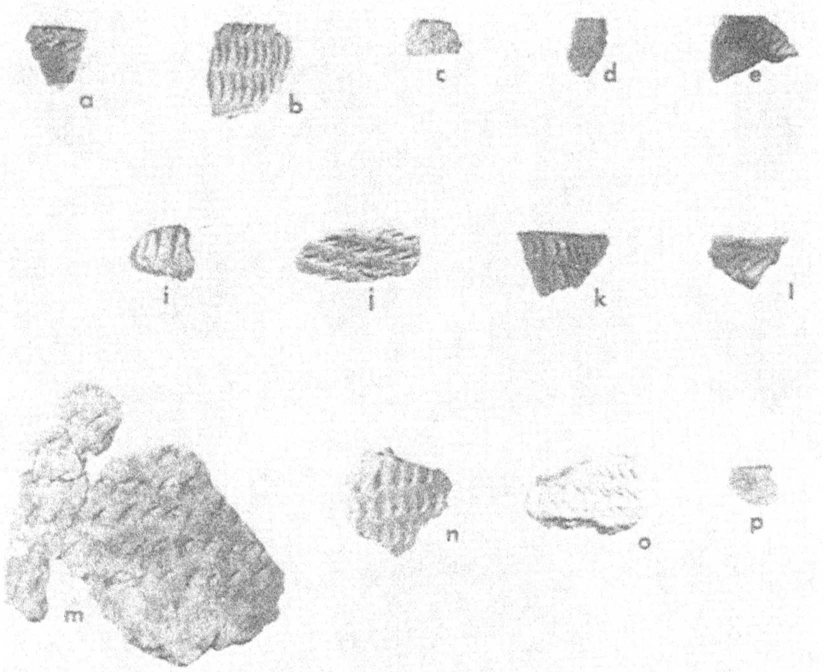

Banked fingernail punctate ceramics. U.M.M.A. Neg. No. 16532.

PLATE XI

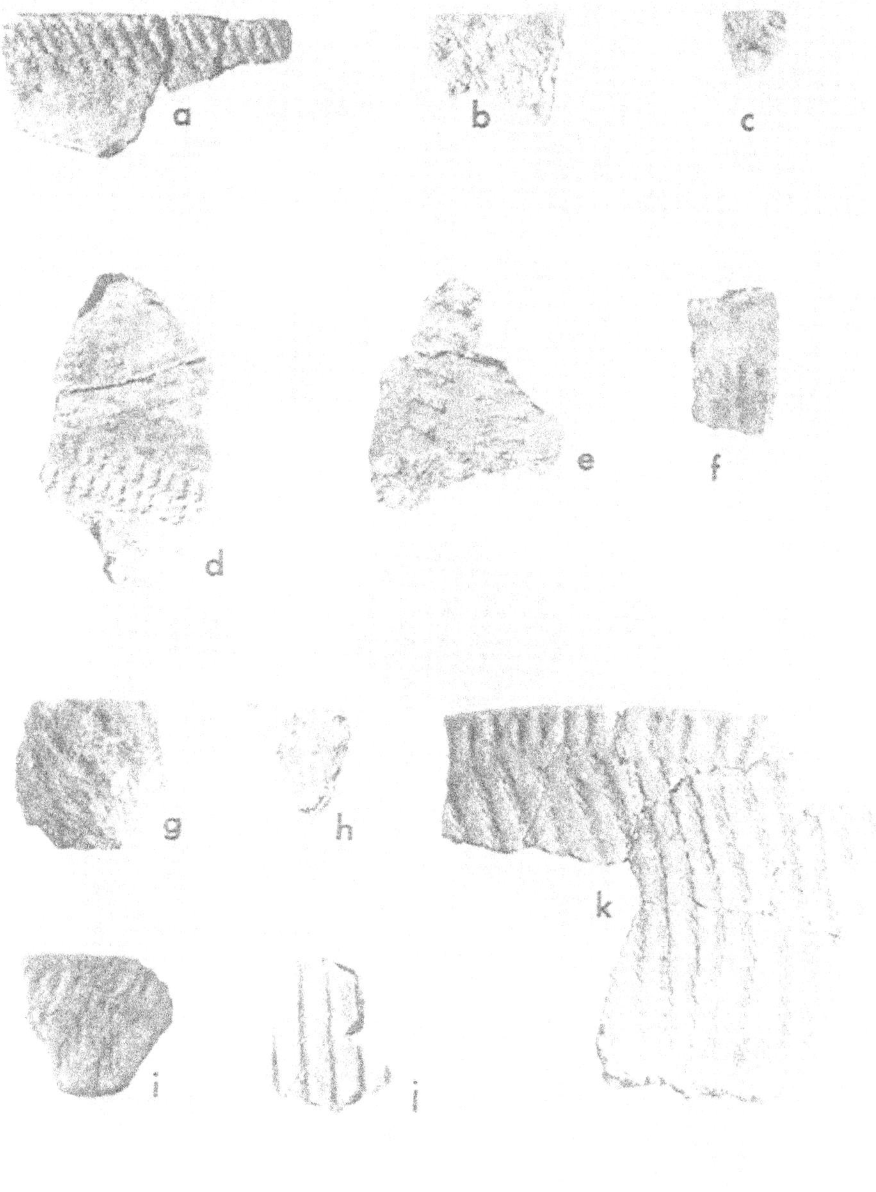

Linear impressed, braided cord ceramics. U.M.M.A. Neg. No. 16533.

PLATE XII

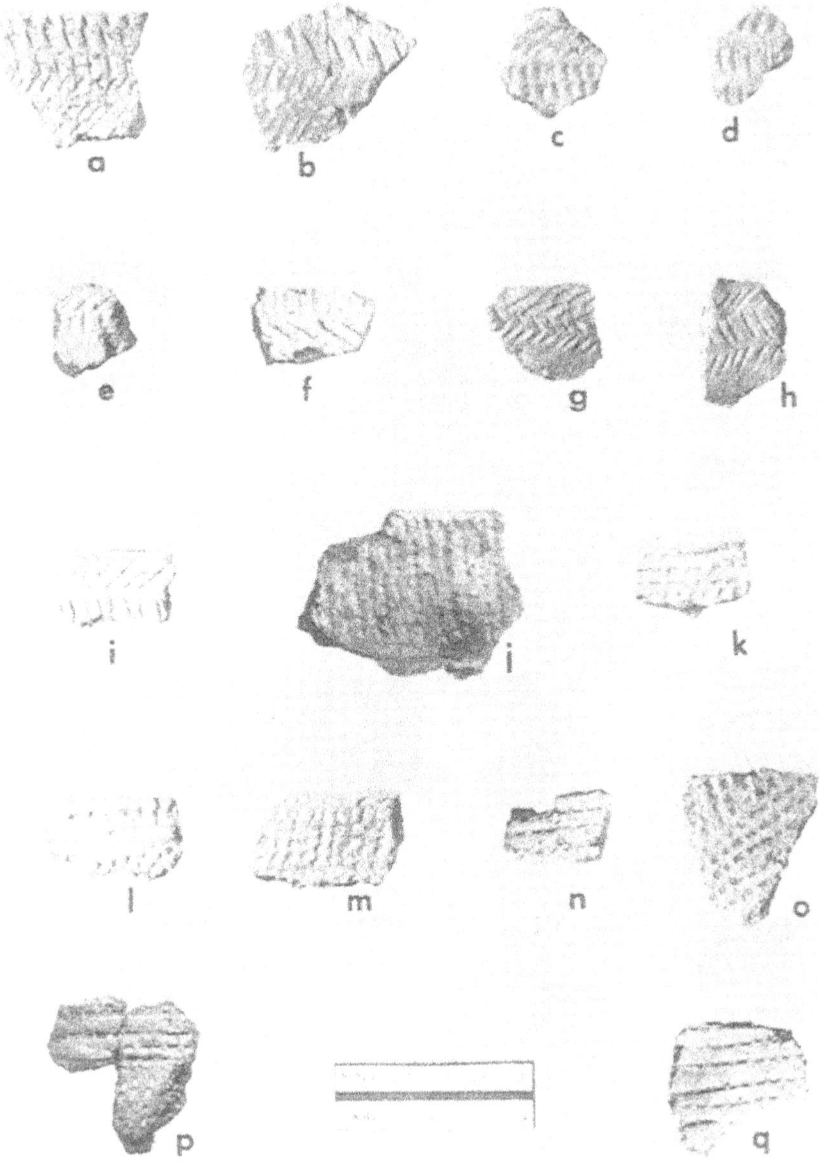

Banked stamp, plain tool and linear impressed, dentate ceramics. U.M.M.A. Neg. No. 16534.

PLATE XIII

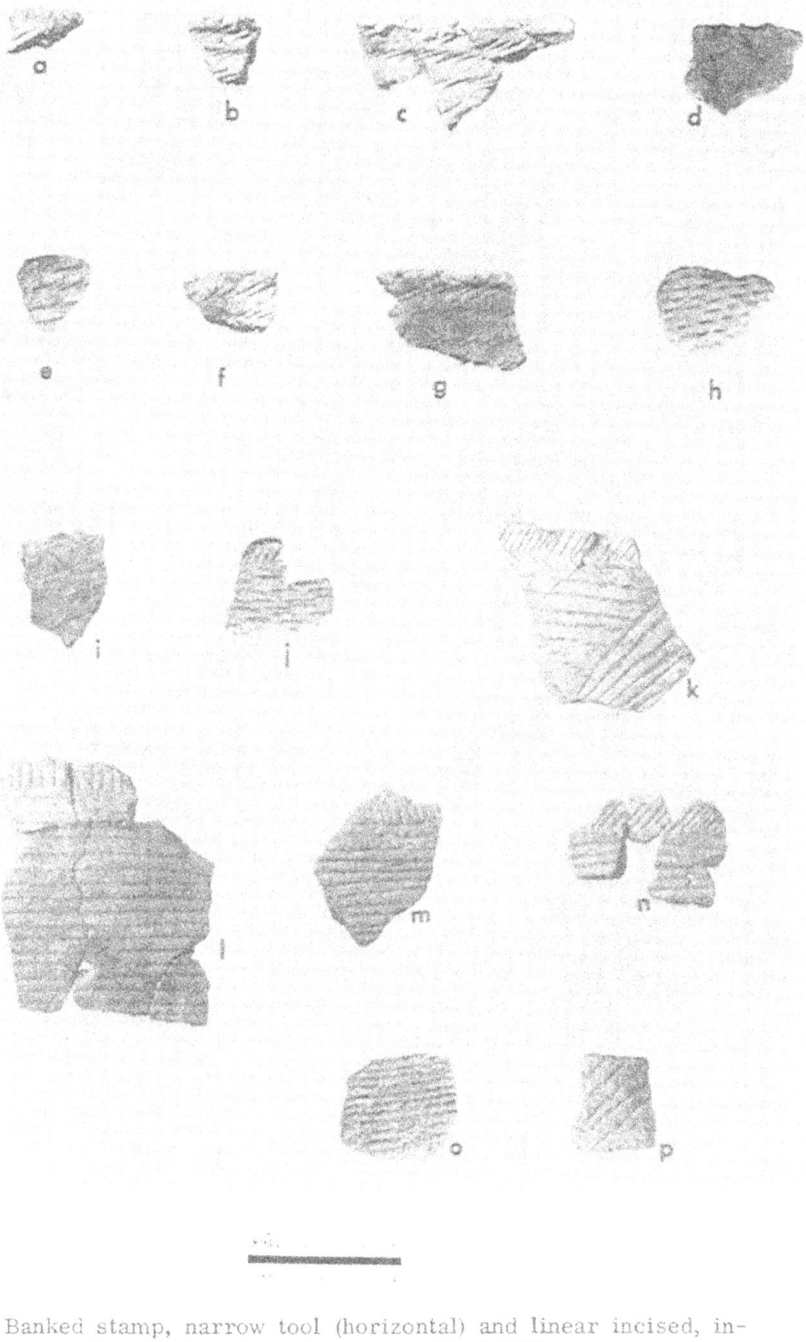

Banked stamp, narrow tool (horizontal) and linear incised, interruped ceramics. U.M.M.A. Neg. No. 16535.

PLATE XIV

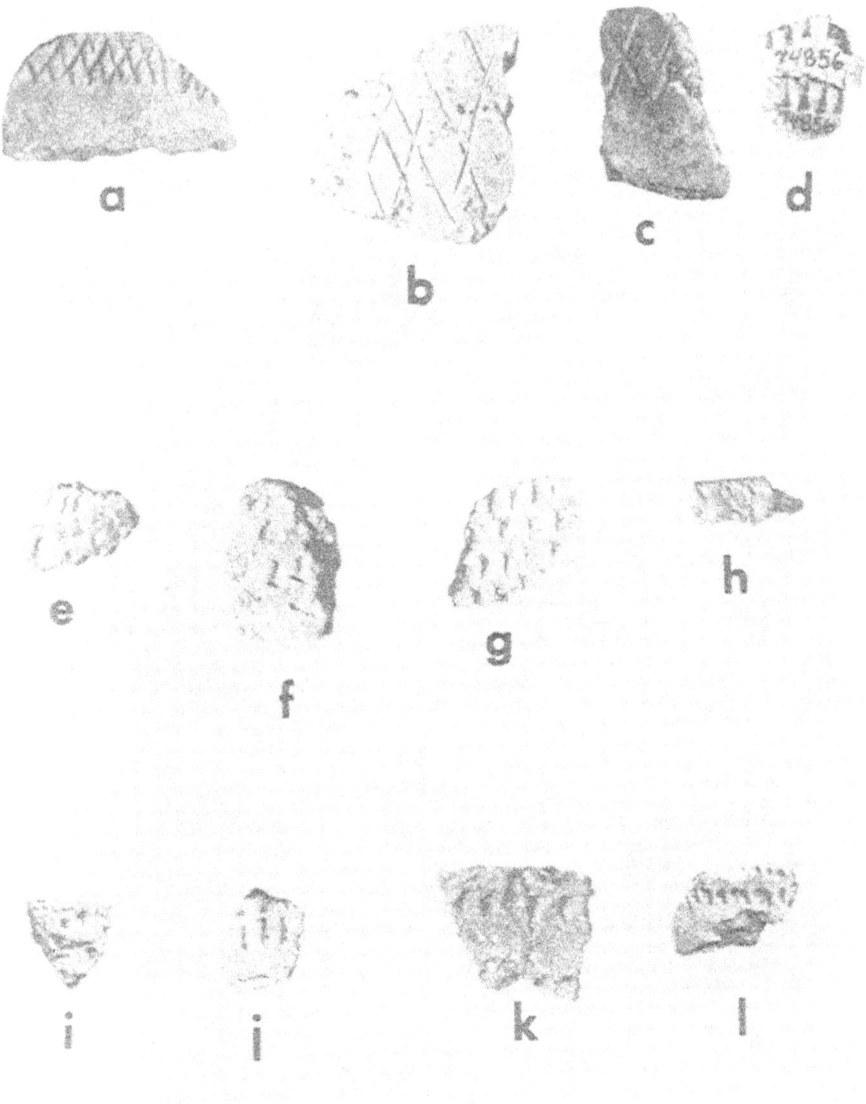

Linear incised, crisscross and miscellaneous punctate ceramics. U.M.M.A. Neg. No. 16536.

PLATE XV

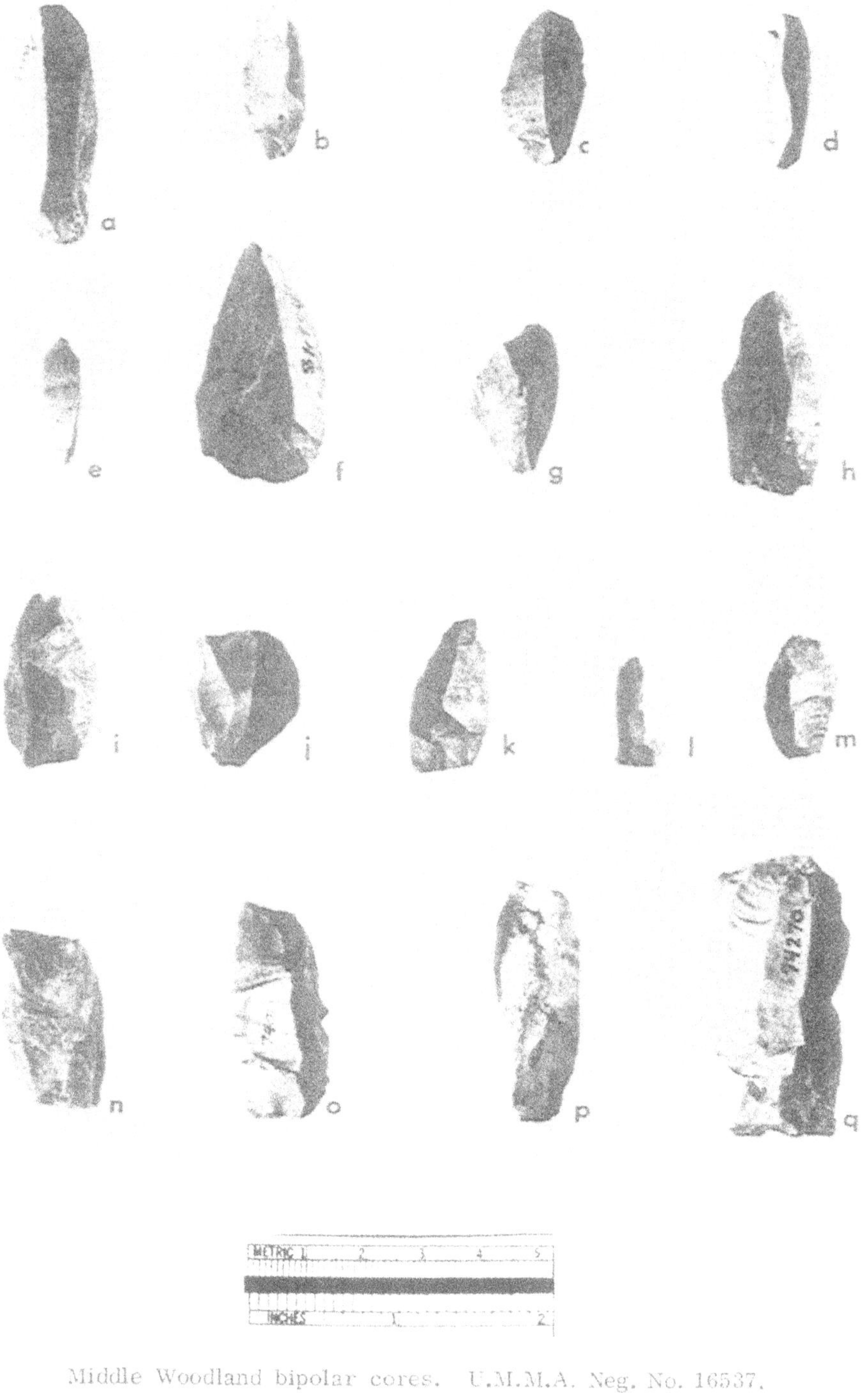

Middle Woodland bipolar cores. U.M.M.A. Neg. No. 16537.

PLATE XVI

Middle Woodland ridge-opposed bipolar cores. U.M.M.A. Neg. No. 16538.

PLATE XVII

Modified bipolar cores and choppers. U.M.M.A. Neg. No. 16539.

PLATE XVIII

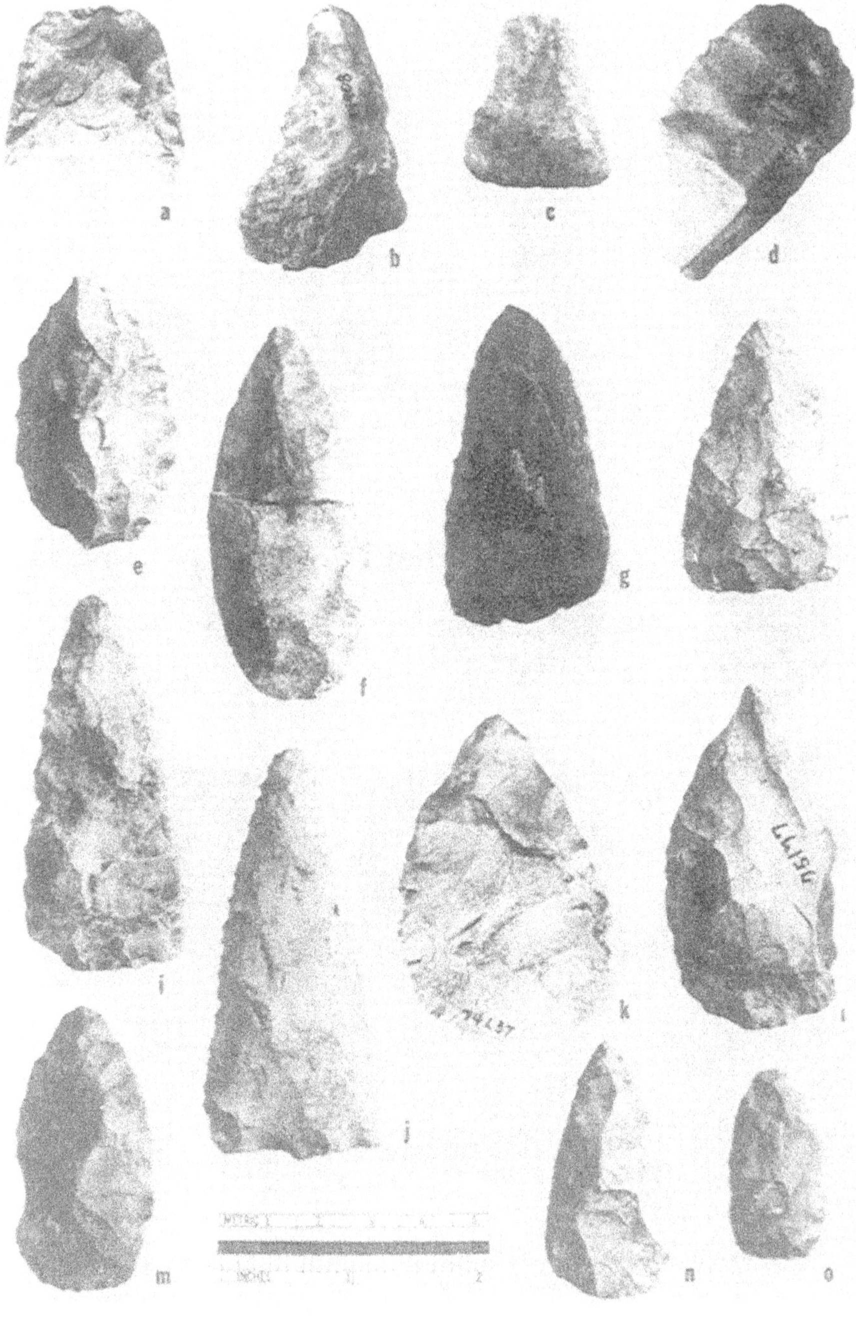

Middle Woodland bifacial scrapers, blades, and blanks. U.M.M.A. Neg. No. 16540.

PLATE XIX

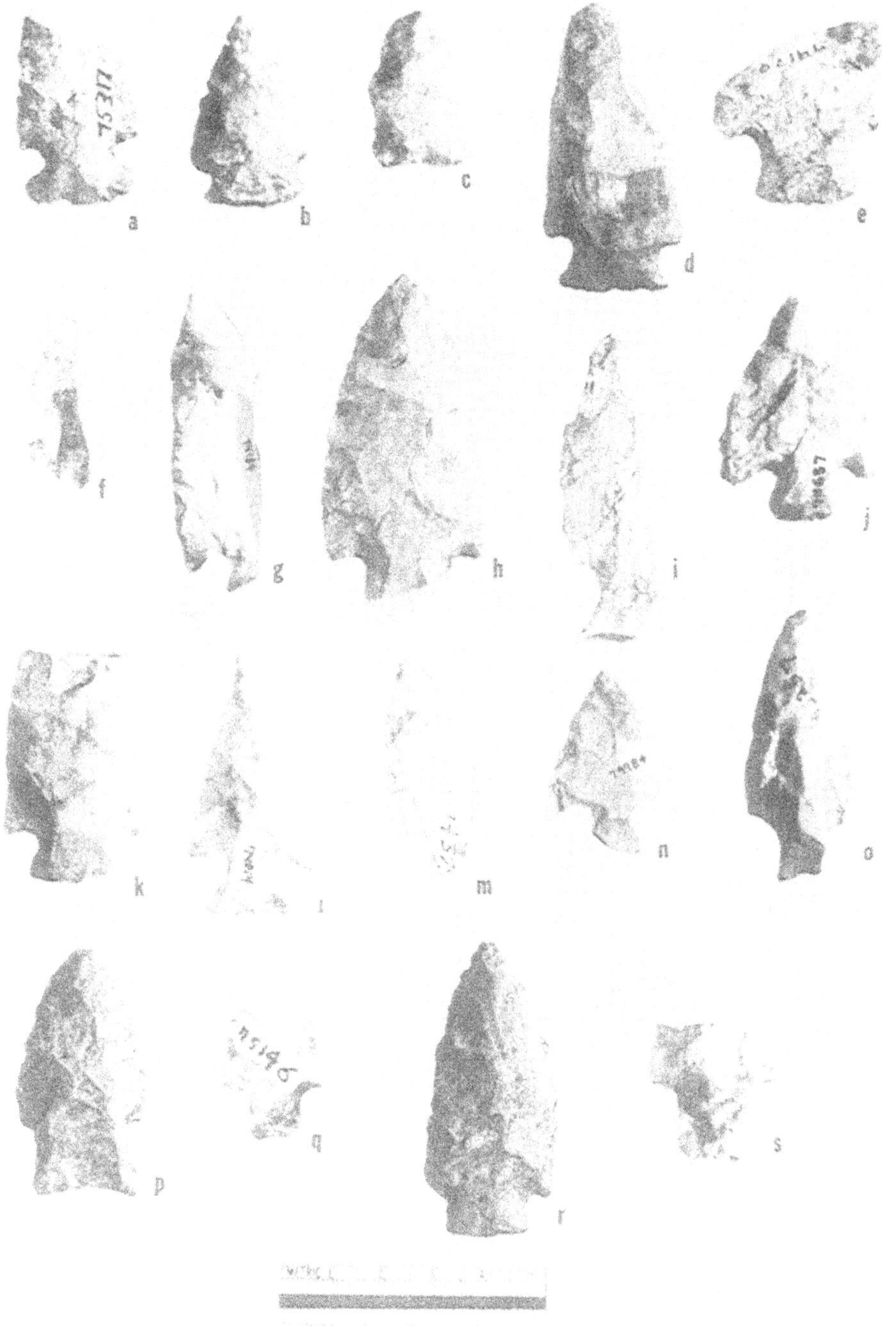

Middle Woodland projectile points. U.M.M.A. Neg. No. 16541.

PLATE XX

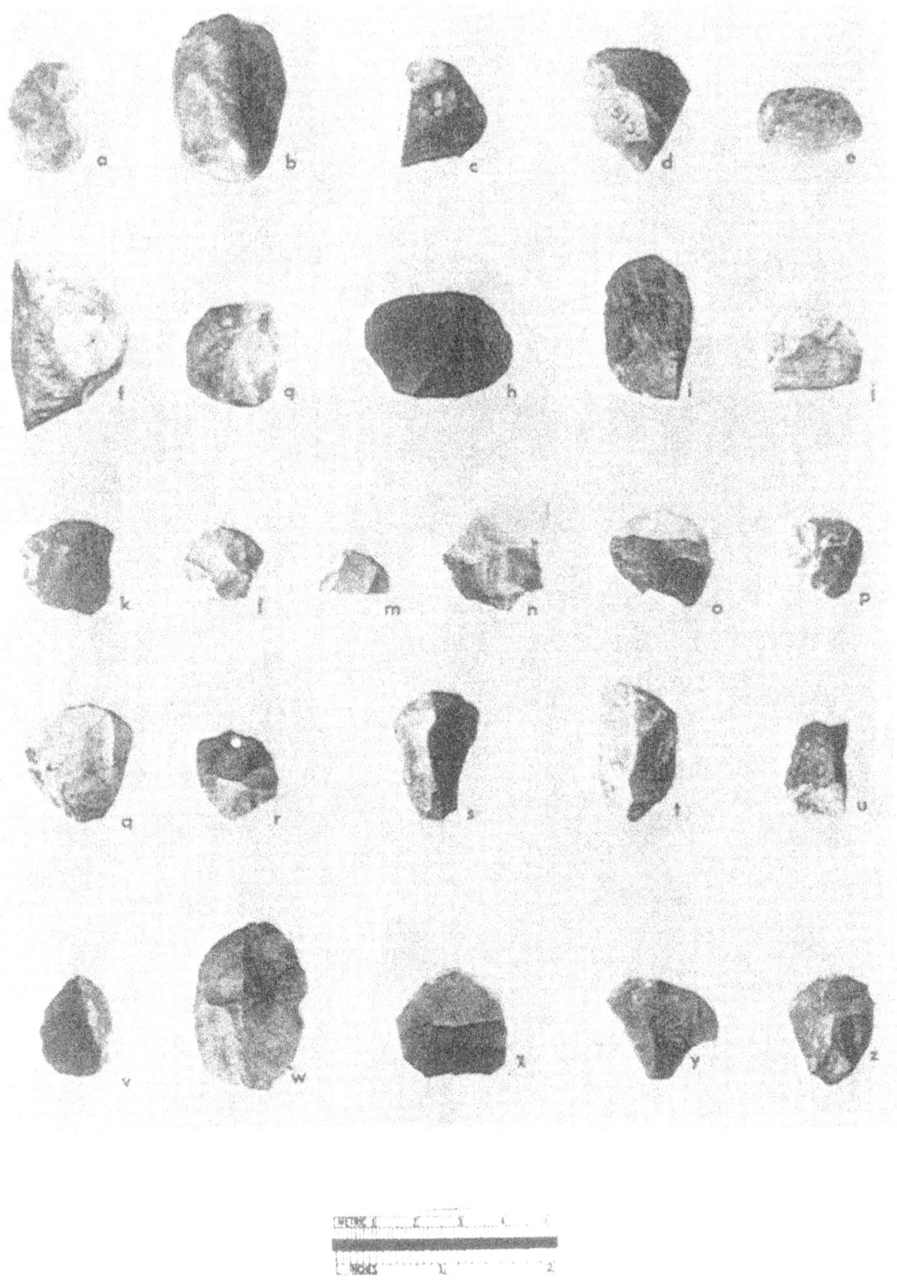

Middle Woodland end scrapers. U.M.M.A. Neg. No. 16542.

PLATE XXI

Other Middle Woodland scrapers. U.M.M.A. Neg. No. 16543.

PLATE XXII

Middle Woodland bladelets. U.M.M.A. Neg. No. 16544.

PLATE XXIII

Middle Woodland rough and ground stone. U.M.M.A. Neg. No. 16545.

PLATE XXIV

Middle Woodland copper artifacts. U.M.M.A. Neg. No. 16546.

PLATE XXV

Middle Woodland bone artifacts. U.M.M.A. Neg. No. 16547.

PLATE XXVI

A

B

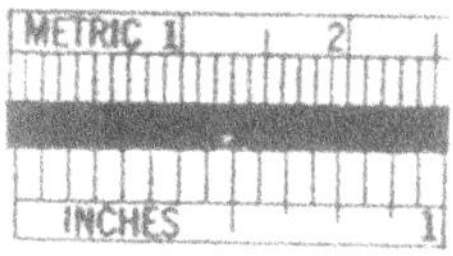

C

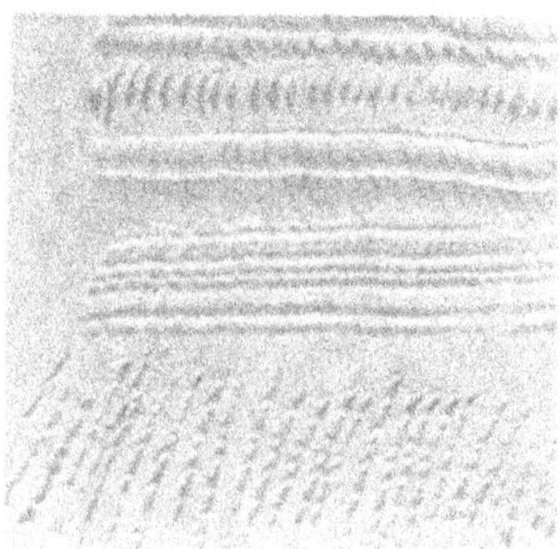

Middle Woodland features, pottery marker, and plasticene impressions. U.M.M.A. Neg. No. 16548.

PLATE XXVII

Ceramics from the Upper Mississippian component. U.M.M.A. Neg. No. 16549.

PLATE XXVIII

Ceramics from the Upper Mississippian component. U.M.M.A. Neg. No. 16550.

PLATE XXIX

Chipped stone from the Upper Mississippian component. U.M.M.A. Neg. No. 16551.

PLATE XXX

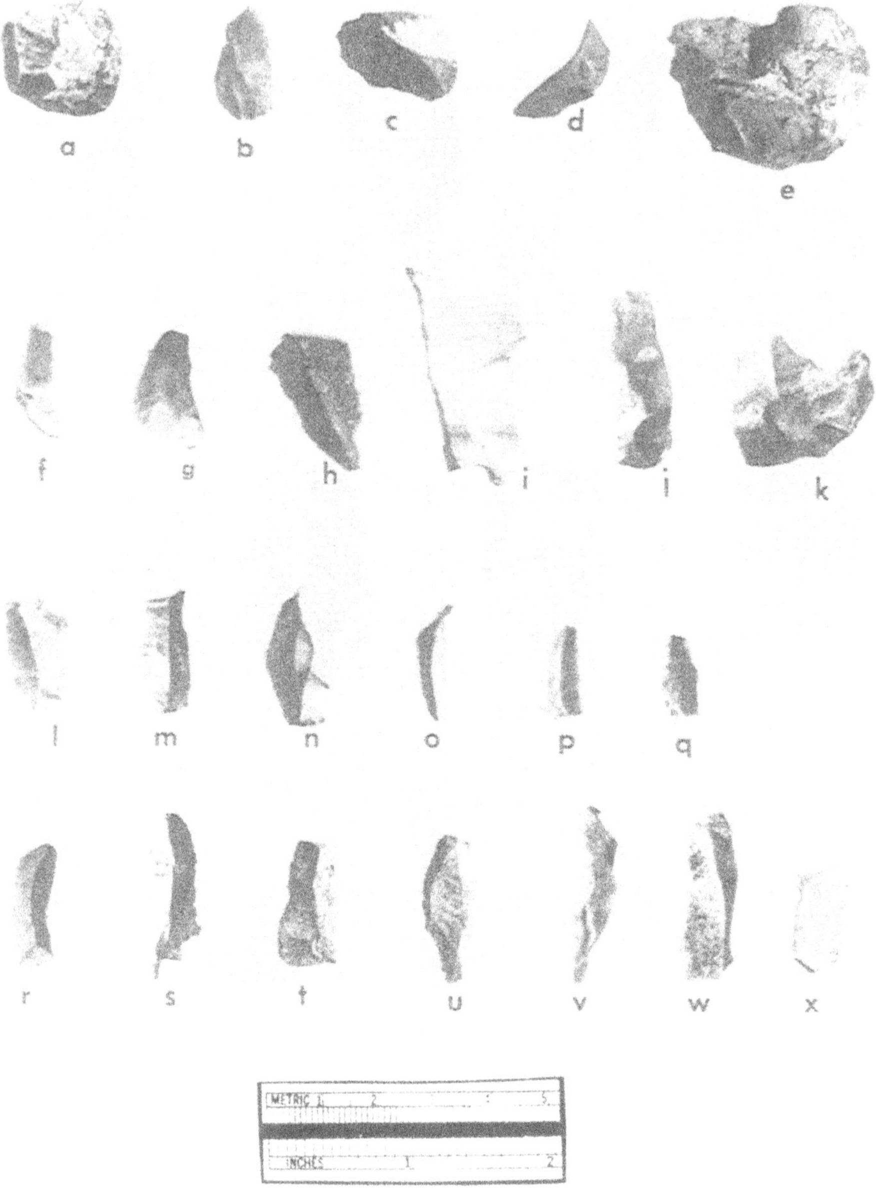

Chipped stone from the Upper Mississippian component. U.M.M.A. Neg. No. 16552.

PLATE XXXI

Ground stone and bone artifacts from the Upper Mississippian component. U.M.M.A. Neg. No. 16553.

PLATE XXXII

Upper Mississippian Feature 11. U.M.M.A. Neg. No. 16554.

PLATE XXXIII

Aboriginal ceramics from the Protohistoric component. U.M.M.A. Neg. No. 16555.

PLATE XXXIV

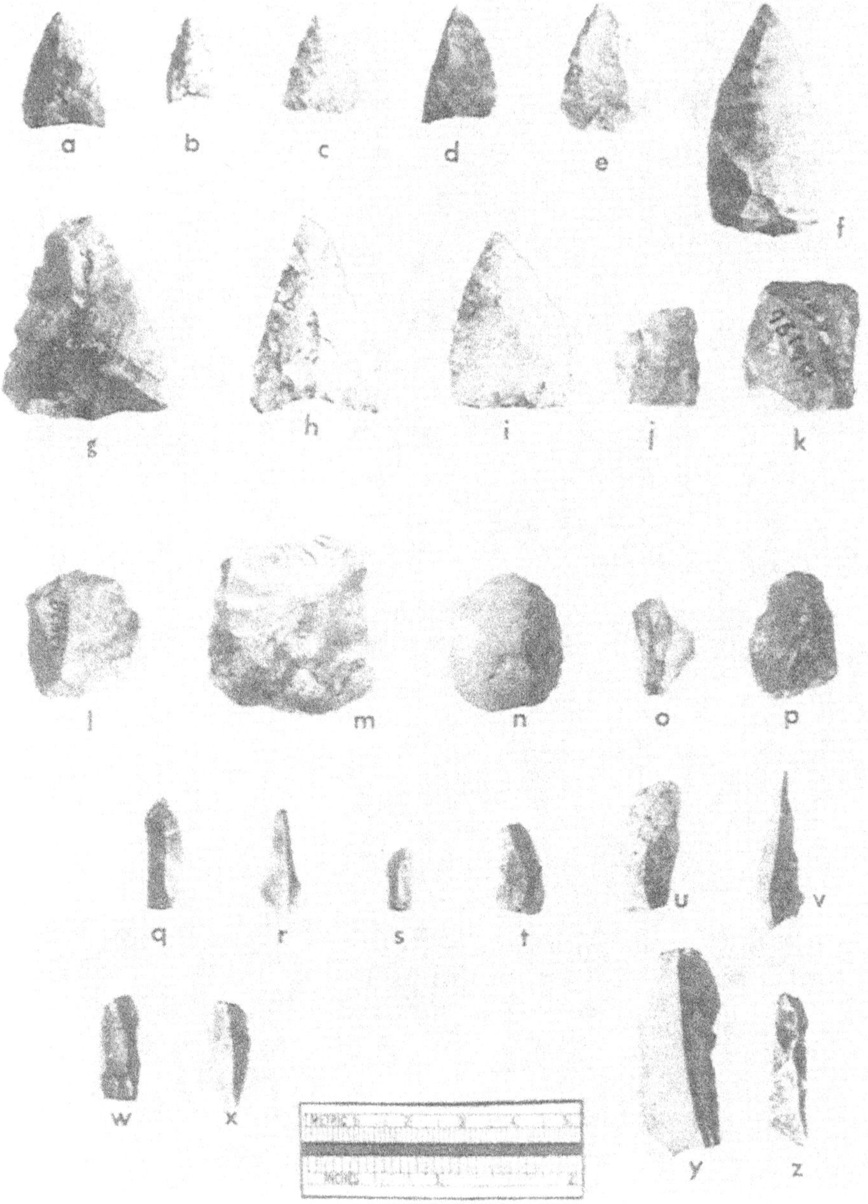

Chipped stone from the Protohistoric component. U.M.M.A. Neg. No. 16556.

PLATE XXXV

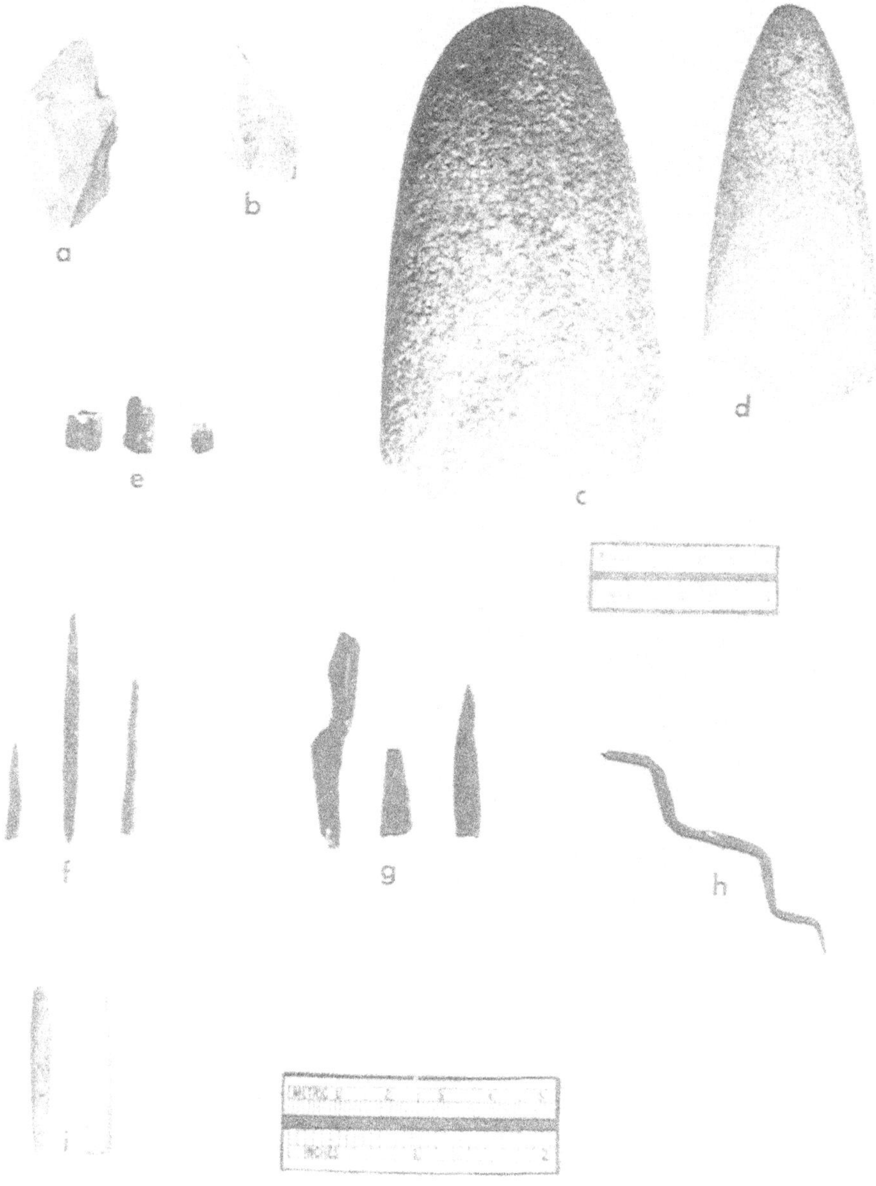

Ground stone, bone, and copper artifacts from the Protohistoric component. U.M.M.A. Neg. No. 16557.

www.ingramcontent.com/pod-product-compliance
Lightning Source LLC
LaVergne TN
LVHW021504270826
846302LV00015B/37